Middle Management in Schools

■ ■ ■

115 - 138
159 - 174

214 - 229.

D0353475

SCHOOL LEADERSHIP AND MANAGEMENT SERIES

Series Editors: Brent Davies and John West-Burnham

Other titles in the series:

Effective Learning in Schools
by Christopher Bowring-Carr and John West-Burnham

Reengineering and Total Quality in Schools
by Brent Davies and John West-Burnham

Strategic Marketing for Schools
by Brent Davies and Linda Ellison

Forthcoming titles:

Managing Quality in Schools
by John West-Burnham

Human Resource Management for Effective Schools
by John O'Neill and John West-Burnham

Management Development
by John West-Burnham

Resource Management in Schools
by Sonia Blandford

Strategic Development Planning in Schools
by Brent Davies and Linda Ellison

Middle Management in Schools

■ ■ ■

How to Harmonise Managing and Teaching for an Effective School

SONIA BLANDFORD

PITMAN
PUBLISHING

London · Hong Kong · Johannesburg · Melbourne · Singapore · Washington DC

To Charlie, John, Paul, Ian and Jack

PITMAN PUBLISHING
128 Long Acre, London WC2E 9AN
Tel: +44 (0) 171 447 2000
Fax: +44 (0) 171 240 5771

A Division of Pearson Professional Limited

First published in Great Britain in 1997

© Pearson Professional Limited 1997

The right of Sonia Blandford to be identified as author of this work
has been asserted by her in accordance with the Copyright, Designs
and Patents Act 1988.

ISBN 0 273 61608 0

British Library Cataloguing in Publication Data
A CIP catalogue record for this book can be obtained from the British Library

10 9 8 7 6 5 4 3 2 1

Typeset by Phoenix Photosetting, Chatham, Kent
Printed and bound in Great Britain by Redwood Books, Trowbridge, Wiltshire

The Publishers' policy is to use paper manufactured from sustainable forests.

Contents

■ ■ ■

Biographical Details

■   ■   ■

Sonia Blandford has taught in primary and secondary schools, and has held a variety of middle and senior management posts including curriculum co-ordinator and pastoral co-ordinator.

Sonia was among the first cohort to gain a taught doctorate in education (EdD) at the University of Bristol.

Sonia is currently a member of the Oxford Centre of Education Management, School for Education, Oxford Brookes University.

Sonia also conducts youth choirs and wind orchestras.

Preface

■ ■ ■

The purpose of this book is to provide advice for practitioners in schools: aspiring middle managers, middle managers, senior managers, teacher educators, governors and inspectors.

Middle management in schools can be compared to being on a roller coaster, travelling at speed through many hoops, having to participate in many teaching and management activities from the 'top-down' and 'bottom-up'. During the journey a middle manager has to assimilate the view from every perspective: pupil, teacher, manager, parent, governor and local education authority. This book attempts to take the reader through the middle management journey progressing forward, presenting ideas, and providing the opportunity to reflect and revise.

Chapter One introduces management and middle management issues, defining and refining the role. This allows the reader to consider his/her own position as a manager.

Chapter Two considers the position of middle managers as player managers; teachers and managers who are led and lead. Practice is placed within the context of leadership theories, management behaviours and accountability. The key themes of motivation and stress management are developed in this section.

Chapter Three focuses on visions and missions, school aims and objectives. Culture is introduced as a means of identifying differences between schools: ethos and organisational structure. Theories are discussed, concluding with models from current practice.

Chapter Four provides practical advice on how to develop communication in schools. The communication processes, written, verbal and non-verbal, are considered. The chapter concludes with recommendations for good practice in creating a positive image for the school.

Chapter Five examines the role of the middle manager in schools. Aspects of team management are introduced within the school context.

Chapter Six defines the administrative process within a practical framework. Timetabling, assessment and inspection procedures are reviewed in detail.

Chapter Seven provides detailed guidance for school and departmental planning. This encompasses strategic and operational planning. Models from current practice illustrate how to approach this complex task. The chapter concludes with an analysis of time management issues.

Chapter Eight prepares middle managers for their resource management responsibilities. It takes the reader from Local Management of Schools (LMS) through to stock-taking procedures. Descriptions of budgetary processes are included as are examples of good practice.

Chapter Nine investigates the management of change in schools. This includes a detailed analysis of resistance factors and methods of approaching change as a middle manager.

Chapter Ten examines staff development issues, encompassing the recent Teacher Training Agency (TTA) initiatives for the Continuing Professional Development (CPD) of teachers. The role of the middle manager in informing team members of development opportunities is also outlined.

Chapter Eleven defines recruitment and selection processes, providing a framework for good practice. This chapter includes: job specification and description, selection techniques, marketing and interviewing.

Chapter Twelve places middle managers within the context of their own career development. Diversity of choice is perhaps unknown to many practitioners. Possible options are described and guidance given on applications and interview techniques. An emphasis is placed on self-reflection and self-assessment.

Sonia Blandford

Acknowledgements

■　■　■

This book would not have been possible without the generous help and support from friends and colleagues. A large number of primary and secondary middle managers provided information which created the framework for the book. Because of the demands of confidentiality these teachers cannot be named or thanked in person.

My thanks are to the 'team' who contributed to the process of creating the final copy: in particular, Rachel Soper and Charlie Eldridge who word processed each draft with speed and accuracy; Dawn Newstead, Clive Cambers, Patricia Sage, Linet Arthur, Nicki McCormack and Michael Ormston for their professional advice and support; and John Wood and Gill Fox for proof reading and valuable comments.

My thanks also to John West-Burnham and Brent Davies for their faith and support.

1
■ ■ ■
Management

Introduction

A manager is someone who gets the job done, through people. Everard (1986) defined a manager as someone who:

- *knows what he or she wants to happen and causes it to happen*
- *is responsible for controlling resources and ensuring that they are put to good use*
- *promotes effectiveness in work done, and a search for continual improvement*
- *is accountable for the performance of the unit he or she is managing, of which he or she is a part*
- *sets a climate or tone conducive to enabling people to give of their best.*

Management is therefore the achievement of objectives through people, managers are responsible for the work of others. Bush and West-Burnham (1994) provide a definition of the principles of management which encompass planning, resourcing, controlling, organising, leading and evaluating. In brief, these involve:

- *leadership* – values, missions and vision
- *management* – planning, organisation, execution and deployment
- *administration* – operational details.

In essence, managers lead, manage and administrate. Critically, managers keep things going, cope with breakdown, initiate new activities and bring teams and activities together.

More specifically the key functions of school management are to manage policy, learning, people and resources. School managers should create, maintain and develop conditions which enable effective learning to take place.

Why management?

The management of schools has changed significantly since the 1988 Education Reform Act (ERA). All school management teams, nursery, primary, special and secondary, now have management responsibilities which hitherto were in the domain of the Local Education Authorities (LEAs). The areas which have had the greatest impact on schools' management are shown in Table 1.1.

Table 1.1: The effects of the ERA on school management

Aspect of era	Affected area of school management
Local Management of Schools (LMS)	Budget
Parental choice	Marketing and development
National Curriculum (NC)	Curriculum co-ordination
League tables	Pastoral and academic
Continuing Professional Development (CPD)	Staff development, appraisal and selection
School Development Plan (SDP)	Strategic planning
Diversity	Grant Maintained (GM) schools, selection and specialisation

These changes set new parameters for management practice in schools. As a direct consequence of the ERA new structures for management of schools evolved, which in turn led to new roles for existing school managers and the proliferation of management teams. In essence someone needed to do the job! Teachers are no longer classroom managers responsible for the delivery of the curriculum; they are managers with responsibilities as diverse as developing the new school prospectus and purchasing carpets. While it is essential to view teachers within the context of learning, the profession was required to develop new skills to accommodate the need to manage policies, resources and people. Spinks (1990, pp.121–2) stated:

It follows from continuing developments in devolution of responsibility for decision-making to schools and communities that schools now have three major tasks:

1. *The development of a relevant curriculum to meet the needs of the students.*

2. *The development of management skills to deliver the curriculum to students in the most effective and efficient ways possible through the resources available.*

3. *The development of approaches through which to manage change as a natural phenomenon in schools.*

Why middle management?

The culture of school management is changing from a top-down hierarchical model to a flatter structure, which will involve the majority of staff in the management of their school. From this scenario evolved the need for middle managers with responsibility points to manage a range of teams including:

- subject teams
- year teams
- curriculum/faculty/department teams
- key stage teams.

The need for middle managers in schools has arisen because of the change to school-based management. In practical terms, existing school managers were unable to meet the demands of the changes in management practice which have been introduced since 1988. Within the profession teachers now have to consider management to be part of their daily practice.

In addition, many schools have created working groups as a means of managing change. These working groups have responsibility for the development, implementation and review of school, LEA and government policies.

As a middle manager in a large comprehensive school, I led or participated in 43 management teams/working groups. The need for rationalisation was self-evident, but no one was available to join the 'Working Group for Rationalising Working Groups and Management Teams'. It is also important to note that many staff who lead working groups are not financially rewarded.

Middle management defined

The process by which teachers become managers is unclear, yet many teachers are now managers. In essence, teachers are managers of their classes and classrooms, but management priorities change when teachers become managers of others.

Central to management and teaching in schools is learning. A teacher is a classroom manager managing the development of knowledge and under-standing, skills and abilities of pupils. A middle manager is a staffroom manager, managing the knowledge and understanding, skills and abilities of colleagues. In both roles the teacher/manager is required to work with other people. This involves working with individual values and beliefs manifested in the ethos of the school. Middle managers are therefore continuously creating, forming and applying practices and policies in order to achieve.

3

A middle manager is also managed and therefore has a role within a team. Team membership and leadership are critical to the function of school management. The middle manager therefore has contrasting roles within management teams. Middle management requires individuals to identify, and identify with, different tasks and different people: teacher, leader, team member. This hybrid role within school management provides the framework for the daily practice of the middle manager. Figure 1.1 places the middle manager in context, as a teacher, leader and team member. Each of these roles are described in full in Chapter Two.

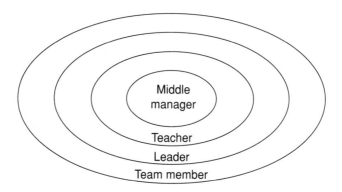

Figure 1.1: Middle management in context

Central to effective middle management is the ability of the middle manager to identify his/her role at any given moment in the school day. An 'effective manager' would, in practice, differentiate between each management role as required. It is therefore essential that a middle manager understands the nature of his/her job.

In defining middle management, this section has also indicated the problems and ambiguities which exist in practice. Middle managers should identify these difficulties in order to determine their role within the school. A more detailed understanding of what management is will lead to a greater understanding of this process.

What is management?

Understanding the purpose of management within the school context is fundamental. Generally school leaders now develop vision and mission statements (school aims and objectives) which identify the purpose and direction of the school. Available to all, these statements provide a starting point for all management activities within the school: practice and policy. However, as will be discussed later in this book, not all educational institutions enjoy shared visions and missions. Occasionally such statements are germinating in the minds of school leaders or safely filed in the headteacher's computer without being circulated for information. Managers of schools as organisations need to participate in the development, implementation and evaluation of vision and mission statements. As will be shown, the shared development of vision and mission statements is critical to determining key objectives and policies, which will provide a framework for education which is specifically suited to each community.

Spinks (1990) identified that the devolution of authority and school inspection procedures has placed the emphasis on school effectiveness and, therefore, the success or failure of schools. Management as an activity is central to the success of schools. In order to achieve desired success, management teams need to collaborate. Caldwell and Spinks (1988) developed a model of collaborative school management as a process which identifies six phases in the management of a school. Spinks (1990, p.123) stated:

> These phases relate to **where** the school is going and **why**, **how** it is going to get there and then checking very carefully to see **if** and **when** it arrived.

The six key phases are:

- goal-setting
- policy-making
- curriculum planning
- resource provision
- implementation of learning programme
- evaluation.

A further consideration in this process is that of personal relationships. As a middle manager you will be in a position where your relationship with the members of your team will be critical to its effectiveness.

A middle manager will participate in each phase as a teacher, team leader and team member. Education management is about getting things done in the right way for each very individual institution (Duignan and MacPherson, 1992).

Framework for practice

To manage is to get things done; school management is to get things done within the framework of practice determined by the school as a community and organisation. Harrison (1995, p.8) commented that *managers live in a practical world*. As a community, each school is self-centred, self-reliant and culturally 'different' to any other school. As an organisation, each school can work within existing structures or create new structures, and as Greenfield and Ribbins (1993, p.54) stated *the self cannot escape organisations.*

A school community will reflect its environment. In contrast, the organisation of the majority of a school will be similar to other schools. Pugh and Hickson in *Writers on Organisations* (1989) collated a variety of definitions applied to the management of organisations, described by management gurus since the mid-1800s. Each focuses on the need to place individuals in the workplace within an identifiable structure. This applies to schools irrespective of cultural, social or community differences. There are generic responsibilities which apply to all schools, from a small nursery, primary, secondary or special school to a large comprehensive school. It therefore follows that a framework for the organisation of schools can apply to all schools. Differentiation will occur in practice; in the 'real world' managers will make choices as to how their schools will be organised. Essentially school managers are responsible for the management of people; each framework for practice can only function as a model to be interpreted by individuals.

Divisions of responsibility within a school are determined by the needs of:

- pupils to learn
- teachers to teach.

These require policies at macro and micro levels of government, LEA and school which, as an example, may include:

- assessment and reporting procedures
- staff development
- curriculum
- learning and teaching styles
- support
- equal opportunities
- pastoral care.

All policies should be available to members of staff. Middle managers should have knowledge and understanding of policies relevant to their practice.

Historically, the leader of a school was as the headteacher, a senior colleague with expert teaching skills who led a team of teachers by example. Today this concept has ceased to exist. Although headteachers may reject the notion of corporate management their position can now be compared to that of a managing director of a corporate company, whose product is education and whose clients are pupils (and parents). School management is now influenced by the owners or patrons of the school: governors, parents, the government and/or LEAs. The organisational structure of the school reflects these changes to professional practice.

Whole school

A middle manager will be required to have knowledge and understanding of whole school issues. These will be determined by the government, LEA, Senior Management Team (SMT) and governors. There will also be other agencies involved in the daily management of the school: support groups, e.g. racial, crisis, social services (educational welfare and probationary officers), educational psychologists, university and other research teams providing academic and management advice, LEA and independent inspection teams, and consultants. A middle manager should know who these people are, how frequently they visit the school, and their roles within the whole school. There should not be a pastoral/academic divide. As a framework, the model might be as shown in Figure 1.2.

In essence a middle manager, as a member of the school management team, needs to have knowledge of all operational aspects of the school which encompass:

- curriculum issues
- pastoral issues
- research and development
- policy and practice.

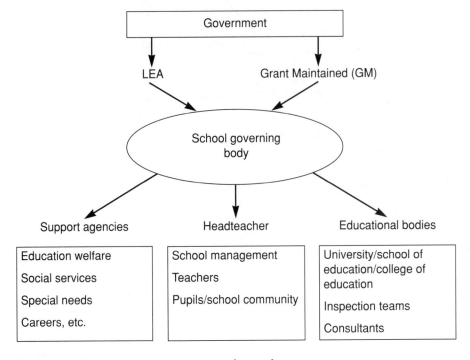

Figure 1.2: School management – external agencies

Participant players in school management differ according to phase and school culture. However, in order to encompass the above, a framework for practice would not be dissimilar to one of the examples of a school management structure shown in Figures 1.3 and 1.4.

In Figure 1.3, pastoral and academic issues are integrated. Differences in practice would be determined not by organisational structures but by professional practice, i.e. a classroom teacher would have pastoral and curriculum responsibilities for the pupils in his/her class and a key stage co-ordinator would be responsible for the management of all pastoral and academic issues. This differs from current practice in many secondary schools whereby the management of key stage initiatives is the responsibility of a member of a curriculum or pastoral team. In contrast Model A emphasises the need for a key stage co-ordinator with full responsibility for all academic and pastoral issues. This would lead to the development of class tutor responsibility for the management of learning.

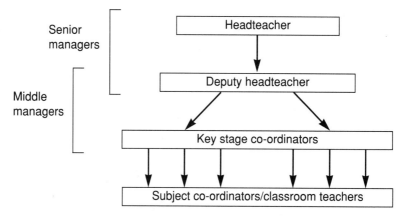

Figure 1.3: Model A – school management structure – nursery, primary and small secondary schools

The organisational structure shown in Model A may not require each position to be filled by an individual. In reality teachers may have shared responsibilities, or have more than one responsibility. The allocation of posts will be determined by local needs, staff availability and financial resources.

Model B in Figure 1.4 indicates the need for a significant number of middle managers within some schools with limited resources. In practice this may lead to dual responsibilities, e.g. head of year and deputy head of academic team. Inevitably there will be 'overlaps' within staff teams, e.g. head of year could be in a position as manager of the head of his/her academic team. From experience, this requires an awareness of the parameters of each position. Clear lines of communication are required, as are good interpersonal skills.

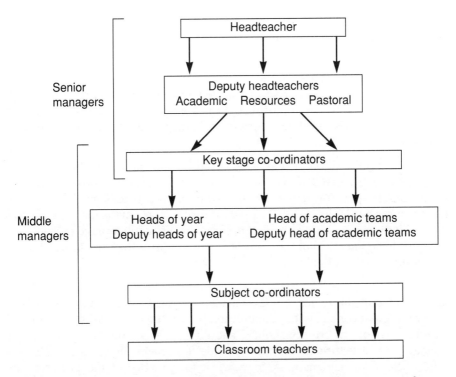

Figure 1.4: Model B – school management structure – large primary or secondary schools

For example, as a pastoral co-ordinator with head of year responsibilities and primary liaison duties in a large comprehensive school, I managed 11 class tutors and liaised with 16 KS2 co-ordinators. I was also chair of a federation of headteachers. There were a considerable number of teachers and senior managers who were affected by me as a manager. In addition, I was a part-time member of the music department, and the head of music was also a member of my pastoral team. We had, I believe, a good working relationship which involved me working for the department, as directed by the head of department and, as class tutor, the head of department working for me as head of year. There was a clear understanding and there were no apparent problems during this period.

Department/faculty

The size of the department or faculty accommodating each subject area will be determined by the size of the school. Formula funding through LMS determines the amount of income for each school, and therefore the number of staff, e.g. while it might be desirable to employ a drama specialist, this may not be affordable in all schools. For a middle manager responsible for a department or faculty, the number of staff within each academic team will reflect the number of pupils attending the school. The size of the academic team will also determine the financial incentive allocated to the post and the level of delegation possible.

In contrast, the tasks of each academic team will not differ according to size. At each key stage, teachers are required to deliver the national curriculum. Each pupil is to be assessed and reporting criteria are to be met. Curriculum support teams, special needs, language support and peripatetic music staff have to be managed.

Communication, written or oral, is essential for the success of the team. As a middle manager you will be a disseminator and gatherer of information, acting as the 'gate-keeper' for your team. Be aware of your team's needs; try not to make assumptions which are unsupported by evidence. In the majority of cases teachers will want to be informed of policies that affect their practice. They will also wish to be informed of staff development opportunities. In essence, try not to be too protective of your staff, there will be a 'need to know'.

A middle manager will be the central person for the team. Every teacher has a pastoral responsibility for pupils. Heads of year manage this area, which involves regular contact with parents, members of the community and external agencies. Areas of responsibility should be well defined within the management structure of the school. This is occasionally a neglected area within school management. A framework for practice of the pastoral care management should (as the above indicates):

- be workable
- recognise the needs of the school
- be understood and acknowledged by all staff
- relate to the school's vision and mission
- allow middle and senior managers to develop knowledge and under-standing, skills and abilities
- allow middle managers to participate in and develop CPD programmes.

Middle management in practice

If the school is to be effective, middle managers need to adopt good practice. The National Commission on Education (NCE) (1996, p.366) stated that school effectiveness involves:

> *leadership, ethos, high expectations of pupils and staff, positive teaching and learning styles, sound assessment procedures, recognition of pupils' participation in learning, parental involvement in the life of the school and a programme of extra-curricular activities.*

Rutter *et al.* (1979) suggested that middle managers should have the following attributes:

- strong positive leadership
- staff involvement
- positive school ethos.

Middle managers should enjoy and encourage good practice directed towards developing and retaining the above if their team (and school) is to be effective.

As stated, middle managers are also teachers; on balance their timetable will have a greater number of contact hours with classes than the number of hours allocated to those employed as senior managers. In order to understand the nature of their job, middle managers need to consider their teaching commitment within the context of their middle management role. This is not merely an issue of time management, but also of the compatibility between the two roles. If practitioner values and beliefs are transferable to management practice, teaching and middle management may co-exist quite successfully. If, however, individuals adopt values and beliefs in their management role which differ from their values and beliefs as a practitioner, this will be problematic. The values displayed by middle managers will determine their management style, and the nature of their relationship with their colleagues.

To know how to manage is an ongoing process. The development of the knowledge and understanding, skills and abilities required to manage others takes time. A middle manager should be aware of the need to reflect on and learn from their practice. Professional managers must constantly evaluate their roles within an institution. This is a two-way process; managers knowing themselves and their team members, and the team knowing its manager. Inconsistency will lead to bad practice; clear direction is respected and valued.

Roles

Being a middle manager does not mean being 'all things to all people'. Middle managers must adopt their own management style which fulfils the requirements of the post. Knowing what is required is the key. It is essential for middle managers to identify their roles in terms of:

- tasks
- responsibilities
- relationships
- working conditions
- external influences.

Middle managers should also have an understanding of their role in relation to others, to avoid management dilemmas. Analysing the design of the job, applying this in practice, reflecting on failures and successes are central to

11

middle management. A middle manager manages a team which can at times stand alone, but can never be separated from whole school policies. The middle manager must be loyal to his/her leader. 'Empire building' is not applicable to teams.

A middle manager has to be able to identify the different influences on his/her job. The structure of the school as an organisation should give a clear view of his/her position within the management system. There will be other influences beyond the role of the middle manager; as an individual member of the community, a middle manager may have community and family responsibilities. It is essential that middle managers maintain their personal and social activities outside the school. Otherwise, their life will move along a single track, with a limited outlook.

Essentially middle managers are responsible for:

1. The implementation of school-wide strategies, structures and intentions. In this process, middle managers 'fine tune' these strategies to suit the real world.
2. Being role models for their staff. A middle manager's daily behaviour must represent the people-centred culture of the school as an organisation.
3. The passing on of practices which are learnt as a consequence of operational wisdom.

Brown and Rutherford (1996) provide a further insight into the role of a middle manager in schools. They applied the following descriptors to secondary school heads of department:

- *servant leader* – serving pupils, teachers and senior management
- *organisational architect* – engaging in professional discussions
- *moral educator* – committed to high educational values
- *social architect* – sensitive to the needs of pupils and staff
- *leading professional* – spending 80 per cent of their time teaching in addition to leading their team.

As a middle manager you should have an understanding of your role as detailed in your job description, negotiated with your senior management team and approved by governors. Clarity is essential if you are to avoid ambiguities which lead to confusion. Resolving management problems early is preferable to watching them grow to unmanageable proportions. In sum the role of the middle manager in schools is to:

- teach
- lead teams
- be a team member.

Dilemmas

For many teachers, involvement in management is not desirable. Whether as a consequence of poor management experiences or the view that management and teaching are not compatible, teachers may prefer to teach and leave others to manage. There is a need within schools to develop opportunities for middle managers to meet and to develop management skills and abilities. Time for such meetings would be desirable for managers as individuals and invaluable to the school. This would also allow middle managers to develop self-evaluation skills within a 'safe' environment.

A middle manager may encounter management dilemmas which generally arise out of the conflict between management of learning and management of people. Hall and Oldroyd (1990a, p.38) identified role strain as a difficult area. Sources of role strain were considered to be:

- *role ambiguity* – when you are unclear about what is expected
- *role conflict* – when one of the roles you have is in conflict with another
- *role overload* – when more is expected of you in a role than you could manage
- *role underload* – when you feel under-utilised in your role.

Handy and Aitken (1986, p.60) suggested a possible method of reducing strains imposed by role problems:

> *The more positive approach would be to reduce the ambiguity by agreeing with everyone what the job is all about [. . .] to reduce the conflict by dropping some roles or at least putting clear boundaries around each so that they interfere with each other as little as possible; [. . .] and to reduce the overload by thinking out the priorities properly instead of coping with the crises as they occur.*

Defining what the job is all about may only go part way to solving the problem, it may also produce its own set of dilemmas. As Holmes (1993) identified, *maintaining a healthy professional community while focusing on learning can create its own conflict.* As a solution Holmes suggested trade-offs when required, which would seem to be a more pragmatic approach to resolving conflict than defining roles.

The job of a middle manager will always have problems and dilemmas. Choices will need to be made and difficult people confronted. While the teaching profession is reluctant to recognise failure, identifying colleagues as 'difficult' can itself be problematic. This is illogical; merely by withholding goodwill and co-operation a 'difficult' colleague can destroy the learning environment. As a middle manager it is important to resolve difficulties as they arise.

Courage, in measured doses, is required to deal with situations in a non-confrontational manner. How a middle manager approaches such situations often reflects his/her own personal integrity. Middle managers are constantly watched by colleagues, so personal integrity is very important. Holmes (1993, p.104) advised:

If the leader misleads, mistreats or misrepresents his or her colleagues in any serious way, he or she forfeits trust, respect and, in extreme cases, collaboration.

Listening skills are critical in the management of others; listen and use information sensitively. Finally, persistence is a valuable tool. As a middle manager has many audiences in his/her role, it may be difficult to resolve dilemmas quickly. Persistence, without being over-bearing, will produce outcomes; changes which will benefit the middle manager and his/her team.

What the job entails

Beyond describing the role of the middle manager in general terms, specifically the job entails the following: knowledge and understanding, skills and abilities which are discussed in detail in this book as follows:

Area	*Chapter*	*Area*	*Chapter*
leadership	2	appraisal	6
participation and delegation	2	strategic planning	7
stress management	2	operational planning	7
conflict management	2	decision-making	7
knowledge of schools as organisations	3	monitoring and evaluation	7
		financial management	8
communication: interpersonal relationships	4	management of change	9
		staff development	10
understanding of teams	5	recruitment and selection	11
time management	6	self-evaluation	12

Summary

The management of schools has changed significantly since the 1988 Education Reform Act. All school management teams (nursery, primary, special and secondary) now have management responsibilities which hitherto were in the domain of LEAs. These changes set new parameters for management in schools.

As a consequence the culture of school management is changing from a top-down hierarchical model to a flatter structure. From this scenario evolved the need for middle managers with responsibility points to manage a range of teams.

The process by which teachers become managers is unclear, yet many teachers are now managers. Central to management and teaching in schools is learning. Schools exist so that:

- teachers teach
- pupils learn.

Middle managers manage people in order to get things done. A middle manager is also managed and has a role in a team. Team membership and leadership are critical to the function of school management. A middle manager is a teacher, leader and team member. Therefore there are problems and ambiguities which exist and can be resolved with a greater understanding of management.

Spinks (1990, p.123) suggested six phases in the management of the school; *goal-setting, policy-making, curriculum planning, resource provision, implementation of learning programme and evaluation*. A further consideration in this process is that of *personal relationships*. As a middle manager you will be in a position where your relationship with the members of your team will be critical to its effectiveness.

School managers get things done within the framework of practice determined by the school as a community and organisation. This requires policies at macro and micro levels of government, LEA and school. All policies should be available to members of staff. Middle managers should have knowledge and understanding of policies relevant to their practice.

A middle manager will be required to have knowledge and understanding of whole school issues. There should not be a pastoral/academic divide, although participant players in school management will differ according to phase and school culture.

To know how to manage is an on-going process. Professional managers must constantly evaluate their roles within an institution. Teaching and management may not be compatible. It is therefore necessary to provide opportunities for middle managers to meet. This could allow middle managers to develop self-evaluation skills within a 'safe' environment.

As a middle manager you should have an understanding of your role as detailed in your job description. However, the job of a middle manager will always have difficulties and dilemmas. Courage and persistence are valuable tools. Personal integrity is essential.

2

■ ■ ■

To be Led and to Lead

Introduction

Handy and Aitken (1986, p. 41) stated:

The assumption behind the promotion structure in schools is that the best teachers make the best managers. Career success means moving upwards to an increasingly managerial role.

When moving to middle management a period of reflection is required in order to analyse the implications of your new position within the school management structure. It is worth repeating that all teachers are managers of the practices which take place in their classrooms; in contrast middle managers are responsible for the policies and practices of their team within the school as an organisation. Middle managers may find it difficult to adapt to their new position – that of manager and teacher. It is helpful to try to identify the knowledge and understanding, skills and abilities required for each, and then place yourself in the role of teacher and manager. As this chapter illustrates, there are no definitive models for those who are in a position to be led and to lead.

Player manager

Middle managers in schools are very much player managers, participating in the daily tasks of teaching while fulfilling the role of team leaders/managers. At an interview for the post of deputy headteacher in a large (over 1000 pupils) rural 11–18 comprehensive I was asked, 'What is the difference between a manager and a leader?' My response:

If the task of the team was to climb a mountain, a leader would climb to the top, throw a rope down and ask the team to join him/her. In contrast, a manager would consult his/her team at every stage of the climb which they would then complete together!

This demonstrates how important it is for a player manager to know the role of a middle manager in relation to both leaders and team. A school middle manager is led by a senior management team, the governing body, advisory/inspection teams and (depending on where the job is in the management structure) their line manager (see Figures 1.2, 1.3 and 1.4, Chapter One).

There is a distinctive status to being a manager. It is important to identify what this means early in your management career. Equally there is a distinct status attached to team membership. As a middle manager, there is every likelihood that you will join teams with responsibility for the management of the school. As an example, if appointed to the post of head of year 8, you may be invited to join the school pastoral team; consequently your role as a player manager may look something like Figure 2.1.

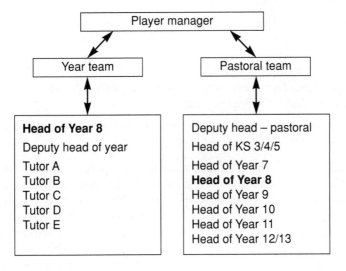

Figure 2.1: Player manager

It is therefore essential to:

• know your role
• know your team
• know your managers.

Critically this requires an understanding of your own needs and capabilities and those of others. You should be able to recognise the initial importance of relevant information for those who lead and those who are led. In essence, the role of a middle manager is a hybrid (see Figure 2.2).

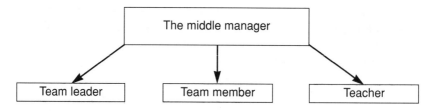

Figure 2.2: The role of a middle manager

What is leadership?

Theories and practice

There are many definitions of leadership in management literature. Increasingly there are many definitions of school leadership in management literature. The backdrop to school leadership is school effectiveness. Educationalists, following intensive periods of research and study, have found that effective school leaders contribute to the development of effective schools. However, as Holmes (1993, p. 9) stated:

> *If you followed all the advice from the available literature on school leadership you would become a very confused and ineffective leader.*

John Harvey-Jones, former ICI chairman, has compared leaders to conductors of symphony orchestras. As a conductor I consider that this analogy is transferable to schools. A conductor is responsible for interpreting the work of others (composer) through a large body of people (the orchestra) who are divided into teams (instrumental sections) with their own team leaders (principal players). The conductor directs and guides his/her subordinates in order to achieve and communicate (through performances) excellence to a diverse and critical audience.

Similarly a school leader is responsible for interpreting the work of others (government at local and national level) through a large body of people (staff, parents and pupils) who are divided into teams (according to task – academic, pastoral, non-teaching and support) with their own team leaders (middle managers) in order to achieve and communicate excellence (through pupil success) to a diverse and informed audience (educationalists, parents, government – local and national). Although the analogy will not be referred to directly it permeates the definitions of management and leadership described in this book.

Before moving on to leadership and management processes, middle managers may wish to reflect on Bennis's (1959) theory of leadership. As an academic industrialist, Bennis's perceptions of leadership came from the context of administrative behaviour. He found (pp. 259–301):

Of all the hazy and confounding areas in social psychology, leadership theory undoubtedly contends for top nomination [. . .] The lack of consensus in this whole area of leadership cannot be blamed on a reluctance by social scientists to engage in empirical research on projects related to these topics [. . .] The problems involved in developing a coherent leadership theory are certainly not new [. . .] As McGregor points out 'The eagerness with which new ideas in this field are received, and the extent to which many of them become fads, are indications of the dissatisfaction with the status quo *in organisational theory.'*

In brief, Bennis found that leadership theory had developed in three phases:

Phase I: Scientific management and bureaucracy

Organisations without people including:

- scientific management – Taylor
- bureaucracy – Weber

Phase II: The human relations approach

People without organisations focusing on:

- wide participation in decision-making
- the face-to-face group rather than the individuals as the basic unit of organisation
- mutual confidence rather than authority as the integrative force in organisation
- the supervisor as the communication agent
- growth of members of the organisation to greater responsibility [. . .]

Phase III: The revisionist

During the *revisionist* phase, a number of management theorists attempted to reconcile phases I and II which led to a new definition of leadership (Bennis, 1959, p. 296):

*Leadership [. . .] involves three major components: (a) an agent who is typically called a **leader**; (b) a process of induction or the ability to manipulate rewards that there will be termed **power**; and (c) the induced behaviour, which will be referred to here as **influence**.*

In essence, theorists define leaders as those within an organisation having power and influence. How this applies to middle managers in practice is described as follows. Middle managers as leaders do things, or as managers get others to do things. How this is achieved is dependent on the leadership style adopted. This will be influenced by:

- previous experience of managers and leaders
- previous experience of managing and leading

- personal qualities and characteristics
- the levels of influence from other agencies
- the function or task.

Individual middle managers will decide on their own leadership style; some will appear charismatic, others less so. This is unimportant. Each individual's qualities will be identified according to their ability to get the job done. In their book *In Search of Excellence*, Tom Peters and Robert Waterman (1982) defined leadership as:

> [. . .] *being visible when things go awry, and invisible when they are working well, it is building a loyal team that speaks with more or less one voice. It's listening carefully most of the time* [. . .] *it's being tough when necessary, and it's the occasional naked use of power – or the 'subtle accumulation of nuances, a hundred things done a little better' as Henry Kissinger once put it.*

Interestingly Peters later argued against middle management in organisations. He considered this element of the management structure to be inefficient, creating dependency from others. The role of a school middle manager is therefore determined by the demands of the situation in which he/she has to function. Each role or situation will have its own demands. As a pastoral manager the emphasis is often an instantaneous decision – on the basis of previous experiences. In contrast, academic managers appear to have more time to reflect, but the demands are no less intensive.

Approaches to leadership may also be determined by styles of management (White and Lippitt, 1983):

- autocratic – leader makes all decisions
- democratic – team makes all decisions
- *laissez-faire* – team works on their own and leader participates when necessary.

In some situations during the school day it would be impossible for a middle manager not to be autocratic. Crises occur and management decisions have to be made. I was faced with a horrifying situation when a pupil's father had been shot. It was of prime importance to limit the threat of violence to the pupil, so a decision was made to remove the pupil from school to a 'safe house'. There was no time to consult colleagues or the pupil's family. The pupil's safety (and that of others) was the priority.

Fortunately events such as the above do not occur regularly in schools. In the majority of situations it is preferable and advisable to adopt a democratic style of management. As a player manager, this is perhaps the most suitable approach to middle management. It is self-evident that a *laissez-faire* approach would not be applicable to school management. As a middle manager you will need to be aware of the difference between collegiality (i.e. working with colleagues) and professional autonomy. Teachers will be autonomous within their classrooms; however the management of professionals requires collegiality.

As shown (Tannenbaum and Schmidt, 1973), management styles will differ according to several factors. These can be identified as:

- *the leader* – his or her personality and preferred style
- *the led* – the needs, attitudes and skills of the subordinates or colleagues
- *the task* – the requirements and goals of the job to be done
- *the contact* – the school, its values and beliefs, visions and missions.

Selection of the 'best or preferred' style appropriate to the individual is critical to the success of the manager and team. A manager should not adopt a style which is inapplicable or unsustainable. 'Sincere insincerity' is easily spotted, be yourself, adapt as required. Remember schools are learning institutions.

Total Quality Management (TQM)

Total Quality Management (TQM) is a holistic approach to management which applies to all levels of an organisation, every relationship, every process. This American concept was originally developed by two statisticians (Deming and Juran) working in the Japanese manufacturing industry (Marsh, 1992). TQM was re-discovered in America during the 1970s, moving to Britain in the 1980s.

In essence, TQM is value-driven, placing a fundamental significance on values and purpose (Ormston, 1996). It is concerned with managing the interpersonal components of all organisations and acknowledges equally the inter-dependence between an organisation and its environment. Within a TQM organisation people are trusted to work as professionals, and there is a strong emphasis on teamwork. In contrast there is a weak emphasis on hierarchy. Critically the organisation sets clear goals which are communicated effectively. As a consequence every member of the organisation has high expectations of themselves, the organisation is 'fit for purpose'.

The customer or the client is central to TQM, defined as the person or group in receipt of a product or service. The organisation only exists for the customer, there is no other purpose. Once the customer's needs are known, systems are established to manage all processes. The emphasis is on prevention of mistakes and poor quality products. The appropriate procedures are defined by those who have the responsibility to implement them within clear organisational guidelines.

There is no one model for the structure of TQM organisations; what is important is that the structure should facilitate the task and process. The theoretical structure of a TQM organisation involves a coalition of autonomous teams able to interact directly with the customer and with each other. These are all linked to senior management teams responsible for strategy.

TQM leaders have a vision which is articulated to the organisation. Leaders are creative and sensitive, empowering people through delegation and training. TQM leaders emphasise change, leading their organisation so as to become changing rather than changed. The organisation becomes a learning organisation, integrating personal and organisational development. The emphasis of TQM is therefore on the development of people, leaders as well as followers, in order to achieve personal and organisational goals.

Teams are fundamental to TQM. Members of TQM teams have explicit and shared values. Leadership is based on function and need rather than power and status. There is pride in belonging to the team, the aims and tasks are clear. Critically the team learns and develops by a process of continuous feedback and review. This process is characterised by a high degree of openness and candour. Essentially decisions are shared. Teams have full commitment, they are action focused. When TQM is applied to organisations teams make things happen!

Whether TQM would be applicable to your school or team would be dependent on its culture and ethos. The philosophy of TQM suggests that profound cultural changes are needed within organisations.

Teams and team leaders make TQM happen and, with full commitment, it works. The extent to which this is possible in education when there are such powerful external influences, e.g. government legislation, is questionable. However, middle managers should consider TQM principles within the context of their own practice. How do you relate to your senior management team? Where are you placed within the organisational structure of the school? How do you ensure the full participation of each member of the team you are leading?

The next section further considers teams and team roles. There is also a detailed analysis of teams in primary and secondary schools in Chapter Five.

Team and team roles: participation and delegation

It is axiomatic that the culture of schools is changing. Rapid changes to the curriculum and the devolution of management responsibilities from LEAs to schools have led to a shift in management styles. As illustrated in Table 2.1 (Knutton and Ireson, 1995, p. 61) a middle manager has to be adaptable – the emphasis is on flexibility, sharing, collaboration and empowerment. Middle managers will be responsible for a team which will have two distinct foci:

1. Day-to-day management of teaching, learning and resources. Collaboration on clearly defined tasks, monitoring and evaluation.

Table 2.1: The changing culture of schools

From:	To:
Fixed roles	Flexible roles
Individual responsibility	Shared responsibility
Autocratic	Collaborative
Control	Release
Power	Empowerment

2. Participation by representation in working groups set up by the senior management team to discuss specific tasks or directives from governing agencies or school policy groups.

How does a team leader lead?

Effective team leadership will produce effective teams and an effective school. A team leader has to be able to work in an open and honest manner. As professionals, teachers should value effective teamwork; schools are dependent on teamwork. As a leader, the middle manager will be concerned with the building blocks of teams. Etzioni (1964) identified indicators of true professionals (quoted in Holmes, 1993, p. 62) as:

- *access to specialised and discrete areas of knowledge and expertise*
- *a degree of control over entry to and discipline within the profession*
- *one-to-one client relationships.*

While these are debatable, the emphasis on the development of client relationship issues identifies teachers as professionals. As such they should develop as professional participants within their teams. A middle manager has a commitment to the professionalism of his/her colleagues.

West Sussex Advisory and Inspection Service (1994) provides a summary of the qualities required for **effective leadership**. These are based on a survey of middle managers and their staff during 1994 (reproduced by permission of the publisher, Advisory and Inspection Service, West Sussex County Council, West Street, Chichester PO19 1RF):

Personal qualities:

- *modelling professionalism, e.g. behaving with integrity, displaying consistency, being open and honest with colleagues, displaying firmness but fairness in their dealings with staff, hard working, committed, putting concern for students' well-being before personal advancement*
- *being well-organised and well-prepared*

- *being personable, approachable and accessible*
- *having a positive outlook and striving to act in a constructive manner, rather than being negative and overly critical*
- *manifesting confidence and calmness*
- *not standing on ceremony or taking advantage of their position; being prepared to help out or take their turn, if necessary.*

Managerial qualities:

- *formulating a vision for the future development of their school based on personal philosophy, beliefs and values*
- *displaying the capacity to think and plan strategically*
- *displaying a consultative style of management, with the aim of building consensus and at the same time empowering others; typically, determining overall direction and strategy, following wide consultation, and then handing over to staff to implement what has been agreed; effectively delegating responsibility to other people, though following through and requiring accountability*
- *ensuring that effective whole school structures are in place*
- *behaving forcefully yet not dictatorially; having the ability to drive things along, yet at the same time displaying sensitivity to staff feelings, circumstances and well-being; maintaining a good balance of pressure and support*
- *being prepared to embrace ultimate responsibility for the school and by manner and actions enabling staff to feel confident and secure*
- *displaying decisiveness when the situation demands*
- *paying attention to securing the support and commitment of colleagues and enjoying their trust; actively shaping the ethos and culture of the school and fashioning a sense of community*
- *being adept at communicating, and being a good listener as well as keeping people informed*
- *being seen to act on information and views deriving from staff, so that consultation was seen to be a meaningful exercise*
- *emphasising the central importance of quality in the school's operations and encouraging colleagues to aim high, discouraging complacency*
- *ensuring that they keep abreast of new initiatives, though taking care not to be seen to be 'jumping on bandwagons'; taking steps to prepare staff for future developments, thereby avoiding ad hoc decision-making and crisis management – though being sensitive to the risk of overwhelming colleagues with new practices*
- *revealing by their statements and actions that they are in touch with the main events in the everyday life of the school, and that they have their finger on the pulse of the school*

- *being proficient at motivating staff, e.g. by providing encouragement or active support, by acknowledging particular endeavour*
- *being able to convey to colleagues that they have their concerns and well-being at heart, and behaving in such a way as to demonstrate this, e.g. facilitating their development as professionals*
- *protecting staff from political wrangling and backing them publicly in any dispute involving external agencies.*

The local authority team also gathered evidence that determined **ineffective leaders**:

Personal qualities:

- *lacking dynamism and failing to inspire*
- *being insufficiently forceful*
- *failing to be at ease with others and to enable them to feel at ease, particularly in difficult and demanding situations*
- *inability to accept any form of questioning or perceived criticism.*

Managerial qualities:

- *being insufficiently decisive; although most teachers were adamant about the importance of consultation, there came a point where a firm decision needed to be taken*
- *either failing to delegate sufficiently or leaving staff too much to their concerns*
- *failing to unite the staff, and to build a sense of a community whose members were all pulling together*
- *failing to communicate effectively, e.g. with respect to their vision, specific objectives or reasons for a particularly contentious decision*
- *lacking proficiency in managing fellow professionals, e.g. being seen to carp at trivialities, behaving in a petty or patronising manner, treating colleagues as if they were children*
- *failing to display interest in and concern for staff, or to praise and celebrate their achievements*
- *being disorganised and insufficiently thorough, especially as regards administration.*

Teams

The process of managing a team is dependent on the task. The characteristics of effective teams are (Hall and Oldroyd, 1990c, pp. 34–5):

- **clear objectives and goals** – *according to task*
- **openness and confrontation** – *dependent on effective communication and interpersonal relationships*

- **support and trust** – *requiring active listening and understanding*
- **co-operation and conflict** – *working together, sharing and developing ideas in a democratic and creative manner*
- **sound procedures** – *enable everyone to contribute to decision-making*
- **appropriate leadership** – *knowing and understanding team members, their beliefs and values*
- **regular review** – *monitoring and evaluating in a rigorous manner*
- **individual development** – *enabling individuals to develop strengths, involving appraisal and staff development*
- **sound inter-group relations** – *a commitment to teaching pupils through openness and trust.*

In practice the emergence of management teams may be a response to the turbulence experienced in schools since the ERA (1988), but they could also provide a much needed career structure for professional teachers.

Participation and delegation

The opportunity to participate in decision-making teams which impact on school management is a relatively new phenomenon. In previous generations teachers were autonomous in their classrooms and, apart from crises, they were responsible for the management of their classroom and not much more. Middle managers must have the freedom to participate in decision-making; senior managers should not manage in a prescriptive manner.

As Caldwell and Spinks (1988, p. 8) described, *a self-managing school is an effective school*. The process is culturally different to previous practice as Knutton and Ireson (1995, p. 61) explained:

> *Leaders and senior managers relocate their 'power', and are then freed to guide new developments. Teachers are given **ownership** in some significant parts of their own working environment and are consequently **empowered** to act.*

This involves participation by team members and delegation from managers. For some middle managers participation and delegation can be difficult to manage. Reliance and dependency on colleagues can be perceived as a weakness. The closer the colleague is to the manager's practice, the more difficult management can become. However, these are not insurmountable problems. If a team is effective and has the characteristics and strengths listed above, participation and delegation will be necessary parts of team management.

Participation

A confident, open middle manager encourages participation which has meaning and relevance to daily practice. Middle managers should interpret participation in a genuine way, the process should not be mechanical. Participation can function in these forms:

- **consultation** – team members are invited to suggest ideas; decision-making remains the responsibility of the middle manager
- **consent** – team members, as a group, can veto any decision made by the middle manager
- **consensus** – team members are consulted, followed by whole team involvement in decision-making through majority vote.

A middle manager should be able to identify which participatory style is applicable to any specific task or situation. Democracy is fine if applicable; equally autocracy is acceptable and can work in the right circumstances. A middle manager will need to decide which style to adopt.

In practice, decisions may be beyond the mandate of the middle manager and his/her team. Senior management may be responsible for the initiation of policies, therefore leaving middle management to implement decisions which have been made by others. In this situation, participation is at an operational rather than strategic level.

Delegation

Both being led and leading will involve the middle manager in the process of delegation. Managers can save time by delegating tasks to colleagues or teams. There are several factors which need to be considered in the delegation process:

- **quality of the result** – will the outcome be good enough?
- **the ability of the individual** – how capable is the individual of completing the task?
- **your relationship** – will you be able to coach the individual or leave him/her to the task? Either could cause problems.
- **time** – have your staff the time to complete the task?

It is essential that any delegated work is clearly understood. As a middle manager, you need to ensure that you have the knowledge and understanding, skills and abilities to complete the task. When delegating, a middle manager should retain control over the work delegated, whether by instruction or participation. The Industrial Society (1982) provided the following advice:

Before beginning, make a job breakdown:
- *what do I do now?*
- *why do I do it?*

- *should I keep it, and why?*
- *to whom could I give the job now?*
- *who else should I be training to do it and how?*

Recognise tasks which cannot be delegated, such as:

- *matters essential to your overall control*
- *discipline over subordinate's own colleagues*
- *confidential, security and policy matters restricted to your own level.*

Prepare delegation plan indicating in detail:

- *tasks to be allocated to subordinate*
- *additional authority and resources needed*
- *additional training/experience needed.*

Instruct/coach subordinate:

- *ensure subordinate understands the limits of the delegation*
- *advise all connected personnel of the delegation*
- *give subordinate confidence by putting trust in him/her*
- *institute occasional spot checks to test effectiveness, but always with subordinate's knowledge*
- *appraise progress and set standards and targets progressively together*
- *revise your own and the subordinate's job descriptions when transfer of task is finally accomplished.*

In essence, delegation will enhance the quality of your work and that of your team. It will demonstrate a move from an autocratic style to a democratic style of management. It is worth noting that reluctant and poor delegation is often worse than no delegation at all. An example of delegation in practice is shown in Table 2.2. Should the member of staff have any problems with this process, (s)he would be able to consult the relevant middle manager.

Management behaviour

In practice, the way managers and their teams behave is dependent on numerous factors which influence individuals and impact on the lives of the people they contact. The majority of management activities involve contact with other people. Much of what is good and bad in management can be categorised according to the knowledge and understanding, skills and abilities of those involved.

Knowledge and understanding can focus the middle manager on knowing human behaviour, both individual and group. Skills and abilities will focus the

Table 2.2: Delegation in practice

Task:	Annual stocktake
Process:	Team member asked to: • audit stock used in current academic year • forecast stock budget for forthcoming year • plan implementation, e.g. stock control and storage
Timescale:	3 weeks
Number of staff:	4
Accountable to:	Subject co-ordinator
Report to:	Subject meeting
Outcome:	Budget plan for stock including: Budget review Budget forecast Budget implementation Stock keeping record procedures

middle manager on the effectiveness of the team, its skills and abilities to complete tasks and deal with situations.

Motivation

Human motivation is central to the management of staff. Middle managers should have the knowledge and understanding of how to provide their staff with meaningful work. School middle managers will have little difficulty in identifying the teaching elements which colleagues find satisfying and rewarding. Identification of motivational factors beyond the classroom will be challenging, involving managerial skills and abilities. In brief, several models exist which can be summarised as follows (from *Writers on Organisations*, Pugh and Hickson, 1989):

The social model (Mayo, 1933):

• people are motivated by social needs, friendship and acceptance; their basic sense of identity is formed through relationships with other people
• people are responsive to peer group pressure
• people are responsive to management if management meets their needs (belonging, etc.).

The rational-economic model (Taylor, 1947):

- people act to maximise their financial and material rewards
- people will perform specialised tasks for high rewards.

Self-actualising model (Maslow, 1943):

- hierarchical needs
- people work to develop skills
- people are self-motivated and self-controlled
- people will integrate their goals with those of the organisation.

A middle manager with knowledge and understanding of the above will have a framework in which to place the members of his/her team. While the advantages of each model can be debated, an awareness of a manager's need to understand what motivates his/her team is both relevant and important.

There is a vast amount of human behaviour literature which focuses on needs and motivational factors without appearing dismissive of alternative theories. Maslow's hierarchy of needs (1943) serves as an introduction to the analysis of human behaviour. The model is also accessible to practitioners who can identify with the developmental approach. He suggested that there are five levels of need that influence an individual's behaviour:

- *physiological needs* – food, drink and shelter
- *safety needs* – protection against danger, threat and deprivation
- *social needs* – to associate, have relationships, affection, belonging
- *'ego' needs* – self-esteem, reputation, status
- *'self-actualisation'* – the needs for realising one's own potential for continual self-development.

According to Maslow, the needs hierarchy means that the lower-order needs have to be satisfied first. In behavioural terms these determine the needs that motivate individuals (see Figure 2.3).

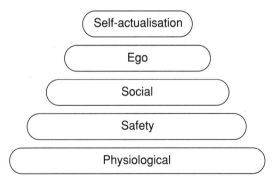

Figure 2.3: Maslow's hierarchy of needs (Maslow, 1970)

Essentially teachers and managers have needs, as Maslow (1943) stated:

> *A musician must make music, an artist must paint, a poet must write, if he is to be ultimately happy [. . .] This need we may call self-actualisation.*

What type of manager are you ?

This leads to the question: 'What type of manager are you?' McGregor as described in Pugh and Hickson (1989, p. 158) defined a model, Theory X and Theory Y, which can be applied to school managers. It is based on the following assumptions:

Theory X:

- the average human being has an inherent dislike of work and will avoid it, if [at all] possible [. . .]
- because of this, [. . .] most people must be coerced, controlled, directed or threatened with punishment [in order to work]
- the average human being prefers to be directed, [. . .] wishes to avoid responsibility, has [. . .] little ambition [and] wants security above all [else].

The antithesis of Theory X is Theory Y:

- [. . .] the ordinary person does not inherently dislike work: according to the conditions, it may be a source of satisfaction or punishment
- [. . .] people will exercise self-direction and self-control in the service of objectives to which they are committed
- [. . .] the average human being learns, under proper conditions, not only to accept but to seek responsibility
- [. . .] many more people are able to contribute creatively to the solution of organisational problems than do so.

When applied to middle management (Hall and Oldroyd, 1990c, p. 35), a Theory X manager will be less likely to be committed to a team approach. McGregor found that, in many situations, managers who used Theory Y assumptions achieved better results. In sum, understanding of the management process and application of knowledge with skill and ability produces team effectiveness.

How do effective teams operate?

Perhaps the most positive model of effective school teams is provided by Caldwell and Spinks (1988) as outlined in Chapter One. Following research into the introduction of collaborative school management, Spinks (1990, pp. 140-1) was able to identify its advantages. In brief:

- *information is readily available to all concerned*
- *policies and learning activities for students are clearly linked together*
- *it is easy for participants to see the relevance of their work to the overall process of providing an education to meet student needs*
- *participants gain satisfaction and develop commitment as they are able to participate in a way that is relevant to them*
- *most of the operations involved already exist in the school – policies, plans, budgets and evaluations*
- *provides a clear method for accountability*
- *openness of information is guaranteed*
- *teams co-operate to benefit each other rather than to compete for resources*
- *the overall process is clear and easily understood*
- *there is inbuilt flexibility within programmes to respond immediately to new or emerging student needs.*

Concerns were also identified by Spinks, namely time and overload. Managers will always face dilemmas and concerns; these are part of the job. Middle managers will need to identify problems before they arise; alternatively they will also need to deal effectively with problems as they arise.

Management accountability

Education reflects society and as society becomes increasingly more complex, education managers encounter many new (and challenging) values and expectations. As their environment changes teachers and teacher managers are increasingly accountable for their actions. A middle manager is accountable to his/her leaders and to those he/she leads. Accountability takes many forms:

- *pupils* – lesson content, examination results and attendance
- *parents* – reporting, consultation and pupil support
- *colleagues* – teaching, management of staff and situations
- *senior management* – participation and delegation, team effectiveness, teaching, results, league tables
- *governors* – results, league tables
- *government* – results, league tables
- *inspectorate/advisors* – all of the above.

Middle management should use accountability in a positive manner, trumpet success, understand accountability. There is little to be gained from viewing the tools of accountability with fear and anxiety.

Managing staff under-performance

Disciplinary procedures

Middle managers should be aware of their responsibilities relating to under-performance of staff in schools. The governing body has full responsibility for the management of staff. In LMS, the LEA has the right to give advice throughout any disciplinary procedures. Critically, governors must be aware of employment protection legislation and statutory rights of employees. The governors of all schools should be aware of the Advisory Conciliation and Arbitration Service (ACAS) code and particularly the essential features of disciplinary procedures. In sum, the governing body:

- is responsible for the school's disciplinary rules and procedures
- and together with the headteacher has the power to suspend staff
- has the power to lift a suspension
- must provide the right of an appeal.

Disciplinary rules set out the standards of conduct including what behaviour is considered by the governors to be misconduct and gross misconduct. The stages of dealing with misconduct are:

- verbal warning
- first written warning (from the headteacher) – no right of appeal
- final written warning (from the headteacher) – right of appeal
- dismissal by a panel of governors
- right of appeal to a second panel of governors.

Each stage of dealing with misconduct will be varied according to circumstances. At each stage, the employee has a right:

- to know the full accusation
- to have the matter properly investigated
- to be heard
- to be accompanied at the hearing and to call witnesses
- a right of appeal to the appeals panel of governors.

Avoiding under-performance

Everyone's performance is variable. Managers should be able to recognise and reverse the downward slide. This will only happen when teachers work in a 'no blame' culture. There is a need to emphasise appraisal and continuous professional development within the context of under-performance. As a manager, you must identify the problem in consultation with the member of staff concerned. The member of staff should then be in a position to comment on their practice in order to contribute to the setting of realistic targets. It is essential to identify who will provide the necessary support, how and when. Professional discussions with colleagues should include identification of:

- the problem
- targets
- review date
- support
- monitoring.

Good relationships will lead to good practice. Identification of a problem in a culture of trust will enable an early resolution. Lengthy processes and negotiations will only lead to stress for all involved.

Stress

A manager is exposed to many dangers in his/her working life. Middle managers are constantly challenged within the workplace. However, challenges are on a continuum from excitement to excessive tiredness (see Figure 2.4).

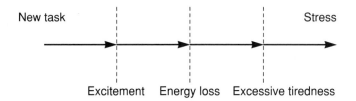

Figure 2.4: Stress levels

A manager's ability to monitor and evaluate is critical within this framework of experience. Individuals should know their energy levels. If a challenge cannot be met and creates energy loss, inevitably stress will occur. The consequences of stress can be debilitating. Stress can be exhibited in many ways, e.g. irritability, tiredness, excessive drinking, depression. Managers should be aware of stress in the workplace; it is important to identify and support those who find work stressful. It is also important to acknowledge personal stress levels.

Stress can be overcome if the imbalances that exist are redressed, e.g. increase low energy levels. Managers must look after their own welfare, and remain in control. Control may also mean evaluating how you use your time, ensuring

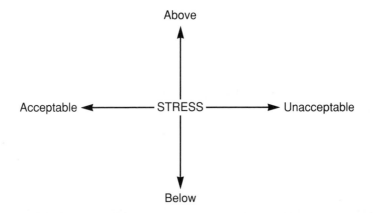

Figure 2.5: A model of stress levels

that no one activity makes excessive demands on your time. Time management, monitoring and evaluation are examined in more detail later in this book.

More specifically, a model of stress will serve to illustrate the effect of stress in a middle manager's working life (see Figure 2.5).

The following levels are described by Lifeskills Associates (1995a):

1. *Optimum level* – when middle managers and teachers are at their optimum level they are likely to be alert and self-confident. In practice, they will think and respond quickly, perform well, feel well and be enthusiastic, interested and involved in the task which they will carry out in an energetic, easy manner.

2. *Over-stressed* – alternatively when middle managers and teachers are over-stressed they are likely to have feelings of anxiety and mental confusion. In this condition they will not think effectively or solve problems clearly or objectively. They will forget instructions, and be inclined to panic. Physically, there will be symptoms such as increased heart rate and blood pressure, excessive perspiration, churning stomach and indigestion. In addition co-ordination will be impaired and reflexes slowed.

3. *Under-stressed* – if middle managers and teachers are under-stressed they are likely to experience a lack of interest or enthusiasm for the task. They can have feelings of futility or depression and believe that nothing matters any more – even a simple job can seem a huge task. They will be bored and lacking in energy. To them the world will look drab and grey and it will be hard to summon up energy to start new jobs or create fresh interests.

In her *Times Educational Supplement (TES)* (16.2.96) review of 'What Really Stresses Teachers', Emma Burstall highlighted the following causes of stress in teachers:

Work	*Home*
• lack of time to do the job	• worries about own children
• lack of parental support	• worries about elderly parents
• lack of resources	• lack of time with family
• national curriculum/irrelevant paperwork	• untidiness of others
	• family illnesses
• rate of change	• housework
• lack of LEA support	• guilt over not meeting all family's demands
• poor status of profession	
• staff relationships	• in-laws
• government interference	• having to take work home
• pressure of meetings	• lack of private space

Having identified the causes, a middle manager should then attempt to manage stress. Brown and Ralph (1995, pp. 95–105) offer the following advice:

1. *Examining beliefs and expectations* – are these realistic and achievable? Is there a need to set more attainable goals?

2. *Time management* – can time be used more effectively? Techniques such as prioritisation, delegation, objective setting can be considered.

3. *Assertion* – learning how to communicate more confidently at all levels and to deal positively with conflict.

4. *Communication* – looking at patterns of interpersonal communication and self-presentation skills.

5. *Relaxation techniques* of all kinds, such as physical exercise, meditation, yoga, aromatherapy and collection of bio-data.

6. *Support networks* – it is important to build and maintain support networks of family, friends and colleagues, both within and outside school.

Brown and Ralph also indicate the importance of how the school as an organisation can help teachers to address the problem of stress. They suggest a variety of ways in which middle and senior managers can approach this issue:

• helping to de-stigmatise the idea of stress by putting it on the agenda for discussion

• encouraging the establishment of self-help groups to explore group problem-solving of school stress factors and to develop appropriate solutions where possible

• developing an empathetic ethos and offering support for self-help management techniques

• identifying and liaising with people who can help within the local education authority and other relevant organisations

- drawing up a school action plan after school-wide staff consultation. Factors to consider might include workloads, resources, discipline, relationships, environment, career progression, future staff development and training needs, parental and community pressure
- providing appropriate staff development, either within the school or at an outside venue
- making available information about counselling services and encouraging staff to use them where necessary.

In sum, Brown and Ralph (1992, 1994, 1995) found that teachers are unable to de-stigmatise stress and that organisational needs must be met before personal needs. Change issues also emerge as a significant factor in contributing to stress levels in schools.

Brown and Ralph (1995, p. 105) conclude that teachers *need to recognise and analyse openly for themselves, signs [of] [. . .] stress [. . .] at work.* They emphasise the need for an organisational approach to the management of stress. In particular, *teachers need to be reassured that they will not lose professional esteem or promotional opportunities by admitting to stress.* This should also apply to middle managers in practice.

Summary

When moving to middle management, a period of reflection is required in order to analyse the implications of your new position within the school management structure. Middle managers in schools are very much player managers participating in the daily tasks of teaching while fulfilling the role of team leader/manager. There is a distinctive status to being a manager; it is important to identify what this means early in your management career. It is essential to know your role, know your team and know your managers.

There are many definitions of leadership in management literature. In essence, theorists define leaders as those within an organisation with power and influence. Middle managers as leaders do things, or as managers get others to do things. Individual managers will decide on their own leadership style. Management styles will differ according to the leader, the led, the task and the context (Tannenbaum and Schmidt, 1973).

TQM offers an alternative model of management practice which should be considered by middle managers: value-driven and team-based.

The culture of schools is changing, and a middle manager has to be adaptable; the emphasis is on flexibility, sharing, collaboration and empowerment.

Effective team leadership produces effective teams and an effective school. Middle managers need to develop personal and managerial qualities related to their position. Effective teams and leaders have clear objectives and sound procedures. They exist in a climate of openness, support and trust. As a consequence there are sound inter-group relations.

Participation and delegation are made possible in such environments. Participation involves consultation in order to gain consent or a consensus. A middle manager will need to decide which participating style is applicable to their team: democracy or autocracy. Delegation will enhance the quality of your work and that of your teams. Should a member of staff have any problems with this process, (s)he would be able to consult the relevant middle manager.

Human motivation is central to the management of staff. There are several theories which focus on analysis of needs. A middle manager should have an understanding of what motivates his/her team.

In order to determine how to motivate your team you will need to define what type of manager you are. McGregor (1966) offers a Theory X and Theory Y model based on an individual's attitude to work. Effective teams will operate with effective management. This will involve an understanding of how to manage under-performance.

Finally, middle managers need to recognise and analyse for themselves, the signs of stress at work.

3
∎ ∎ ∎

Vision and Missions

Introduction

A vision will move an organisation forward from where it is now to where it would like to be. A precise goal is more credible than a vague dream. A vision should be realistic and attractive to all members of the organisation. As a condition, a vision should be more desirable in many important ways than that which currently exists. A specific definition of vision within the context of schools would be the schools aims. These are notably achievement orientated and, as such, should be shared by all members of the school community.

Missions will provide a clear sense of direction and purpose. These are a means of creating operational plans: objectives or targets to be met by members of the school community.

To anyone who has worked in a number of schools it is evident that each will have its own atmosphere, characteristics and personality. An understanding of the culture of schools is required before considering the purpose of visions and missions. Schools are often referred to in much the same way as people. However, schools do not consist of homogeneous groups of people with shared identities; in contrast some schools are collections of individuals within a shared culture. The culture of each school is determined by sets of values and beliefs. Values and beliefs are at the root of a school's vision. Structure and systems provide the way in which a school chooses to carry out its activities or vision. The vision for the school is contained in policy statements which emerge from the collective values and beliefs held by the school's population.

Although policy statements may appear to be static and dry, with little relevance to the daily routine of staff and pupils, they provide the rationale for practice. Vision statements and policy documents will also provide an insight into the ethos of the school – that which is distinctive in character, often intangible. As a middle manager you will have an image of how you would like your team to operate, a vision that will reflect the vision for the whole school.

A School Development Plan (SDP) will define and describe how the school will operate as an organisation. The SDP reflects the vision, encompassing the values and beliefs of those participating in the daily management of the school: teaching and non-teaching staff. SDPs are discussed in more detail in Chapter Seven.

Cultures

The culture of a school is its 'personality', the way that work is done. Every school is different and has slightly different expectations of its management. In her article, 'To strengthen the mixture, first understand the chemistry', Nancy Foy (1981) suggested reasons why managers should try to understand the culture of their organisation. In brief:

1. Managers will be better able to relate to the organisation if they appreciate its nature.

2. Managers may be able to predict the behaviour of people in the organisation, thereby making the managers more effective.

A school culture will manifest itself in many forms:

- **practice** – rites, rituals and ceremonies
- **communications** – stories, myths, sagas, legends, folk tales, symbols and slogans
- **physical forms** – location, style and condition of the school buildings, fixtures and fittings
- **common language** – phrases or jargon common to the school.

Within each culture, sub-cultures exist with their own sets of characteristics. The school culture may be the dominant culture. In contrast, subject or year teams may create their own sub-cultures.

Handy offers a means of understanding the culture of organisations by identifying common characteristics. Handy (1993) in *Understanding Organisations* identified three concepts of organisations: power, people and politics. Handy believed that the concepts should:

- *help to explain the past, which in turn*
- *helps to understand the present, and thus*
- *to predict the future, which leads to*
- *more influence over future events, and*
- *less disturbance from the unexpected.*

He stated that the analytical task of the manager is to:

- *identify the key variables of any situation,*
- *predict the probable outcomes of any changes in the variables*
- *select the ones [s/]he can and should influence.*

More specifically, Handy perceived organisations as:

- *collections of individuals*
- *political systems*

joined together by:

- *power and influence.*

Handy (1993, p.182) described how organisations differ according to the way they work, levels of authority, formality and control, how much planning, financial matters, rules and results. Handy also described the impact of the building; schools can certainly offer variety here.

Most significantly, Handy focuses on the people within organisations, as it is people who create and work within the culture of an organisation. Handy (pp. 183–91) defined four cultures which could provide a framework for analysing practice:

- power culture
- role culture
- task culture
- person culture.

Each list may contain elements that apply to your school. There may be other characteristics which could be applied. Equally, the characteristics may be more observable at different periods of the school day, week or year!

1. The power culture

- small entrepreneurial organisations
- web shape in design
- patron god would be Zeus – the god of the broad light of day
- culture depends on a central power source, rays of power and influence spreading out from the central figure

- organisation dependent on trust and empathy for effectiveness
- communication dependent on telepathy and personal conversation
- if whoever is at the centre of the web chooses the right people, they can be left to get on with the job
- few rules and procedures – little bureaucracy

- control is exercised by the centre, by occasional forays from the centre or summonses to the centre
- proud and strong, can move quickly in response to threat or danger – the type of movement will depend on the person(s) at the centre
- the quality of the person(s) at the centre is of paramount importance
- individuals employed by them will prosper and be satisfied, if they are power-orientated, politically minded and rate risk-taking as important
- resource power (financial and human) is the major power base
- limited security
- size – the web can break if it seeks to be involved in too many activities
- faith in the individual not in committees
- judges by results and is tolerant of the means
- low morale and high turnover in the middle layers – too competitive.

2. *The role culture*

- stereotyped as bureaucratic
- can be pictured as a Greek temple
- patron god is Apollo – the god of reason
- logic and rationality
- strength is in its pillars

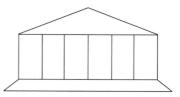

- the work of pillars, and the interaction between the pillars, is controlled by:
  - procedures for roles (job descriptions, authority decisions)
  - procedures for communications (required sets of memos)
  - rules for the settlement of disputes
- co-ordinated at the top by a narrow band of senior managers
- role or job description is more important than the individual
- individuals are selected for satisfactory performance in the role
- performance over and above the role is not required
- position power is the major power source
- personal power is frowned upon and expert power is only tolerated
- rules and procedures are the major methods of influence
- needs a stable environment, e.g. civil service
- offers security and predictability – clear career path
- economies of scale are more important than flexibility
- slow to perceive the need for change
- change may lead to collapse and the need for new management.

3. *The task culture*

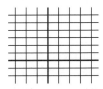

- job or project orientated
- structure best described as a net
- some strands of the net are thicker and stronger than others
- emphasis on getting the job done
- influence is placed on expert power more than on person power
- utilises the unifying power of the group to ensure that individuals identify with the objective of the organisation
- groups, project teams or task forces for a specific purpose
- high degree of control over work
- easy working relationships within the group with mutual respect based upon capacity rather than age or status
- appropriate where flexibility and sensitivity are important
- limited depth of expertise
- thrives where speed of reaction, integration, sensitivity and creativity are important
- control is difficult – by allocation of projects
- little day-to-day management
- preferred by middle managers
- lack of resources can lead to political problems
- not always the appropriate culture for the climate and the technology.

4. *The person culture*

- unusual, individuals may cling to its values
- the individual is the central point
- it exists only to serve and assist the individuals within it
- structure best described as a cluster
- control mechanisms are impossible
- influence is shared; the power-base is usually expert, individuals do what they are good at
- generally only the creator achieves success
- individuals may exist in other cultures – not easy to manage
- little influence can be brought on them, not easily impressed.

Managers should note that each culture is as bad as it is effective. Essentially, organisational culture will vary; schools are complex organisations with management structures that are determined by and are a reflection of the dominant culture.

In most schools, middle managers will need to understand the culture in the same way that they need to understand their own personalities. Middle managers will need to identify the culture of the schools in which they work; they should also identify the culture in which their team works. This will be according to the collective beliefs and values of the school community and their relationship to the community's own beliefs and values. As a sub-culture, do the characteristics and practice of the team reflect the culture of the school or do they differ in any way? Middle managers represent school management within the context of their team. These must be compatible in order to succeed.

As a middle manager it is unlikely that you will be in a position to change your school's culture. However, as a manager of a team or department, you will be in a position to influence or change its sub-culture.

Effective schools require collective practices. Individuality may generate creativity; however, if the individual's values and beliefs are the antithesis of the organisation's values and beliefs, this will result in anarchist behaviour. Conflict will inevitably ensue!

Organisational structure

Organisational design or structure is essential for the efficient and effective management of a school. This applies to all schools, small or large. The organisational structure of the school will determine levels of responsibility. Laurie Mullins (1993) described organisational structure:

Structure is the pattern of relationships among positions in the organisation and among members of the organisation. The purpose of structure is the division of work among members of the organisation and the co-ordination of their activities so they are directed towards achieving the goals and objectives of the organisation. The structure defines tasks and responsibility, work roles and relationships, and channels of communication.

There are several models of organisations which are pictorial representations of an organisation's formal structure. As a middle manager you should know which model applies to your school and where you are within the structure. Poor or inappropriate structures will generate poor practice.

As a manager you will also be part of the school's organisational structure. Theorists suggest that an interlinked span of control is the most effective structure for schools. This contrasts with tall and flat structures currently found in schools.

To elaborate, an over-emphasis on management through the creation of excessive numbers of working groups and management teams can result in bad practice. Alternatively, good practice is shown in Figure 3.1. Work is interlinked, therefore management of tasks, control and direction can be difficult. Further models of school management structures illustrate the diversity of practice that exists in schools (see Figures 3.2 and 3.3).

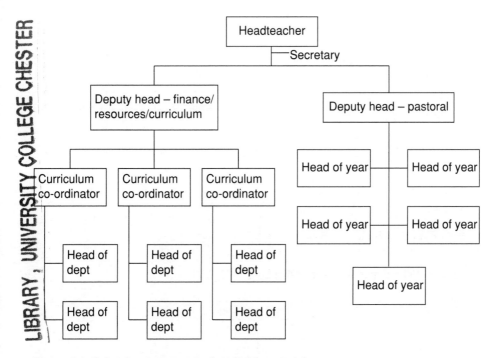

Figure 3.1: School management – interlinking model

A tall structure is hierarchical in practice (Figure 3.2). The antithesis of a tall structure is a flat structure (Figure 3.3). This limits the need for pastoral and academic managers, thus reducing the number of middle managers employed. As a model, this may be more representative of a primary school structure and practice.

In recent years, models of school management have tended to become flatter. This avoids the problems of tall structures, where there are too many layers of management and there is a tendency for needless bureaucracy. Flatter organisations can change and react more quickly in the increasingly dynamic and ever changing working environment of education. Interestingly, flatter organisations have a tendency to force managers into delegation, because of the enlarged managerial span of control.

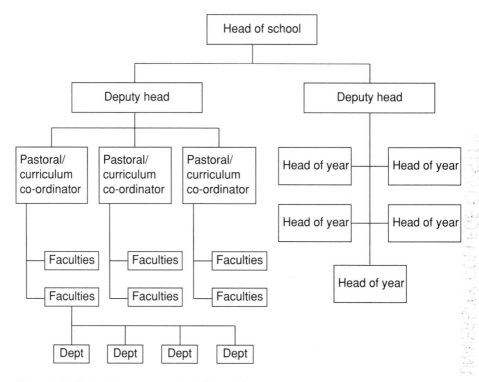

Figure 3.2: School management – tall model

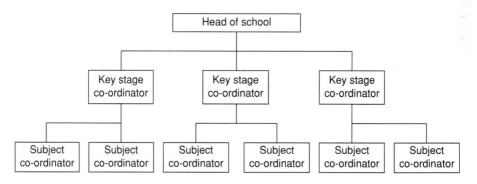

Figure 3.3: School management – flat model

Collaboration framework

A collaborative framework has been designed by Caldwell and Spinks (1988) in Chapman (1990, p. 124) and shown in Figure 3.4. The specific purposes to be achieved in collaborative decision-making at school level are (Spinks, 1990, p. 122):

- *to provide an approach to school management which clearly focuses on learning and teaching (the central issues of any school)*

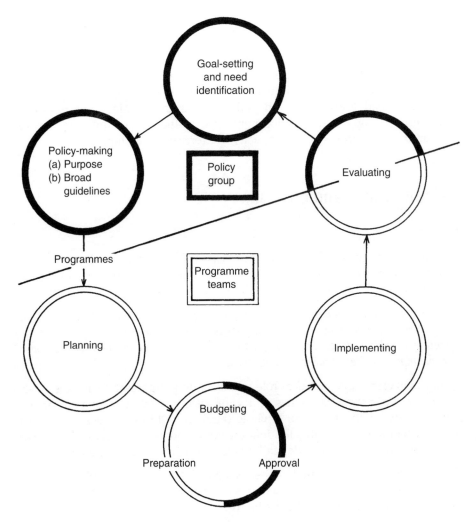

Figure 3.4: Collaborative framework (Caldwell and Spinks, 1988, p. 37. Reproduced by permission of the publisher, Falmer Press Ltd, Taylor & Francis Group, 1 Gunpowder Square, London EC4A 3DE.)

- *to facilitate sharing in the decision-making processes and the involvement of all possible participants in appropriate ways*
- *to identify clearly the management tasks and to provide direct and easily understood links between them and information about them*
- *to identify clearly responsibilities for decision-making and activities, and to demonstrate lines of accountability*
- *to provide a means to relate resource allocations of all kinds to learning priorities for students*
- *to facilitate evaluation and review processes with the emphasis on further improving opportunities for students*

- to limit documentation to simple, clear statements that can easily be prepared by those involved in their already busy schedules.

In the context of management structures for school cultures, the above model is more flexible and would be appropriate to the majority of schools. As Spinks (1990, p. 145) stated, *the model* is just a starting point. If managers are to make it work they need knowledge and skills related to 'learning and teaching', curriculum design and development, the gathering of information for programme evaluation and the capacity to exercise leadership.

Defining vision and mission

Vision

Although management literature emphasises the need for vision in organisations, vision is often an intangible, difficult and ambiguous concept. Bennis and Nanus (1985) in Caldwell and Spinks (1988, p. 174) describe a vision:

> as a mental image of a possible and desirable future state of the organisation [. . .] as vague as a dream or as precise as a goal or mission statement [. . .] a view of a realistic, credible, attractive future for the organisation, a condition that is better in some important ways than what now exists.

School managers have a critical role in articulating organisational goals. These will reflect your personal values and your vision or mission for your area of responsibility, or the school as a whole (Hall and Oldroyd, 1990a, p. 29). The headteacher has responsibility for defining your school's vision or aims. Your participation in this process will depend on the culture and management practices.

This stresses the relationship between what is desired and the defined goals as a route to achieving it. As each school's culture is distinctive, school vision or mission statements will also be distinctive.

When preparing the school prospectus, headteachers may create statements which fail to reflect the culture of the school. Headteachers may also fail to consider seriously the implications of such statements (Holmes, 1993, p. 18). Statements about the purpose of the school must be meaningful to teachers and must be explicit in professional practice (Holmes, 1993, p. 35).

In order to become a reality, vision statements must be realistic and attainable, a summary of what is achievable within the culture and climate of the school. Hoyle (1986, p. 103) states that to be effective, the school manager or leader must:

> [. . .] grasp the configuration of forces at work in the environment, to construct an achievable mission[/vision] – the art of the possible – to convey this mission to others often through the skilful use of language and symbol, and to obtain commitment to the mission.

If a school is to be successful, it has to be effective. A measure of a school's effectiveness is the ability of the staff to work towards achieving the school's vision, i.e. working towards a shared set of values and beliefs. The vision statement should be succinct and should contain, within a few words, the philosophy underlying professional practice within the school.

A vision must be clear and comprehensible to all: teachers, parents, pupils, governors, visitors, etc. A school's vision statement is not a party political statement, it does not require the fervour and charisma of political rhetoric. School vision statements should direct the school's population towards a common purpose.

Identifying shared values is central to generating a vision for the school. Based on past and present they should reflect what is good within the school. A genuinely good school with shared values and beliefs will be an effective school. Characteristics such as openness and trust are attainable within a culture of openness and trust.

Visions must be shared; it is the headteacher's responsibility to share the creation of a vision for the school with colleagues. It is the responsibility of managers to ensure that visions 'happen'. Knowledge and understanding of a school's vision by staff is central to the success of the school. A shared vision will provide a framework for practice. When shared, the vision can be debated and developed. Monitoring and evaluation of values and beliefs through the sharing process should be common practice in schools.

Vision is fundamental to the success of the school. Figures 3.5–3.8 show examples of effective vision statements that are representative of special, primary and secondary schools.

The school is able to meet the many varying needs of the hearing impaired child by offering a wide range of provision that includes departments located in mainstream schools, an individualised integration scheme, an advisory teacher service and an administrative and resource centre.

The school believes that the development of communication, learning and awareness through education and integration enables the child to play a full and successful part in society.

The school aims to ensure that equal curricular opportunity is genuinely available to both boys and girls and believes that all children should be educated for living in a multi-cultural, multi-racial society.

All pupils are encouraged to develop their full potential whatever their capacity to learn, through an understanding of the world, the acquisition of knowledge and the development of skills relevant to life.

Figure 3.5: School A – school and service aims

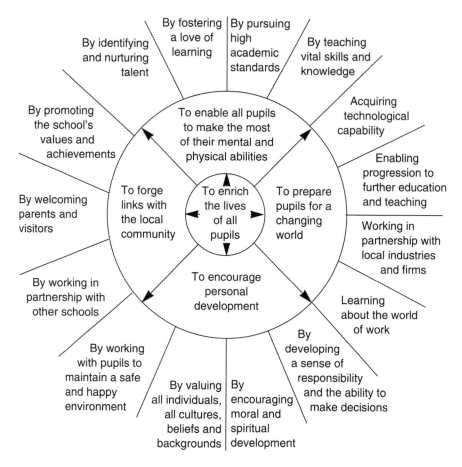

Figure 3.6: School B – aims

Mission

A school's mission statement will provide the framework in which a vision can become a reality. A mission statement is therefore operational. In practice, it is very easy for a school to lose its overall direction because it is unsure about what kind of school it is, and what it is trying to do. Middle managers have a significant role in the realisation of mission statements, ensuring that things get done and that targets are achieved. Figure 3.9 is an example of good practice outside education, the Grampian Health Board adopted a 'management approach' to their mission statement (Fullerton and Price, 1991).

We seek to:

1. Create a happy, friendly, caring and welcoming school that will provide for pupils' needs in a sensitive way.
2. Foster a positive self-image in pupils, building self-confidence through praise and encouragement.
3. Encourage a positive attitude to life and learning, enabling each pupil to reach his/her full educational potential.
4. Prepare pupils for leaving and participation in society by teaching the appropriate social, independence and academic skills.
5. Ensure that all pupils and staff feel valued, and that any prejudice is challenged on all levels.
6. Promote an atmosphere of co-operation, with governors, staff, parents/carers and pupils working together as a school.
7. Develop links with the wider community, exploring integration for pupils wherever possible.
8. Provide a broad curriculum which encourages aesthetic, physical, academic and social development while meeting the requirements of the national curriculum.

Figure 3.7: School C – aims

We try to be a caring school where every child will feel secure, happy and valued and where purposeful learning can take place. We want the children to be happy at school and we want learning at school to be a positive experience [...] We aim at happy and hardworking children who are proud of their achievements.

Figure 3.8: School D – prospectus

A mission statement describes the way in which an organisation has chosen to conduct its activities. The extent to which the middle manager participates in this process will be determined by:

- how much authority the manager has to make decisions
- how many staff each manager has to manage
- level of staff specialisation
- clear job descriptions for all staff
- clear lines of communication relating to the manager's team.

As managers we are committed to:

- improving the quality and delivery of care
- ensuring that staff are briefed on the board's objectives and are clear about their own limits of authority
- utilising to the maximum the skills of our staff
- encouraging staff to take decisions for themselves within the limits of their authority
- concentrating on achievement
- encouraging individuals to find solutions rather than putting forward problems
- fostering the building of teams to promote achievement
- increased participation in 'Resourcing Grampian' (a performance improvement training programme)
- encourage a sense of belonging to a unit/department
- being supportive to staff in their endeavours, allowing them an opportunity of putting forward their views and encouraging their initiative.

Figure 3.9: Grampian Health Board mission statement

The National Commission on Education (NCE) identified 11 effective schools in disadvantaged areas of England and Wales. The subsequent report, *Success Against the Odds* (1996), includes examples of good practice for teachers and managers, primary and secondary. The curriculum statement given in Figure 3.10 from a Welsh primary school stresses the importance of matching work to the ability, needs and readiness of children, of ensuring that the skills taught are both extended and applied, and of having expectations of pupils' performance which are realistically high. As a mission statement, it sets out aims to help all children realise their potential (NCE, 1996, pp. 80–1). Essentially the school staff recognised that the translation of ideas and principles in the practical day-to-day task of teaching demanded extensive curriculum planning.

Informal Structures

Before concluding visions and missions, there are aspects of school culture and management which are less formal than those described so far. Middle managers need to be aware of the impact of informal structures on formal activities.

Burns, as described in Pugh and Hickson in *Writers on Organisation* (1989), suggested that the effect of an organisation's structure goes well beyond the allocation of work and management. Burns noted the importance of political

- to ensure that each child has a command of language and the ability to communicate effectively and confidently in reading, writing, speaking and listening
- to develop a knowledge and understanding of basic mathematical facts and concepts and of how to use them
- to encourage scientific curiosity and to organise observational studies, particularly in the local environment
- to awaken children's awareness to their heritage, both local and national, and to give some understanding of their place in the world
- to give an understanding of moral and ethical codes, religious beliefs and ideas, and of how to live with others
- to teach skills and the appreciation of aesthetic qualities in the creative arts: art, craft, music and drama
- to develop and maintain a healthy body by providing enjoyment in physical activities
- to create a happy school environment
- to help children learn that courtesy, good manners and consideration for others are very important qualities and to make each child a responsible member of the school community and also of the wider community
- to encourage children to develop a habit of learning and to develop a lively enquiring mind and a co-operative attitude towards all the people who are working for the successful achievement of these aims.

Figure 3.10: Welsh primary school mission statement

and career structures. Political structures inside organisations tend to be informal – corridor and staffroom politics, networks which develop organically between those who share contacts or information and advice. This may occur without the knowledge of those involved!

Equally, career structures can be formal or informal. Although the Teacher Training Agency (TTA) plans to develop a programme for the Continuing Professional Development (CPD) of teachers, past practice has been less structured. Middle managers should develop career planning skills for the benefit of themselves and their teams.

Every member of staff in a school will have his/her own agenda, a career to pursue, a team to manage, a view or an interpretation of what the school should be doing – their own beliefs and values. People think and sometimes act in different ways. Managers will have to be aware of the inevitability of such differences.

Summary

A specific definition of vision within the context of schools would be the school's aims. A vision will move an organisation forward from where it is now to where it would like to be.

Missions provide a clear sense of direction and purpose. These are means of creating operational plans, objectives or targets to be met by members of the school community.

The culture of a school is its 'personality', the way that work is done. Every school is different and has slightly different expectations of its management. A school culture will manifest itself through practice, communication, physical forms and a common language. Handy (1993) defines an organisation according to its culture. His definitions of power, role, task and person culture provide a framework for the middle manager. It is highly unlikely that you will be able to influence or change the culture of your school.

As a manager you will also be part of the school organisational structure. Theorists suggest that an interlinked span of control is the most effective structure for schools. This contrasts with tall and flat structures currently found in schools.

Visions are set within the culture and organisational structure of a school. Vision statements must be realistic and attainable. Visions must be shared; the monitoring and evaluation of values and beliefs through the sharing process should be common practice in schools.

A school's mission statement will provide the framework in which a vision can become a reality. A mission statement is operational, it describes the way in which an organisation has chosen to conduct its activities.

The effect of an organisation's structure goes well beyond the allocation of work and management. Every member of staff in a school will have his/her agenda. Managers will have to be aware of the inevitability of such differences.

4

■ ■ ■

Communication

Effective communication

Middle managers will communicate with colleagues, parents, pupils and other agencies; therefore communication is central to effective school operations. According to Hoy and Miskel (1991) in National Policy Board for Educational Administration's (NPBEA) *Principles for our Changing Schools* (1993, 16–4):

> *communication underlies all organisational and administrative situations, and is essential to decision-making and effective leadership. [. . .] At the heart of communication lies the opportunity to resolve contradictions, quell rumours, provide reassurance, and, ultimately, instil meaning in the complex but engaging task of education (National Leadership Network, 1991).*

In schools, teachers and managers use different methods of communication for different purposes; some are more successful than others. Why is it that communication always seems to flow more smoothly in some schools, teams and departments than others? One reason is the current and/or established communication climate. The conditions in which ideas, information and feelings are exchanged directly influence the extent to which communication is a positive or negative force in a school. In practice, middle managers may make decisions 'on the hoof' without consulting colleagues. While necessary, this may not always be the appropriate means of managing your team.

An open or supportive communication climate promotes co-operative working relationships, leading to effective information-gathering and transfer. Supportiveness is communicated most clearly by the following kinds of responses (NPBEA, 1993, 16–4):

- **descriptive** – statements are informative not evaluative
- **solution-orientated** – there is a focus on problem-solving rather than on what cannot be done
- **open and honest** – even if criticism is expressed, there are rarely hidden messages; the aim is to help and improve

- **caring** – emphasis on empathy and understanding
- **egalitarian** – communications value everyone, regardless of their role or status
- **forgiving** – error is recognised and minimised
- **feedback** – a positive and essential part of maintaining good working relationships and high levels of performance.

In an open supportive communication climate, staff feel valued, crises are dealt with and staff are more open themselves. They will feel trusted, secure and confident in their jobs and in the organisation as a whole. Effective teamworking, flexibility and a sense of involvement all contribute to, and benefit from, an open and supportive climate.

The closed communication climate is the antithesis of the above. Where the environment is highly 'political', competition for approval, promotion or resources is high on the hidden agenda. Control is often maintained through the suppression of open forms of communication.

Communication behaviours that are likely to predominate in a closed communication environment include the following (NPBEA, 1993, 16–4):

- **judgmental** – emphasis on apportioning blame; feedback is negative; people feel inferior
- **controlling** – people are expected to conform to certain types of behaviour
- **deceptive** – messages are manipulative and hold hidden meaning
- **non-caring** – communication is detached, impersonal with little concern for others
- **superior** – interaction emphasises differences in status, skills and understanding
- **dogmatic** – little discussion, unwillingness to accept other points of view
- **hostile** – a predominantly negative approach, placing little importance on the needs of others.

A closed climate may be a direct outcome of management style. As a middle manager, you will need an open and positive climate within your team or department. Some methods of communication may be more effective than others, depending on the situation.

Communication is the exchange of information, which can range from an informal discussion with a colleague to a full report to school governors. Channels of communications in school can be summarised as shown in Table 4.1.

There are advantages and disadvantages to each channel of communication, which are not mutually exclusive. Meetings may fulfil social needs as well as more formal requirements. In addition, schools may have briefings, newsletters (information sheets), noticeboards, prospectuses and informal conversations

Table 4.1: Communication channels

Communication channel	Descriptors
Oral – spoken word	Most preferred – direct and personal
Written	Letters, memos, reports, e-mail, therefore consistent and available for future reference
Meetings	Two or more people, formal/informal, planned/unplanned, structured/unstructured
Telephone calls	Immediate, time-consuming, a degree of personal contact

(chats). Any passing of information between two people will involve communication.

The aims of communication also focus on seeking information, instructing, motivating, encouraging, supporting and persuading (Hall and Oldroyd, 1990d, p. 10). As a manager you will need to decide on the purpose of your communication – the message and the most effective means of communicating. An understanding of the communication process will produce effective results (NPBEA, 1993, 16–9). It involves:

- **message** – can be intended or unintended, needs to be clear
- **encoding** – the ability to put thoughts or words into actions
- **setting** – as appropriate: classroom, boardroom, conference room, office
- **transmission** – to communicate effectively, messages must be well organised, clear and must make appropriate use of words and body language
- **decoding** – the process of interpreting messages
- **message received** – this may happen simultaneously to the giving of the message
- **feedback** – as a message is decoded the receiver responds to it, listening is critical.

Some people appear to have an innate ability to communicate; many others acquire skills through study and practice. Potential barriers to communicating according to the NPBEA (1993, 16–13) are:

- **filtering of information** – not telling the 'whole story'
- **organisational structure** – inappropriate administration
- **information overload** – inappropriate timing and content
- **semantics** – different words have different meanings
- **status differences** – status/roles can interfere with the meaning of the message
- **over-interpretation** – reading too much into the message
- **evaluative tendencies** – qualitative judgments

- **stereotypes** – negative stereotypes based on race, sex, age, role, etc.
- **cultural and gender differences**
- **arrogance and superiority**.

Verbal and non-verbal communication

Verbal and non-verbal communication requires person-to-person contact, formally or informally. As a manager, you will be required to receive and send information. As a consequence of your role and status within the school, non-verbal cues will be important to your team and other colleagues. Non-verbal cues may include:

- **vocal cues** – tone, pitch and general expression
- **body posture** – the way in which you stand or sit
- **body gestures** – what you do with your hands, head and body to explain or support what you are saying
- **eye contact** – how much you look at the other person and for how long
- **body contact** – a gentle touch on hand or arm
- **orientation** – facing the other person or at an angle
- **personal space** – the distance you maintain between yourself and the other person
- **appearance** – the image you create through clothes and grooming.

The above are as relevant for the receiver of the message. When giving and receiving messages a middle manager has to be an active listener. Being an effective listener is a skill that can be developed and practised in each new situation, whether it be a meeting, a consultation, a telephone conversation or a chance encounter in the corridor. Listening is not just hearing; it is understanding. Knowledge can be gained through active listening. This will lead to appropriate feedback.

The skill of effective listening involves: listening for message content, recognising the barriers, listening for feelings, responding (non-verbal cues), checking to avoid contradictions, encouraging and reflecting. It is essential to concentrate on the general theme and flow of the message as well as the facts. Try to be positive, looking for points of agreement and attempting to understand the feelings of others. Finally, managers should check under-standing with a quick summary at the end of the conversation.

Networking

Networking, the activity of developing personal contacts, is the most acceptable form of politicking as it is endemic to organisations. It is a positive and useful activity for managers to be involved in; at its most informal, networking is barely distinguishable from friendship. If two colleagues have a chat before a meeting and agree a strategy, this is networking. Clearly networking is a broad term and there are many different types of network.

Networks offer the support and the opportunity to share information. It may be easy to enter networks if you have something that other people want. Networks may exclude as well as include; you should be aware that by identifying with a group there may be negative effects.

Written communication

Middle managers in schools require the ability to communicate clearly in writing. There will be occasions when you will use both spoken and written communication in order to convey a message. As leaders and role models, managers are in a position to improve communication by their quality of writing as well as by providing an example to teachers and students. Managers also have an impact on student education, teacher outlook and school image (NPBEA, 1993, 17–5). There is a strong relationship between written skills and job effectiveness.

Identification of audience is important for all forms of communication. Before writing, you need to consider your audience, to be clear what it is you are trying to communicate and feel confident that you have the writing skills necessary to convey your message to your intended audience. The process of writing will also be dependent on the purpose. A memo to a colleague, for example, will not involve the same amount of detailed preparation as a report for the senior management team or governors. It is essential that middle managers identify their audience in order to adopt the appropriate style of written communication.

As the National Policy Board for Educational Administration (NPBEA) states, every type of document has it own format. The following advice is based on the NPBEA (1993, 17–13 to 17–14):

1. **Memos and letters:**
   - knowing the appropriate audiences for memos and letters
   - composing letters that include heading, inside address, salutation, body of the letter, complimentary close and signature
   - writing memos that demonstrate the correct form: introduction, body and conclusion

2. **Reports:**
   - accurate content
   - structure – title page and text, table of contents and references
   - organising headings, sub-headings, the body of the report and graphs

3. **Grants and proposals:**
   - sources of grants
   - basic components for developing a grant proposal: evidence of need, activities/objectives, method of evaluation and project budget

4. **Public announcement:**
   - demonstrating basic writing format
   - planning the layout of a newsletter, effective headlines and captions
   - developing surveys to gather information from the community
   - publishing articles in professional journals

5. **Summaries and plans:**
   - preparation of summaries of articles, disseminations and meetings in as few words as possible
   - preparing comprehensive plans: objectives, descriptions of current status, strategies, method of evaluation and dissemination of results.

Middle managers require technical proficiency in order to complete the above, which includes:

- **no errors**
- **the ability to correct errors**
- **correct tense** – past tense in formal documents
- **correct 'voice'** – according to document and voice
- **grammar** – correct use of verbs and pronouns
- **correct spelling**
- **appropriate writing style according to audience**.

The tools of written communication are sound grammar, accurate spelling, structure and punctuation. Each sentence will need to be effective, forming part of the message. The NPBEA (1993, 17–14) suggests the following stages of the writing process:

1. Pre-writing.
2. Drafting.
3. Revising.
4. Editing.
5. Final product.

In detail:

1. *Pre-writing*: the generation of ideas and gathering of data as shown in Figure 4.1.

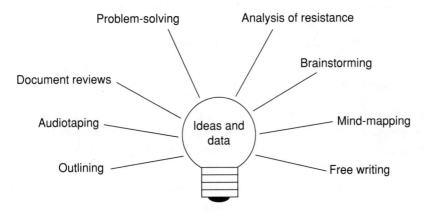

Figure 4.1: Communication ideas and data

Then organise the material:
- chronologically
- by topic area
- formats

in order to:
- highlight cause and effect
- compare advantages/disadvantages
- identify personal relationship with written text.

2. The next stage is *drafting* which involves;
- identifying the objective of the communication
- identifying the audience
- selection of appropriate format
- focus on broad issues – develop and fine tune objectives
- present/construct final format – produce document.

3. The following points should be considered for *revising*:
- revision differs from editing, focusing on evaluating the document to determine whether it delivers its intended message to its intended audience
- whether the document fails to achieve its objectives and whether changes should be made

- coherence and fluency: paragraphs may be re-organised, sentences may be lengthened or shortened
- additional information or the deletion of unnecessary or irrelevant information
- changing educational jargon (not everyone will have the same understanding of jargon)
- positive tone – documents should be positive.

Revising and editing will be more effective if there is a break between the drafting and revision stages.

4. The final stage in the writing process is *editing* which aims to produce an accurate, sensitive and concise piece of writing. This phase includes:
   - careful review of the document, checking spelling, grammar, punctuation, word choice and tone
   - remove redundant words and expressions
   - check the spelling of unfamiliar names and words
   - clarify abbreviations.

5. The *final product* can then be printed and distributed as required. Keep a copy for reference.

The process of writing can be summarised as follows:

- establishing ideas – 'jotting down'
- planning of ideas – planning relevant order
- selection, de-selection – omitting data
- identifying audience – in order to determine style and format.

For documents to be read in detail, they should be easy to read and visually appealing. The choice of format will enhance the document's message. The presentation of the text should do justice to its content. The following are key features for effective presentation:

1. Clear title which identifies the content and meaning of the text.
2. Appropriate headings and subheadings.
3. Visual impact, do not overcrowd each page.
4. Double space.
5. Use a simple type font (size 12).
6. Use numbering when necessary (titles, paragraphs, pages).
7. Summarise key points by using lists.
8. Label as appropriate.
9. Use capitals, bold, underlining and italics.

10. Longer documents should have:
    - contents table
    - introduction
    - summary
    - index
    - appendix
11. Binding – use an attractive folder and/or cover.

Middle managers should ensure that team members follow good practice when preparing written documents. Development of 'house-style' would enhance the effectiveness of a schools/team communication with its audience.

Information technology

Information technology is increasingly making information easier to access and share, enabling middle managers to engage in the communication chain in schools. The Schools Information Management System (SIMS) encompasses such areas as attendance (registers), finance (records and budgeting systems), examination results (records) and curriculum (timetabling and modular pathways).

Information technology is also crucial to the empowerment of front-line staff. It is a key tool in providing information to middle managers and staff and is fundamental to the flattened organisational structures adopted by many schools.

Information can be used as a personal power weapon by many managers (and staff); modern computer and communication technology ensures that this weapon is increasingly ineffective. Middle managers and their teams should have access to all information relevant to their position in the management of the school.

Middle managers require adequate training in order to access and process information. Schools, as organisations, require comprehensive communication systems: site networks, computers available for all managers and adequate information technology management. There is also a responsibility for those designing and contributing to the site network to comply with relevant legislation.

Meetings

A significant difference to a teacher newly appointed as a middle manager is the importance of meetings. The number of meetings held in a school will reflect the size and culture of the school. Whatever the number of meetings, practitioners and managers often have the impression that meetings are a waste of time!

Before planning a meeting it would be useful to reflect whether a meeting is necessary. The advantages of meetings should be considered:

Advantages

- communication
- improve staff skills in communication and decision-making
- sense of involvement and ownership among staff
- democratic – improves job satisfaction
- keep managers and staff in touch.

Disadvantages

- time – meetings take longer to reach decisions and take teachers away from preparation, marking and contact with pupils
- expense – is this the best use of non-contact time?
- limited control – can be dominated by the most senior or the most vocal
- decision-making and communication dependent on the quality of the meeting.

If the quality of school meetings is to improve, it is necessary for all staff to understand the function of each meeting. Middle managers are required to plan, lead and participate in meetings which may have one or more of the following functions:

- to communicate information – giving and receiving
- to take decisions
- to influence (and understand) policy
- to monitor and evaluate
- to problem solve
- to plan
- to develop co-operation and commitment
- to motivate.

In their study of 24 Manchester secondary schools, Torrington and Weightman (Hall and Oldroyd, 1990c, p. 38) show the extent to which meetings are used as a co-ordinating device and as a means of contributing to group cohesiveness (Table 4.2). It is interesting to note the different practices from school to school, for example, School 6 appears to hold very few meetings.

As stated earlier the size and culture of the school will determine the number of meetings. Similarly the culture and style of each meeting will determine its effectiveness. Understanding the culture and style of meetings will help teachers and managers to:

- make better use of the opportunities
- alter the culture and style, when appropriate.

Meetings develop according to the membership of the team or group, sometimes producing a change in culture and style; this may need to be part of more radical changes in the school as a whole.

There are usually two key roles in formal meetings: chair and secretary (minute taker) (Hedge *et al.*, 1994, pp. 42–62). Middle managers may be required to chair team meetings and act as secretary to senior management or staff meetings. It is not advisable to chair and take minutes simultaneously. The collective functions of the chair and secretary are:

- to progress the meeting efficiently
- to maintain the meeting as a viable working group.

In addition, chairs will decide whether a meeting is to be formal or informal, generally dependent on the function and/or purpose of the meeting. A chair or secretary will then:

Before the meeting:

- prepare an agenda in advance of the meeting to allow members to consider each point and allow other points to be added to the agenda
- distribute the necessary papers.

During the meeting:

- open the meeting
- state the purpose of the meeting
- take the meeting through the agenda
- close the meeting
- ensure fair play
- stay in charge
- control length and depth of discussions
- summarise discussion
- end discussion
- ensure decisions are taken in the appropriate manner, i.e. conduct a vote, check consensus
- encourage participation.

Table 4.2: Co-ordinating meetings in the MOSS 24 schools

	Senior staff meeting	Head of department/ faculty meeting	Head of year/ house meeting	Other
1.	Weekly	Weekly	None	
2.	Daily	None	Weekly	4-week cycle, management organisation open to all
3.	Weekly	None	Weekly	
4.	Weekly	Half-termly	Half-termly	Weekly senior management team, 2 ad hoc working parties on curriculum, faculty teams
5.	Weekly	Half-termly	None	
6.	None	None	None	2 per week senior management team, 1 standing committee on curriculum, 2 working parties, faculty teams
7.	As required (Academic Board)	None	As required (Pastoral Board)	
8.	As required	None	As required (weekly more or less)	Full staff – open agenda, open interest meetings, 2 working parties, faculty teams
9.	Monthly	None	As required (without head!)	
10.	Weekly head + 3 deputies; Weekly 3 deputies + 2 senior teachers	Monthly	Monthly and 2 briefing meetings per week	Staff consultative committee and staff management
11.	Weekly, incl. union reps	None	None	Staff development committee and ad hoc working parties
12.	Weekly with 2 deputies	None	None	Full staff meeting monthly and new support team meetings
13.	Weekly head + 2 deputies	Monthly	As required	Termly staff meeting

14.	Weekly head, heads of faculty + heads of year	None	1 as required but none while there	Full staff meeting, 2 per term
15.	As required	Monthly	Monthly	Full staff meeting, 2 per term
16.	Weekly	None	None	Weekly staff briefing – school teams, e.g. expressive arts, lower school unit
17.	None (but three quarters met weekly)	None	2 per team	
18.	Weekly	None	2-weekly but flexible	Senior staff meeting – open attendance, head of faculty/department/year expected to attend weekly briefing
19.	Weekly	Monthly	Monthly	Curriculum working parties
20.	Weekly	Half-termly	Half-termly	Half-termly
21.	2 per week	Half-termly	Half-termly	Curriculum working parties monthly or *ad hoc*
22.	Most mornings	As and when necessary	None	2 working parties, open curriculum meetings
23.	Weekly	None	Head of house – occasional	Working parties
24.	Weekly	Half-termly, more often if necessary	Half-termly	None

(From Torrington and Weightman, 1989, pp. 58–9; reproduced by permission of the publisher, Stanley Thornes Publishers Ltd, Ellenborough House, Wellington Street, Cheltenham GL50 1YD)

67

After the meeting:

- pursue discussions/actions
- represent the team at other meetings.

When preparing to chair a meeting, a middle manager should:

- read the necessary papers
- obtain briefing from colleagues, when required
- think through the process (mentally rehearse each item)
- anticipate conflict
- contact speakers/participants to ensure that they are aware of when (and for how long) they are required to speak
- check procedures and rules – know to whom the meeting should report.

Effective chairing of meetings will require effective interpersonal skills. It is the chair's responsibility to ensure that the atmosphere of the meeting is conducive to discussion and that members feel valued. Middle managers need to develop skills in managing teams during meetings – take the lead, talk to people, establish acceptable behaviour and set a good example. Haynes (1988, pp. 62–5) suggested that if conflict arises it can be dealt with by:

- clarifying objectives
- striving for understanding
- focusing on the rational
- generating alternatives
- postponing the issue
- using humour.

A chair with a sense of humour may be able to diffuse the situation. Detailed planning may also avoid possible areas/items of conflict. Problems will arise if meetings have unclear objectives and lack leadership. Avoid holding meetings with large groups of people. Have a clear agenda and keep to time.

Middle managers will be required to participate in meetings. Aim to become a valued member. The hardest part of managing meetings is arriving at group decisions. This will be discussed later. In sum, a group consensus can be reached if appropriate behaviour is practised in meetings. It is essential for chairs and secretaries to evaluate their practice and to change if required. With good leadership, meetings can be effective.

Public events

Many schools have events when staff and pupils present their work. As schools become more self-sufficient, creating a positive image is a high priority (Hall and Oldroyd, 1990d, p. 14). Parents, as clients, need to be attracted to the school and convinced that the school will offer a quality education for their child. Public relations are therefore important. All staff need to be aware of how to promote the 'corporate image', and each team within the school will need to participate in creating the image. Middle managers will find that they have an additional role, related to how the school communicates to the outside world.

Presentations

Presentations are events at which members of the school community are presented with awards and/or examination certificates. As an event that involves large numbers of pupils and parents, management has to be good. Points to consider:

- numbers – visitors, participants
- staging – levels
- programme – include all names where possible
- guest speaker – essential to get this right!
- refreshments.

Guidelines given for open evenings and concerts later in this section will also apply.

The importance of a relevant amusing guest speaker cannot be over-emphasised. The speaker will set the tone of the presentation. Participants and your audience will need to relate to the speaker and s(he) will also need to be able to relate to his/her audience. The following suggestions may help:

- actors
- politicians
- journalists
- managers from industry
- key educationalists (Chief Education Officer)
- sports people.

All of the above will be experienced public speakers with an understanding of what is involved and their audiences' expectations. Do not be too restrictive, aim for an eminent public figure who lives locally. You may be very pleasantly surprised at the response you receive.

A middle manager may have responsibility to act as the school's press officer, feeding accounts of school events to the local press, television and radio stations. You will need to have a reliable and trusted contact in each media. Heads of years will have regular contact with parents and other agencies. Effective communication is critical to the generation of a positive image for the team and school.

Notice boards/displays

Middle managers will have notice boards which are used to communicate with parents, pupils and colleagues. Schools are often visited by members of the public and outside agencies in addition to their own clientele. It is therefore necessary for staff to consider:

1. Who will see the message?
2. Who is the message for?
3. What will be communicated by the quality of the message/display and its presentation?
4. How involved are the pupils?
5. Should parents/pupils/other agencies read the message – what other means are there to communicate the message?
6. Is there a 'house-style' that should be adopted?

Open evenings

Schools hold many open evenings during the course of the academic year. These may be to deliver reports, select examination courses, the annual governors' meeting, and to 'market' the school to prospective parents and pupils. Whatever the purpose, it is essential to communicate the 'right' message. Middle managers often have a critical role in the preparation and management of such events. The following advice may be useful in the planning stages:

1. What is the purpose of the event? Has this been communicated to the appropriate audience?
2. How many room/chairs/tables will be required?
3. Do staff require name tags or place names on each table/desk?
4. Are all notice boards used effectively, e.g. announcements/messages/ positive results/sports scores/photographs of active learning?
5. Do all staff know what to do? Newly Qualified Teachers (NQT) and new staff will need additional support and guidance.
6. Has the caretaker been notified? Rooms will need to be cleaned before and after the event.
7. Is the furniture in the right place?
8. 'Front of house' – who will be responsible for greeting visitors to the school?
9. Dress – are staff/pupils aware of the appropriate 'dress code'?
10. Refreshments – have arrangements been made?
11. Will visitors require a map of the school?
12. Is the school site clear of rubbish?

13. How will the event affect the school timetable? Have staff been approached regarding any possible intrusions and/or interruptions to their schedule?

14. Create a positive atmosphere, formal or informal as appropriate.

15. Microphones and amplification, if required, should work efficiently.

16. Visual impact – does the school 'look good'? Flowers, etc. may be required.

17. Have car parking arrangements been agreed with police/school caretaker?

Middle managers should not take full responsibility for all of the above, the list is too long for any one person. Delegation is critical, therefore advanced planning will be required. Middle managers may also be responsible for the induction of new staff in the appropriate protocol and practices involved in open evenings. The following may assist this process. Teachers should:

- keep a record of parents' appointments
- keep a record of letters sent to parents and responses
- know where heads of department, heads of year and senior managers will be for consultation/emergencies
- keep a list of problems/actions following parents' comments
- know who to consult and the appropriate times for consultation.

A NQT or new appointee will need to know and understand the above as applied to your school. Expert advice is best given in advance of such events.

Public performances: school productions/carol services/concerts

The majority of schools will produce a public performance during the academic year. The key to success is planning and preparation. Regardless of the level of performance, the standard of hospitality will provide the base-line from which the school will be judged. The list of requirements is not dissimilar to the above with the following additions:

1. Health and Safety – Environmental Health (District Council) and the local Fire Officer should be informed, as they may wish to inspect the premises prior to the performance. Each will provide their own list of requirements.

2. Changing rooms/warm-up area should not be within visual/hearing distance of the audience!

3. Hospitality – as above, those providing hospitality will need to know the approximate interval time.

4. Programmes and tickets should be printed in advance of the performance. Acknowledgements need to be checked; include everyone who has contributed, even in the smallest way.

5. Disruption – events are often *very* disruptive to colleagues, so ensure that everyone who needs to be contacted is approached *before* the event.

6. Rehearsal timetable – parents will need to know when their children are required, and when to collect them.

7. Seating – plan the hall according to the event. It may not be necessary or appropriate to follow the same seating plan for each event.

8. Be aware of deaf/disabled members of the public.

9. Have a first aider available with access to the hall.

10. Discuss all plans with a member of the senior management team.

11. Invite governors, LEA inspectors and members of the senior management team to all events.

Presenting the school in a positive manner is the responsibility of the whole school community, i.e. involve appropriate departments for ticket design (design and technology), refreshments (home economics) and setting up chairs (tutor/PE group). As a team leader, a middle manager should express this clearly.

School visits

School visits encompass all school activities which take place off school premises. Visits involve a great deal of planning. The value of a visit for pupils should be measured carefully against the problems of:

- classes left in school by staff absent on visits
- disruption of classes when significant numbers of pupils are absent on visits
- pressure on staff substituting for colleagues.

All visits should be self-financing, including the cost of insurance. Organising staff are responsible for the collection of money and insurance.

The DES Circular 2/89 details requirements for schools and LEAs regarding charging and remissions. Activities which take place mainly in school time should be free to pupils. In order that trips are self-financing, voluntary contributions may be requested from parents, but this approach should not preclude pupils from taking part if they do not wish to pay or are unable to pay. A letter to parents/guardians may be worded:

> We would ask for a voluntary contribution of £... to cover the cost of the trip and insurance. In the event that insufficient voluntary contributions are received, the trip may have to be cancelled. Cheques should be made payable to ...

This leaves open the possibility that the school could subsidise or pay for pupils who require assistance.

Where the activity is a requirement for a public examination or part of the national curriculum no charge can be requested at all – not even voluntary contributions. However, for a field study trip that may be a requirement for GCSE geography the cost of accommodation may be charged, provided that a remission is made for pupils whose parents receive income support or family credit. Where there is an enhancement parents may be offered the opportunity to make voluntary contributions. Organisers must check LEA policy regarding:

- approval of visits and journeys
- levels of supervision (police screening)
- communications with parents/guardians
- insurance
- charging policy
- first aid
- prior experience and knowledge
- organiser's checklist of venue
- activities of a hazardous nature.

Once a visit has been approved a letter should be sent to parents/guardians giving appropriate details of:

- total cost
- deposit required (whether deposit is returnable)
- dates
- accommodation/venue
- supervised/unsupervised activities
- clothing requirement
- number of pupils
- number and names of staff
- pocket money.

The appropriate parental consent form should be attached to the letter and held by the visit organiser. Medical forms, dietary details and contact names/ numbers should also be completed by parents prior to each visit and retained by the organiser. Emergency procedures should be known and understood by all staff accompanying the visit. Figure 4.2 is an example of good practice.

APPLICATION FOR A NON-RESIDENTIAL SCHOOL VISIT

Part 1 (*To be submitted for approval of Headteacher before visit is notified to parents or pupils*)

Proposed Day & Date: _____ Time: Depart: _____ Return:_____

Alternative Date(s): _____

Year Group or Form/Teaching Group(s) involved: _____

Venue: _____

Contact name & phone of venue: _____

Purpose of visit: _____

Names of adults supervising (or at least number of same):

_____

Financial arrangements, including rules on participation:_____

Method of travel (school minibus, coach hire, etc.): _____

Signature of member of staff responsible: _____ Date:_____

Signature of Deputy Heads: (1)_____ (2)_____

Notification of visit approved (Headteacher): _____ Date:_____

Figure 4.2: School visit – application

Part 2 (*Please re-submit to Deputy Head with Action Checklist, at least 10 days before visit and attach copy of parents' letter which should include the above details*)

Name of adults participating:

_____ (Leader)_____

_____ (First Aider) _____

Number of pupils:_____ 'Cost' per pupil: £_____

Name & tel. no of coach company etc.: _____

OR Route & itinerary (attach if necessary): _____

- -

I confirm that I have carried out all the appropriate procedures listed in the Staff Guide

Signed: _____ (Party Leader)   Date: _____

Action Checklist confirmed:_____   Date: _____

(Deputy Head to sign)

Further action required? Yes/No: _____   Date: _____

(Headteacher to sign)

Figure 4.2: continued

75

Having received approval for the trip, organisers should write to parents with details as shown in Figure 4.3.

---

28 February 1996

Dear Parent,

During the past year, your son/daughter has been following a GCSE course in geography. A valuable (but not compulsory) component of this is fieldwork visits which enable students to see some of the places and explore some of the processes studied in the course.

The physical geography fieldwork visit in Year 10 is to Seven Sisters Country Park near Eastbourne, East Sussex, which provides an excellent location for the study of coastal and river processes as well as a study of the issue of the conservation and management of a country park. There will also be stops at the coastal town of Seaford and at the port of Newhaven (if time allows).

The visit will take place on WEDNESDAY 12th JUNE. Students will need to be in school at the normal time of 8.35 a.m., but due to the travelling time and nature of the visit, will not be back at school until approximately 8.15–8.30 p.m. It is essential that arrangements are made for the students to be collected from school at this time.

Students will be transported by coach and will be closely supervised at all times during the day by five members of teaching staff and a welfare assistant. I have led several school trips to this location in recent years and will personally re-visit the location before the visit.

Should you wish your son/daughter to attend the visit, we would ask for a voluntary contribution of £8 to cover the cost of coach hire and County School Journey insurance. In the event that insufficient contributions are received, the trip may have to be cancelled. Cheques should be made payable to ...

Students on the visit will not be required to wear school uniform but are requested to dress sensibly (jeans, shirt, warm jumper and strong walking shoes/trainers are ideal). Students will also need to bring a waterproof coat, a packed lunch and plenty of liquid to drink.

If you wish your son/daughter to take part in this visit, please sign and return the slip below as soon as possible. Please also enclose a completed medical form (attached).

Yours faithfully,

Head of Geography.

- -

I wish/do not wish my son/daughter _____ to attend the geography fieldwork visit on Wednesday 12th June to Seven Sisters Country Park, East Sussex. I enclose/do not enclose a voluntary contribution of £8.

Signed: _____   Parent/Guardian

Figure 4.3: School visit – letter to parents

It will then be necessary to plan the content of the trip, including as much relevant information as possible (see Figures 4.4–6).

YEAR 10 VISIT TO SEVEN SISTERS COUNTRY PARK

Wednesday 12th June 1996

Introduction

Your visit is to one of the best locations for anyone studying geography. In this area of chalk downland (South Downs) near Eastbourne there are many interesting things to study such as river, coastal and valley processes as well as the human geography – how people affect and have been affected by the area . . . and all in one location.

A day such as this takes a great deal of planning by the staff involved and much hard work on the day. Please ensure that you remember this and behave courteously and sensibly at all times. Most of all we want you to enjoy the day but remember that it is a school visit and that you will be expected to work hard so that you get maximum benefit from the experience – remember those GCSE's!

Safety and Environmental Awareness

- NO stone throwing, especially on the beach.
- TAKE CARE not to slip on the wave-cut platform.
- NO trampling on vegetation, especially on shingle. Keep to paths.
- Last person must close gates. If in doubt, CLOSE IT!

Figure 4.4: School visit – pupil information

PLAN OF THE DAY

(may be subject to change)

Time:	Activity:
8.25–8.35	Assemble in dining area
8.35–8.50	Register/briefing
8.55	Board coach
9.00	Depart
11.00	Estimated time of arrival – Exceat village car park – use visitors centre toilets/brief snack
11.20	Assemble
11.35	Walk to coast
12.00	Divide into groups
13.15	Lunch on beach – must not wander
13.35	Introduction to afternoon session
15.00	All groups reach second field sketch site
15.30	Management of a Country Park session
16.30	To Seaford
16.50	Arrive Seaford
17.30	Depart for home (including chance to buy food)
20.15–20.30	Arrive school

Figure 4.5: School visit – timetable

Geographical enquiry

Geomorphic land forms at Seven Sisters Country Park

1. This enquiry counts for 15 per cent of your final GCSE mark.

2. It will be based on first hand collection of data during fieldwork. This fieldwork will take place at Seven Sisters Country Park.

3. After the fieldwork, the enquiry will be completed in class and for homework for three weeks, and then as homework until the end of term. The completed enquiry must be handed in at the beginning of the Autumn term. Make sure you make full use of the class and homework time and keep to the deadlines given.

4. Use A4 size paper and when complete, number the pages and include a contents page. Include a bibliography at the end with details of the sources of information you have used.

5. Present all your work neatly and with care. Remember that 5 per cent of the marks for the enquiry will be awarded for spelling, punctuation and grammar; and for the correct use of geographical terms.

6. If you are going to use IT to produce any part of this unit, check with your teacher that its use is acceptable.

7. Remember that cheating in any way, especially copying, is strictly forbidden. Part of the fieldwork will be done as a group and you are permitted to use the data collected in this way but you must present and interpret this data yourself.

8. Your enquiry will involve you in a lot of work. It may also prove to be the most interesting and rewarding part of your school geography course. This is because you will have to take an active part in your own learning. You will be finding things out for yourself and producing a piece of work which is original.

In the course of your enquiry, you will be required to investigate the following four questions:

1. How has the structure of the rock affected the past and present processes acting upon it?

2. What are the geomorphic processes which contribute to the development of valleys and coasts?

3. What evidence can you find of the processes which have given rise to land forms and landscapes including weathering, erosion, transport and deposition?

4. What evidence can you find of the effects of human activity on geomorphic processes?

Figure 4.6: School visit – general instructions

Summary

Communication is central to effective school operations. In schools, teachers and managers use different methods of communication for different purposes. An open and supportive communication climate promotes co-operative working relationships, staff will feel valued, trusted, secure and confident.

Communication is the exchange of information, which can range from an informal discussion with a colleague to a full report to school governors. Channels of communication include: oral, written, meetings and telephone calls.

Problems that arise during the communication process are generally focused on: the message, encoding, the setting, transmission, decoding and feedback. Some people appear to have an innate ability to communicate; many others acquire skills through study and practice.

Verbal and non-verbal communication involves listening and observing. Being an effective listener is a skill that can be developed and practised in each new situation. Networking, the activity of developing personal contacts, is the most acceptable form of politicking in organisations. Networks offer support and a means to share information.

Middle managers require the ability to communicate clearly in writing. The NPBEA (1993) suggest that the stages in the writing process are pre-writing, drafting, revising, editing and the final product.

Information technology is increasingly making information easier to access and share, enabling middle managers to engage in the communication chain in schools. Middle managers require adequate training in order to access and process information. There is also a responsibility for those designing and contributing to the site network to comply with relevant legislation.

A significant difference to a teacher newly appointed as a middle manager is the importance of meetings. Middle managers are required to plan, lead and participate in meetings. Understanding the culture and style of meetings will help teachers and managers to make better use of the opportunities.

Middle managers should aim to become valued members of meetings; prepare, think and listen, then speak and encourage others. It is essential to know your audience. With good leadership, meetings can be effective.

Many schools have events when staff and pupils present their work. As schools become increasingly more self-sufficient, creating a positive image is a high priority (Hall and Oldroyd, 1990d, p. 14). Middle managers have a role related to how the school communicates to the outside world.

5
■ ■ ■

Management Teams

Introduction

There are many features common to all school management teams, across all phases of education. These include: management structures, management roles, size of team and team roles. Wallace *et al.* (1996, p. 8) in their study of primary and secondary school senior management teams found that the key differences between the two phases were a consequence of the differential in funding. This led to lower staffing levels and a lower resourcing level in primary schools. In practice this created technical constraints on the operational ability of primary school senior management teams.

The study also found that secondary school managers tended to focus on school-wide responsibilities which contrasted with the multiple responsibilities of primary school managers. As an example, a secondary school middle manager may be responsible for a subject area or year group, whereas an equivalent post-holder in a primary school may be responsible for a subject area, year group and special needs throughout the school. Wallace *et al.* (1996) commented on the lack of status of middle and senior managers in primary schools. In sum, primary school deputy headteachers do not have the luxury of pastoral, curriculum and administrative teams. This research concluded that the cultural and political (power) perspectives of primary and secondary schools are incompatible, which contrasts with the similarities between the structure and management roles.

This chapter identifies the generic structures and management roles of primary and secondary school management teams. Specific attention is then given to primary and secondary phases.

Generic structures and management roles

In the majority of schools middle managers work in teams (Figure 5.1). The size of each team will reflect the size of the school. Subject co-ordinators in small primary/secondary schools may be in a department of one: themselves! Ultimately the place of the middle manager within the structure of the team is as team leader.

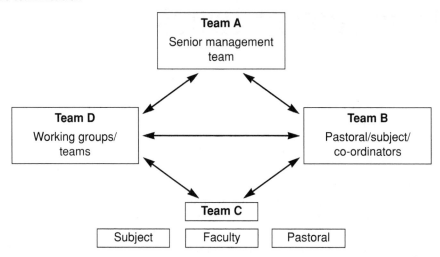

Figure 5.1: School management teams

Trethowan (1985, pp. 3–4) in Coleman and Bush (1994, p. 265) offers the classification of teams shown in Table 5.1 (reproduced by permission of the publisher, The Industrial Society, 48 Bryanston Square, London W1H 7LN).

Table 5.1: Membership of management teams

Team	Membership
Senior management teams	Headteacher and deputy headteacher
Middle management teams	Head of department, heads of year
Staff teams	Subject or pastoral staff
Project teams	*Ad hoc* groups established to achieve short-term goals
Interdisciplinary teams	Comprise members from various departments to deal with long-term issues

It is axiomatic that teams are necessary within the context of schools as organisations and that schools as organisations should value effective teamwork. Everard and Morris (1990, p. 172) stated:

A team is a group of people that can effectively tackle any task which it has been set to do. The contribution drawn from each member is of the highest possible quality, and is one which could not have been called into play other than in the context of a supportive team.

As a middle manager, it is critical to understand that teams do not act as teams simply because they are described as such. Teams need to work together on a common task. Bell (1992, p. 45) defined teamwork as a group of people working together on the basis of:

- shared perceptions
- a common purpose
- agreed procedures
- commitment
- co-operation
- resolving disagreements openly by discussion.

Middle managers in schools will inevitably work in two types of team: structured teams (Teams A, B and C in Figure 5.1) and those created for specific purposes (Team D). Determining the purpose of the team is critical to effective management. Handy (1993) suggested the following functions or purposes of teams which can be applied to schools as organisations:

- distributing and managing work
- problem-solving and decision-making
- enabling people to take part in decision-making
- co-ordinating and liaising
- passing on information
- negotiating or conflict resolution
- increasing commitment and involvement
- monitoring and evaluating.

Essentially, successful teamwork depends on a clearly defined set of aims and objectives, the personalities of team members and the team manager. Teamwork is, as with all aspects of effective management, time-consuming.

Tuckman (1965) defined the stages of team development as:

1. **Forming:** the team is not a team but a set of individuals. The focus is on the team's purposes, composition, leadership and lifespan. Individuals are concerned to establish their personal identities in the team and make some individual impression.

2. **Storming:** having reached a consensus on the team's purpose, conflict arises as assumptions are challenged. Personal agendas are revealed and some inter-personal hostility may be generated. Successful handling enables the team to reach fresh agreement on purpose, procedures and norms.

3. **Norming:** the team seeks to establish its norms and practices – when and how it should work. As working procedures are established there will be a communication of feelings, mutual support and sense of team identity.

4. **Performing:** solutions to problems emerge, the team is mature and productive. Individuals and team are relaxed and confident.

Developing middle management skills will involve a balance between concern for the team, concern for the task and developing the individual. Few middle managers are able to achieve this effective balance. Adair (1988, p. 44) warned that if the team fails to function, task achievement is impaired. West (1995, p. 84) produced the model shown in Table 5.2.

A middle manager may find identifying the characteristics of his/her team difficult. The nature of the task and the culture of the school will influence the working habits of team members. Equally, pressure from external agencies will affect the quality of teams in schools. Family commitments, hobbies and political initiatives are areas of influence on teachers' lives; these, in turn, will influence the individual's commitment to the team. In essence, the quality of the relationships within the team will determine the quality of the task.

Middle managers should aim to lead and participate in effective teams which agree aims, share skills, realise potential and reduce stress and anxiety. A middle manager should avoid the pitfalls of weak management. These are discussed in detail in Chapter Two and include:

- over-emphasis on people
- over-emphasis on task
- over-emphasis on agendas, not processes
- reacting to events, not anticipating them
- failure to celebrate success, individual and team.

The complexity of the middle manager's role is further illustrated by West-Burnham's nine components of team effectiveness as presented in Coleman and Bush (1994, pp. 279–80):

1. **Explicit and shared values:** no team can operate effectively unless it is working in a context where the values are clear and agreed, and translated into a mission.

2. **Situational leadership:** the team is sufficiently mature to base leadership on function and needs rather than power and status. Skills are more important than hierarchical factors. This requires a willingness by the designated leader to stand back and allow other team members to assume control according to the needs of the situation.

3. **Pride in the team:** this implies commitment and involvement and is manifested in high morale and loyalty. Team members have self-belief, and confidence in others and the team as a whole.

Table 5.2: Management tasks

Key functions/actions	Task	Team	Individual
Define goals	• clarify goals • establish timescale • gather information • identify requisite resources • establish parameters of authority	• select/assemble team • explain goal and rationale • generate commitment • encourage questions	• check that individuals understand goals • respond to questions and expressions of concern • involve each person
Plan and decide	• identify options • investigate how to make best use of skills of members • plan timing of events • check resource needs • identify success criteria • generate ownership of plan	• consult with team • brainstorm ideas • list suggestions • agree priorities • agree success criteria	• listen to suggestions • identify/assess abilities relevant to the task • coach relevant skills as required
Organise and brief	• establish procedures • draw up brief and action plan • check individual understanding of roles and tasks • listen to and respond to feedback	• set up appropriate structures and agree on sub-tasks • communicate agreed plan • take questions and queries • delegate tasks • finalise plan	• check understanding of individual roles • reward commitment and enthusiasm • reward good ideas • invite feedback
Control, support and monitor	• report progress to key stakeholders at agreed intervals • amend action plan as necessary • set examples • maintain commitment to goals	• co-ordinate work of sub-groups • check resources are in use • provide feedback on tasks • deal with disagreements/conflict • celebrate sub-goal achievement • resolve emergent problems	• provide support to individuals • encourage disclosure of problems • recognise individual achievements • reassure where necessary • check agreed deadlines are on course
Evaluate/review	• evaluate goal achievement by applying agreed success criteria • report on team performance • consider future action • note potential improvements • recognise and celebrate achievement	• give feedback on achievement • invite team to review their effectiveness • identify learning/insights gained	• provide individual feedback on goal achievement • recognise individual development • recognise contributions made to the team • gather individual perceptions of team's effectiveness

(From West, 1995, p. 84. Reproduced by permission of the publisher, David Fulton Publishers Ltd, 2 Barbon Close, London WC1N 3JX.)

4. **Clear task:** the outcome which the team is created to achieve is clear, realistic and understood. Teams are motivated by tangible goals, clear outcomes and a firm time-scale.

5. **Review:** effective teams learn and develop by a process of continuous feedback and review. Team review is a permanent feature of every activity and leads to more effective working.

6. **Openness:** teams achieve a high level of candour in review and exchange. There are no 'hidden agendas' and there is praise and criticism. The latter is frank and direct, but constructive rather than negative.

7. **Lateral communication:** team members are able to communicate with each other without reference to the team leader. Networks are formed and nourished by the team.

8. **Collaboration:** decisions are shared and have full commitment. Quality decisions emerge from the full utilisation of the knowledge and skills of team members.

9. **Action:** team decisions are expressed in terms of action. Each team member knows what has to be done, by whom and when. Effective teams issue agreed actions after their meetings.

(Adapted from West-Burnham, 1992, pp. 121–4)

Motivation

Perhaps the most important element of team leadership is the ability to motivate others. Staff who are motivated and committed to educational excellence create an environment which motivates pupils. Managers who know and understand this will enable staff to develop professionally. Team leaders should create conditions which focus on achieving excellence. A middle manager should encourage participation and facilitate teamwork. As a team leader, a middle manager will serve as a role model to his/her team members. Middle managers should inspire and motivate others to achieve high standards and to work towards fulfilment of the school's aims. In practice this will require middle managers to:

- provide staff with challenges and intellectual stimulation
- celebrate the positive impact staff are having on children
- practise participatory decision-making
- encourage teamwork and collegiality
- develop positive appraisal systems
- enhance individuals' self-esteem
- articulate performance expectations

- be aware of and use the rewards that staff members value
- be aware of and use various types of feedback systems.

Clearly motivation is more than satisfaction; it also requires knowledge and understanding of what is expected. The most important aspect is sharing a common goal which is highly valued by the team.

The National Commission on Education (NCE) (1996) study of effective schools in disadvantaged areas provides several examples where good practice and a common goal can motivate teachers. The NCE refers to the ten features of success in *Learning to Succeed*, (1995), which formed the basis for the proposals for raising achievement in schools:

1. Strong, positive leadership by the head and senior staff.
2. A good atmosphere or spirit, generated by shared aims and values and by a physical environment that is as attractive and stimulating as possible.
3. High and consistent expectations of all pupils.
4. A clear and continuing focus on teaching and learning.
5. Well-developed procedures for assessing how pupils are progressing.
6. Responsibility for learning shared by the pupils themselves.
7. Participation by pupils in the life of the school.
8. Rewards and incentives to encourage pupils to succeed.
9. Parental involvement in children's education and in supporting the aims of the school.
10. Extra-curricular activities which broaden pupils' interest and experiences, expand their opportunities to succeed, and help to build good relationships within the school.

NCE researchers (1996, p. 179) visited a school in the West Midlands which had a positive, highly motivated staff. The research team was able to observe each of the above in practice:

> *We were impressed by the positive attitude of staff, including teaching support staff, and by their dedication. It is surely a central part of successful school management to create the conditions to enable the staff to make this kind of commitment. One example of the school's success in this respect is the range of after-school provision which is provided by teachers out of sheer commitment to the school.*

A further example of good practice cited by NCE researchers (1996, p. 139) was that of a dynamic primary school which is moving forward and making progress. While neither the headteacher nor the staff felt that they had achieved their goals, staff morale was high and this has placed the school in a position where everyone can move forward on teaching and learning. The headteacher stated:

The minute I feel the school has gone as far as it can, I should go. The minute we say we have achieved our vision for the school we should do some soul-searching.

Primary school middle managers

This section is based on the work of Bennett (1995) and West (1995) who have examined the issue of middle management in primary schools. West (1995, p. ix) defines middle management thus:

The words 'middle management' and 'middle manager' are used [. . .] to refer to members of staff in primary schools who have oversight of a designated area of the curriculum or an aspect of the work of a school such as a key stage, pupil assessment, parent-school liaison, special needs, links with industry.

Bennett (1995, p. 72) casts doubt as to whether primary schools and middle management are compatible. Bennett (1995, pp. 72–3) supports his argument with three key observations:

1. *Most primary schools have ten or fewer full-time equivalent teaching staff and under three hundred pupils [. . .]*

Consequently, the number of responsibility points (or increments) available is limited and the absence of promotion affects the career expectations of primary teachers.

2. *Primary schools are usually organised on the basis of one teacher taking responsibility for all the learning of a class of children for the whole year [. . .]*

As a result individual teachers can become isolated. A teacher's involvement with pupils could be all-embracing and time-consuming. The classroom and its pupils can become his/her 'domain' to the exclusion of the rest of the school.

3. *Primary schools have a majority of female staff [. . .]*

Bennett concludes that as a consequence many primary teachers will have experienced a 'career break' and have extensive family commitments. As Bennett points out, literature focusing on primary school management prior to 1987 refers to primary schools as if they are the property of the headteacher (Alexander, 1984).

Generally, primary school middle managers are curriculum leaders or curriculum co-ordinators. Responsibilities will involve leading professionals in the delivery of the curriculum.

In essence, middle management in primary schools should not be seen within a hierarchical model. West (1995, pp. 6–9) refers to *Primary Matters, A Discussion on Teaching and Learning in Primary Schools* (OFSTED, 1994a) and *Handbook for the Inspection of Schools* (OFSTED, 1994c, revised 1996a) for information concerning the management of the curriculum in primary schools. The former publication reports the findings of a survey *focusing on primary matters related to the quality of teaching and from that basis raises a number of important general issues, mainly concerned with curriculum and staff management and development.* Examples of co-ordinator practice cited in the report included:

- involvement in the long- or medium-term planning of topics and subjects
- acting as a semi-specialist teacher, teaching every class in the school his/her own subject for a block of three weeks out of twelve
- giving demonstration lessons
- working alongside colleagues
- preparing and introducing a series of lessons for a whole year group
- writing policies and schemes of work
- leading staff meetings
- providing INSET
- attending courses
- auditing, purchasing and organising resources
- advising teachers
- supporting or leading planning.

The report suggests, that in all but the smallest primary schools, headteachers are able to delegate the management of particular subjects to individual members of staff. As West (1995 p. 10) commented, *this represents a major shift in practice from headteacher curriculum management to subject specialists.*

There are other areas of management in primary schools for which responsibility points are allocated (West, 1995, pp. 12–13). These involve such processes as: policy formation, implementation and/or review; formulating or revising schemes of work; assisting the planning process by leading or advising year group teams as they construct units of work, lesson plans, projects and themes; working and advising colleagues; INSET-based initiatives; School Development Plan (SDP); and preparation of relevant LEA or OFSTED documentation.

In sum, the emergence of middle managers in primary schools has been a response to the needs of primary teachers, who have experienced immense curriculum change and associated administrative burdens. As a consequence, there has been a need to promote the development of common understanding and good relationships (Knutton and Ireson, 1995, p. 60). While Bennett (1995, p. 84) describes the practice of middle management in primary schools as *confused,* new initiatives have to be addressed by headteachers. These focus on the need to facilitate the development of middle managers in their institutions. Bradley *et al.* (1983) comment on the need to support school leadership by:

- *fostering a collaborative and participative approach*
- *making maximum use of the talents of each member of staff, by creating an efficient structure of responsibilities within the school and then delegating effectively*
- *encouraging staff to take responsibility for their own development.*

As a primary school middle manager, you will need to understand the processes involved in developing management skills. This section has shown, albeit briefly, that there are general skills which can be identified in primary and secondary schools. The key difference between management of primary and secondary schools is that secondary schools perceive management posts as points on a hierarchical scale. In contrast, primary colleagues perceive management as curriculum-focused and task-orientated.

Secondary school middle management

An analysis of middle management in the secondary school is provided by Earley and Fletcher-Campbell (1989). Bennett (1995, p. 101) sustains the view that many middle managers deny the validity of the concept. Bennett (pp. 101–4) does, however, acknowledge that there are five characteristics that generate a need for middle managers. Briefly:

1. *The size of the school*, the smallest secondary school is larger than *most* primary schools. In addition to the teaching staff, there is a body of technicians and support staff. The organisation is larger, needing greater administrative and managerial support. There is also the need for communicating information to a larger number of pupils, parents, outside agencies and employees than the number involved in primary schools. Some arrangement has to be made to communicate.

2. *The nature of the work,* is different to that of primary schools. Ball and Bowe (1992) found that as the national curriculum has been implemented, the status of the subject area, or department, has increased.

3. *How the work is organised.* The pastoral system with a combination of guidance and disciplinary functions has a significant role in secondary schools. There has been a move during the 1980s and 1990s to strengthen the guidance function and develop a teaching focus through programmes of personal and social education, passing the disciplinary function to subject departments as a teaching issue. In contrast, a primary school teacher will have to relate to all subject co-ordinators of the subjects they teach, thus creating a complex web of formal relationships. In both primary and secondary schools, teachers can be both superordinate and subordinate to each other. However, in secondary schools teachers may work in isolated teams and are less likely to experience close collegial working relationships with the whole staff.

4. *The national funding structure for schools* has also had a significant impact on secondary school middle management. Since the ERA (1988), schools are funded on a formula based largely on the number of pupils of particular ages on the roll. Subject departments are similarly funded to a formula encompassing the number of pupils for each age being taught and its subsequent resourcing needs. As a consequence, departments will compete with each other to gain the maximum number of students.

5. *Teachers' status.* Teachers' salaries, status and promotion prospects are also affected by the size of the school. Changes to school management have created the need for teachers to be responsible for the sub-units of the school.

Middle management in secondary schools applies to a form of tier authority which attempts to co-ordinate the day-to-day work of teachers in various sub-units and integrate them into the totality of the school. Senior management should therefore recognise the integration function of the middle manager.

Middle management responsibilities

Secondary school middle managers should have specific responsibilities identified in the job description for each position within the structure of the school. A framework for each post is specified in the Teachers' Pay and Conditions Act 1987 (Schedule 3: Conditions of Employment of School Teachers), which lists the main duties of a Main Pay Grade (MPG) teacher, described by Armstrong *et al.* (1993b, pp. 26–7; reproduced by permission of the publisher, Folens Ltd, Albert House, Apex Business Centre, Boscombe Road, Dunstable LU5 4RL):

1. **Teaching:**
   - planning and preparing courses and lessons
   - teaching, setting work and marking
   - assessing, recording and reporting development, progress and attainment.

2. **Other activities:**
   - promoting general progress and well-being of individual pupils, groups or classes
   - providing pastoral and careers guidance and advice
   - recording and reporting personal and social needs of pupils
   - communicating and consulting with parents
   - communicating and co-operating with persons or bodies outside the school
   - participating in meetings for any of the purposes described above.

3. **Assessments and reports:**
   - providing or contributing to oral and written assessments, reports or references relating to individual pupils and groups of pupils.

4. **Appraisal:**
   - participating in any arrangements within an agreed national framework for the appraisal of his/her performance and that of other teachers.

5. **Review: further training and development:**
   - reviewing from time to time his/her methods of teaching and schemes of work
   - participating in arrangements for further training and professional development.

6. **Educational methods:**
   - advising and co-operating with the headteacher and other teachers on the preparation and development of courses of study, teaching materials, teaching programmes, methods of teaching and assessment and pastoral arrangements.

7. **Discipline, health and safety:**
   - maintaining good order and discipline and safeguarding pupils' health and safety when they are authorised to be on school premises and when they are engaged in authorised school activities elsewhere.

8. **Staff meetings:**
   - participation in meetings relating to the curriculum, administration or organisation of the school, including pastoral arrangements.

9. **Cover:**
   - supervising and, so far as is practicable, teaching any pupils whose teacher is not available to teach them in accordance with government/ LEA/school guidelines on cover.

10. **Public examinations:**
    - participating in the preparation and assessment of pupils for public examinations; recording and reporting such assessments and taking part in the supervision of examinations.

11. **Management:**
    - contributing to the selection for appointment and professional development of other teachers and non-teaching staff, including the induction and assessment of new and probationary staff
    - co-ordinating or managing the work of other teachers

- taking part in the review, development and management of activities relating to the curriculum organisation and pastoral functions of the school.

12. Administration:

- participating in administrative and organisational tasks, relating to duties as described above, including the management of supervision of persons providing teacher support and the ordering and allocation of equipment and materials
- attending assemblies, registering attendance whether before, during or after school sessions.

As a middle manager you will also have additional responsibilities as described by Armstrong *et al.* (1993b, p. 28–9; reproduced by permission of the publisher, Folens Ltd, Albert House, Apex Business Centre, Boscombe Road, Dunstable LU5 4RL):

1. Staff (teaching and non-teaching):

- selection, including job specification in consultation with the headteacher, compilation of advertisements, selecting the short list and interview procedure
- deployment, including equitable distribution of classes and timetabling
- appraisal
- support, including induction of new staff and students on teaching practice
- staff development and in-service training including contribution to School Development Plans (SDPs)
- maintaining morale
- supervision
- organisation of departmental meetings.

2. Curriculum development:

- aims and objectives: their statement, evaluation and modification
- syllabus, selection and design
- monitoring, including the recording of progress of new courses
- evaluation
- methodology
- responding to national and local initiatives
- implementing school policies and curriculum statements, for example, equal opportunities, information technology, language across the curriculum and special needs.

3. **Curriculum management:**
   - schemes of work
   - examination administration – internal and external
   - setting cover work for staff absence
   - continuity and progression – KS2 to KS3 and KS4 onwards.

4. **Resources:**
   - management of financial resources
   - management of equipment and stock
   - maintenance of specialist accommodation
   - security, especially of hazardous substances
   - organisation of field trips and visits
   - development of teaching resources.

5. **Pupil progress:**
   - assessment – development and supervision of formative and summative profiling systems, including those related to national testing
   - internal and external moderation procedures
   - grouping – organisation of student groups to encourage effective learning and progression
   - motivation, discipline and welfare.

6. **Record-keeping:**
   - co-ordination and upkeep of departmental records, group lists, staff and pupils' records, including profiles and records of achievement
   - compilation, collation and security of records of examination assessments
   - administration of national tests.

7. **Liaison:**
   - with members of the department
   - with parents, employers, industry, etc.
   - with senior management, heads of year, other departments, ancillary staff
   - with feeder schools and colleges
   - with officers, advisers and inspectorate
   - with external moderators and assessors
   - with governors.

8. **Safety:**
   - overall responsibility with the department
   - checks on implementation of LEA policy

- reporting problems to the headteacher and LEA
- liaison with Schools' Safety Officer and LEA Safety Officers.

The above refers to a department or subject-based area; secondary schools also have highly complex pastoral teams. Calvert and Henderson (1995, p. 70) explain:

> [...] pastoral [care...] places special demands on managers to provide a supportive framework, which will equip pupils to cope with the ever-increasing pressures of life. Often under-valued and misunderstood, inadequately resourced and prepared for, pastoral provision can be patchy.

All teachers are involved in pastoral areas as it permeates every aspect of school life. Formally there are two pastoral roles experienced by the majority of teachers and co-ordinated by middle managers: heads of year and Personal and Social Education (PSE) co-ordinators. Form tutors have responsibility for administration, discipline and welfare of pupils. PSE teachers (who may be the form tutor) are responsible for teaching a set syllabus encompassing a range of issues: personal, social, vocational and moral.

As Calvert and Henderson (1995, p. 71) describe, *the pastoral domain is not straightforward; complexities and conflict may arise.* Pastoral co-ordinators will need to be aware of these (pp. 71–2):

- *a lack of shared understanding and agreement* as to the purposes and nature of pastoral provision
- the existence of an *academic/pastoral divide* – misunderstanding [...] of the complementary nature of the two [...]
- a resulting *inferior position of the pastoral curriculum,* [...] with an over-emphasis on academic results [...]
- pressures of an *overcrowded curriculum* and reduced funding [...]
- *teacher overload* – an increase in workload and expectations [...]
- the difficulty of encouraging teachers to take on an enhanced pastoral role [when] increased demands are being made [in other areas (academic and management)] and [when] *high levels of stress* are reported
- *a lack of pastoral care for staff* under such circumstances [...]
- *a lack of commitment and confidence* in the pastoral domain on the part of many teachers [...]
- *a lack of consensus as to the aims, nature, content, skills and processes* of PSE work [...]
- *a lack of appreciation as to the value of PSE* on the part of teachers and pupils [...]
- *a lack of suitable materials and ineffective use of available resources* [...]

- *a lack of a clear role of management* [. . .], [middle managers], form teachers and teachers of PSE
- *inappropriate management structures* for developing pastoral care
- *difficulties in providing adequate preparation for Newly Qualified Teachers* in initial teacher education and induction [. . .]
- *difficulties of monitoring and evaluating pastoral work* and measuring success [. . .]
- *lack of support* for pastoral care at national levels.

This analysis reveals the need for a strong framework to co-ordinate those involved in the different aspects of pastoral care. Middle managers of pastoral teams need to be good managers, capable of building teams, resolving conflicts, counselling and providing support. Pastoral teams will need to have a shared commitment to the needs of pupils and teachers. If senior managers are to recognise the developmental needs of pastoral co-ordinators and teams, training should be provided.

Summary

There are many features common to all school management teams, across all phases of education. In the majority of schools middle managers work in teams. The size of each team will reflect the size of the school. It is axiomatic that teams are necessary within the context of schools as organisations. As a middle manager, it is critical to understand that teams do not act as teams simply because they are described as such.

Middle managers in schools will inevitably work in two types of team; structured teams (Figure 5.1 – Teams A, B and C) and those created for specific purposes (Team D). Essentially, successful teamwork depends on a clearly defined set of aims and objectives, the personalities of team members and the team manager. Developing middle management skills will involve a balance between concern for team, concern for the task and developing the individual. A middle manager may find identifying the characteristics of his/her team difficult.

Middle managers should aim to lead and participate in effective teams which agree aims, share skills, realise potential and reduce stress and anxiety. Perhaps the most important element of team leadership is the ability to motivate others. As a team leader, a middle manager will serve as a role model to his/her team members. Middle managers should inspire and motivate others to achieve high standards and to work towards fulfilment of the school's aims.

Bennett (1995, p. 72) casts doubt as to whether primary schools and middle management are compatible. Literature focusing on primary school manage-ment prior to 1987 refers to primary schools as if they are the property of the headteacher (Alexander, 1984). Generally, primary school middle managers are curriculum leaders or 'curriculum co-ordinators'. In essence, middle management in primary schools should not be seen within a hierarchical model.

In sum, the emergence of middle managers in primary schools has been a response to the needs of primary teachers, who have experienced immense curriculum change and associated administrative burdens. As a primary school middle manager, you will need to understand the processes involved in developing management skills.

Middle management in secondary schools applies to a form of tier authority which attempts to co-ordinate the day-to-day work of teachers in various sub-units and integrate them into the totality of the school. Secondary school middle managers should have specific responsibilities identified in the job description for each position within the structure of the school. All teachers are involved in pastoral areas as it permeates every aspect of school life. As Calvert and Henderson (1995, p. 71) describe, the pastoral domain is not straight-forward, complexities and conflict may arise. Middle managers of pastoral teams need to be good managers capable of building teams, resolving conflicts, providing counselling and support.

6

■　■　■

The Administrator

Introduction

Brighouse (1991) states:

> *How well the school is organised and maintained – the administration of the school – vitally affects the lives of teachers. If there are constant foul-ups in the administration, it is almost impossible to avoid staff stress and loss of morale accumulating during the school year; moreover it saps the highest common factor of shared values and common purpose which should be that of a good school.*

There are 'peaks and troughs' of administrative activity that occur in every academic year. Timetabling, assessment and inspection are key events in each school's programme. Identifying when such events occur is essential to the successful management of a department or school. This chapter starts with general advice on how to control documentation and then highlights three important events:

- timetabling
- assessment and reporting
- inspection

Middle managers need to understand the administrative processes involved if they are to operate effectively as a manager and teacher in a school. There are few differences between primary and secondary practice. After more than a decade of externally imposed changes to schools as organisations, all middle managers need to develop the administrative skills and abilities required to manage their team.

At the start of each working day, a middle manager will have a number of administrative tasks to complete. The first section suggests ways in which documentation can be tackled.

Documentation

An observable difference between classroom teachers and middle managers is the amount of paperwork that accumulates in their staffroom pigeon holes. A feature of good management practice is the ability to identify the relevant, urgent and important documentation. In order to prioritise, a middle manager needs to know and understand the purpose of each document. As a middle manager you should always keep administration under control and not let it control your actions.

Types of documentation

What documentation will a middle manager be expected to process?

- School Development Plan (SDP)
- school policy documents
- department/year handbook
- prospectus
- contributions to newsletter and senior management meetings
- financial strategic plan
- timetable allocations
- resource material
- curriculum/pastoral papers
- LEA papers
- pupils' reports
- assessment papers
- league table information (Form 7)
- department/team development plans
- staff appraisal
- examination results.

To begin with, set aside a period in each day for administrative tasks. This may involve arriving 30 minutes earlier for work. Try to find a window in which you can work without interruptions by pupils, colleagues and the telephone. Process all documentation by categorising each paper according to importance. The action plan shown in Table 6.1 may help.

Practical advice

In-service training should be provided for middle managers. The following suggestions will help:

Table 6.1: Documentation action plan

Category	Responses	Paper e.g.	Consultation (list of who to contact, e.g.)	Action
A	Within 24 hrs	Team matters/pupils requiring immediate response	Pupils, parents, headteacher, staff	Read and write
B	Within 48 hrs	Team matters/pupils, senior management papers	Team member, SMT	Meetings: read and write
C	Within 1 week	Meetings/agendas/ reports – dept/school/ LEA	LEA/SMT	Meetings: read and write
D	Within 2 weeks	Reports	Government/ SMT	Read and write
E	Within 1 month	Documentation *not* requiring a response, but could be useful at a later date		Read only / research

1. **Diary** – keep an up-to-date diary in which you identify busy periods during the term.

2. **Filing cabinet** – always file away information. Check through files regularly discarding any out-of-date or irrelevant information. You may need to obtain a filing cabinet for your classroom/office.

3. **Computer** – use and develop your computer skills. Preparing responses/ reports in advance saves time. Keep a catalogue of programmes and files for easy reference.

4. **Current folder** – a useful 'litmus test' for each document is to create a 'current' folder which you will refer to several times throughout the day. If a document is not relevant it can be filed away.

5. **Things to do** – add documentation to your daily 'things to do' list; where possible complete all responses in advance of the date requested.

6. **Team delegation** – there may be a specific area of work in which a team member has an interest. Develop his/her skills in this area and delegate some of your paperwork.

7. **Reading** – when reading documentation, highlight key words and points of action. This avoids unnecessary reading and could provide the framework for your written response.

8. **Response** – when responding to a document ensure that your points are relevant and relate to specific areas of the document (see "Written Communication" in Chapter Three for further advice).

9. **Keep a copy!** – always keep a copy of responses, filed with related documentation.

Timetabling

Since the national curriculum (DES, 1988a), middle managers have had increased responsibility for the timetabling of subjects. Timetabling is both an administrative and team management process. The national curriculum provides a curriculum framework for all schools. Guidelines are given on the number of subjects taught and recommendations of allocated time.

This applies to all schools across all phases. The final decision as to how the time is distributed is at the discretion of all school management teams. How the school is managed will determine the degree of staff involvement in timetabling. Middle managers need to be able to know and understand the concepts and procedures involved in timetabling and curriculum planning.

The timetable is the plan by which the curriculum is delivered according to:

- subjects
- teachers
- pupils
- time
- rooms.

1. The number of **subjects** is determined in part by the national curriculum. This is a framework which stipulates which national curriculum subjects should be taught within five key stages (see Table 6.2). The content of a school's curriculum should also reflect the ethos of the school. Schools may place an emphasis on technology, sport, expressive arts or languages. This

Table 6.2: School structure – key stages

Key stage	Year	Age
Compulsory		
KS1	Years 1, 2	5–7
KS2	Years 3, 4, 5, 6	7–11
KS3	Years 7, 8, 9	11–14
KS4	Years 10, 11	14–16
Post-compulsory		
KS5	Years 12, 13	16–19

will be reflected in the number of additional periods on the timetable which are allocated to those subjects.

2. **Teacher availability** will also determine the content of the curriculum and timetabling. There would be little point deciding to place an emphasis on music without a music specialist. Staff availability is important. The majority of schools employ part-time staff; team leaders need to identify when his/her staff are available.

3. **Pupils** need to be organised into groups prior to timetabling. Policy decisions will need to be made, i.e. are pupils grouped according to age? Such decisions will reflect the ethos of the school. In larger schools, middle managers and their teams may elect to organise pupils differently to other subject/pastoral areas in the school. This will need to be considered in the timetabling process.

4. **Time** is important! The use of time on a timetable is often neglected. How the school day is divided is relevant to how pupils learn. Equally relevant is when pupils are taught. Practical considerations should also impact on the timetabling process, e.g. movement around the school site and changing for physical education. The carrying of kit, books, materials for technology and musical instruments to school on the same day may be a physical impossibility for some children.

5. **Rooms**. Middle managers may have responsibility for a suite of rooms within the school. The availability of each room and the position of the room will be relevant to delivery of the curriculum. Shared rooms will only 'work' if managed sensitively. Staff needs should be considered. The availability of relevant equipment and access for preparation are both necessary considerations for timetabling.

Before scheduling the timetable, middle managers may be approached by the senior management team to identify timetabling needs. Keep copies of memos and details of conversations held. Timetabling is a detailed process, aspects of which even the most efficient deputy headteacher may forget!

Team leaders should always consult with staff to establish their requirements.

Middle managers will need insight into the process of translating the curriculum into the timetable to avoid any possibility of making irreversible decisions which have negative implications (Armstrong *et al.*, 1993a, p. 56). As team leaders, middle managers need to identify the needs of their colleagues and communicate these to senior management.

The process

A timetable for the next academic year will be written during the summer term. Managers should have a clear summary of subjects, teachers, pupils, time and rooms. In order to gather this information, senior management should consult with middle managers who, in turn, meet and discuss all issues and their implications with their team. Analysis of staff needs is essential. All requirements should be listed and presented in a clear format to the senior manager responsible for writing the timetable.

Middle managers should copy any details sent to their team, e.g. responses and memos to senior managers. Try to prioritise, as this will ease the decision-making process and avoid rejection of your team requirements. The key to the process is *negotiation*. It may be necessary to manage changes to the timetable over a number of years. The national curriculum and assessment practices are legislated for and must therefore take priority. For example, in a music department, additions/changes may include those shown in Table 6.3.

Table 6.3: Timetable changes (music department)

Area	Change(s)	Implications
Subjects	• integrated courses • modular curriculum	• 'blocked' timetable • additional staff
Teachers	• additional Special Educational Needs (SEN) support • increased music provision	• financial (LMS) • staff development • team building • management
Pupils	• re-grouping mixed ability teaching • additional subjects	• rooms • financial development • management
Time	• increased music provision	• reduction of time allocated to other subjects • staff • rooms • management
Rooms	• specialist rooms, e.g. music, computers, labs, workshops	• financial • need for rooms • non-sharing • management

As Table 6.3 indicates, the ramifications of change to the structure of the timetable in any of the five areas are considerable. Middle managers need to know the component parts of the timetable and understand the effect their decisions will make on other subject areas. 'Defending your corner' may not be the most profitable way of approaching timetabling. Compromise is essential; there may be more than one approach to achieving your aim. Work with the timetabler; appreciate the enormity of his/her task.

Curriculum plan

Final decisions as to how the curriculum will be timetabled will be made by senior management. Middle managers should be involved in the process of planning the delivery and content of the curriculum. The process is as shown in Figure 6.1.

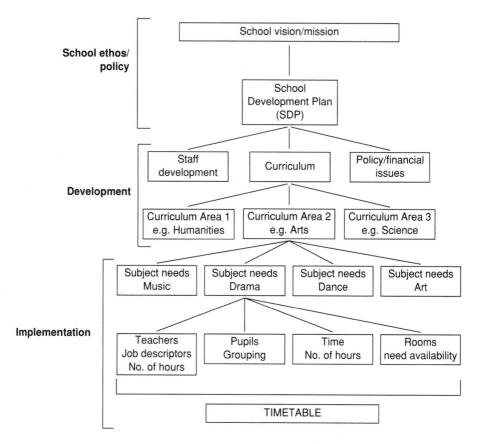

Figure 6.1: Timetable – process of development and implementation

Having completed this process, estimates of the number of periods will be required. This should then be checked with staff who will be able to identify potential problems. For example, in secondary schools there will be the added dimension of examination options. The role of middle managers is critical to the successful development and implementation of an effective curriculum plan.

External influences will have an impact in pupils' education. Recent changes to the examination structure, i.e. the introduction of General National Vocational Qualifications (GNVQs) have had a tremendous impact on curriculum planning in secondary schools. Equally, the need for specialist subject teachers in the primary sector has led to significant changes to the structure of the school day in both infant and junior schools.

Management

A final consideration in timetabling is the allocation of time to manage. With increased responsibilities and the development of staff management posts in primary and secondary schools, there are timetabling implications. Agreement is needed as to how much time should be negotiated for middle and senior management posts. The time allocated should reflect the requirements for each responsibility and/or task. Non-contact time is always a contentious issue between staff. The allocation of hours for management tasks is critical to the effective management of schools.

As a pastoral manager, I was allocated significantly more hours than curriculum managers. This reflected the school ethos and the needs of staff, pupils and parents. It also reflected the number of tasks I had to complete on a daily basis, and the impact of my post on the running of the school. Such details should be considered in relation to curriculum commitments. I would have found it impossible to fulfil my pastoral role with a significant teaching commitment.

Detailed job descriptions will assist the timetabler. If a member of staff has a clearly defined role which relates to hours on the timetable, there can be no doubt as to how the timetable at an individual level can be constructed. Areas of indecision, or lack of definition, will hinder the process.

Middle managers should therefore aim to be involved in the curriculum planning process. It is essential for effective planning to identify individual and team needs. Copies of all correspondence should be kept. Negotiate and compromise; aim to resolve problems. Middle managers should have clear knowledge and understanding of the curriculum planning process. With the necessary skills and abilities, middle managers should be in a position to plan ahead.

Assessment and reporting

In recent years there have been many debates focusing on assessment and reporting issues in education. This section will not attempt to engage in any school debate. As a middle manager you will be required to process documentation related to assessment and reporting.

Assessment

The purposes of assessment and reporting are:

- to assist the pupil in the process of learning
- to assist the teacher in curriculum evaluation
- to provide information for third parties.

At the end of each key stage, a headteacher must fully comply with the arrangements for assessing pupils. While this is the headteacher's responsibility, in practice middle managers will be employed to complete each task which includes:

- identification of arrangements for each pupil
- ensuring that all pupils are assessed
- ensuring that the school's standards conform to national requirements
- moderating the final levels for each pupil
- ensuring that all pupils are accurately assessed and final levels are ascribed.

The statutory assessment arrangements involve Teacher Assessment (TA) of each pupil's achievements in each Attainment Target (AT), based on the pupil's school work over the course of the key stage, and national curriculum tests administered to each pupil and marked by his/her teacher.

Teacher assessment is an assessment of pupils' school work in relation to the ATs set for each national curriculum subject. The process of building up evidence of pupils' attainments over the course of a key stage is fundamental to good practice. Middle managers are required to work with colleagues to develop the key elements stipulated by DFE Circulars 12/92, 13/92 and 1/95. Evidence is now collated by teachers. Samples of pupils' work at different levels are then moderated by external moderators. The fundamental principles of the orders are:

- assessment over each key stage
- integrating assessment, teaching and learning
- drawing on evidence from
  - ongoing school work
  - observation
  - homework
  - written classwork
- record keeping
- retaining evidence
- school policy on assessment.

Good assessment practices should therefore be established which may include:

- involving pupils in their own assessment
- formative marking
- assessment-based learning activities
- clear learning objectives explicit to each pupil
- individual portfolios
- adapting mark books to identify evidence
- focusing on achievement.

Schools may want common systems across subjects but may prefer to let faculties, curriculum areas or departments develop their own systems to agree principles as stated in the school policy. Middle managers may also be required to develop assessment practice within their teams. The following key questions may assist in this process:

- how can marking be made purposeful and useful for assessment?
- how can previous experience be shared between year groups and subject areas?
- what recording systems in place can be adapted to current needs?
- how can the breadth of pupil achievement be celebrated, recorded and supported by evidence?
- what mechanisms can be set up to use the same work as evidence to support assessment in more than one subject?
- what is the role of the tutor/class teacher in co-ordinating assessment?
- how can secondary practice build on what partner primary schools are doing?
- how can common cross-phase practices be achieved?
- how accessible/useful will the records and evidence be to parents and pupils?

In addition to end of key stage assessment, the government post-ERA (1988) introduced the National Record of Achievement (NRA) (1991). The more recent introduction of GNVQs (1992) led to the bringing together of the NRA and the National Record of Vocational Achievement. The former was designed to focus on summarising achievement, while the latter was designed to facilitate planning, assessment and recording. The bringing together of the two approaches ensures that the single record is a useful tool for training and development, while providing a picture of achievements to date and as a basis for credit accumulation.

Reporting

Having established good assessment practice, middle managers need to be aware of the legal requirements for reporting. As an administrative task, report-writing is time-consuming; however, pupil reports should be an invaluable tool to teaching and learning. The Education (Individual Pupils' Achievements) (Information) Regulations 16/93 (DFE, 1993a) and Reports on Pupils' Achievements 1/95 (DFE, 1995) provide the legal framework for current reporting practices. The regulations can be summarised as follows:

Introduction

The Education (Individual Pupils' Achievements) (Information) Regulations came into force in December 1993. They require:

1. **Reports to parents:**
   - a written report must be sent out **at least annually** to the parents of **each pupil** for their retention
   - the report should contain at least the minimum information required by the regulations
   - the report must be sent by the required deadlines.

2. **Reports to receiving schools:** when a pupil moves school, a report containing at least the minimum requirements must be passed on to the headteacher of the new school within 15 school days.

3. **Reports to school-leavers:** information covering at least the minimum requirements is given to every school-leaver using mandatory format (NRA).

Details

Reports to parents

The report must include:

- 'brief particulars' of the pupil's progress in all subjects and activities studied as part of the school curriculum, written in the form of *succinct narrative comments* highlighting strengths and weaknesses
- the results of all public examinations, qualifications achieved or credits towards qualifications gained; results received after the report has been dispatched must be sent on to parents as soon as possible
- details of the arrangements under which the report may be discussed with teachers at the school
- separate 'brief particulars' for all NC subjects studied; where the pupil has been assessed under statutory assessment arrangements, these particulars must amplify and explain the NC assessment results
- a record of the pupil's attendance during the year, including the total number of school sessions and the number for which the pupil was absent without authority.

KS1, 2 and 3 – all pupils assessed under statutory arrangements to be reported at the end of each key stage:

- in the **core subjects, history, geography and a modern foreign language**, the pupil's level of attainment on the NC 1–10 scale by subject and both the teacher assessment and, where relevant, test level in each attainment target
- in **technology**, the pupil's level of attainment on the NC 1–10 scale by subject, profile component, and both the teacher's assessment and, where relevant, test level in each attainment target
- in **music, art and PE**, a commentary on the pupil's progress in relation to the end of key stage targets
- comparative information about the levels of attainment of other pupils in the school and nationally at the end of KS3.

KS4 – all pupils assessed under statutory arrangements to be reported at the end of KS4:

- details of subjects in which the pupil has been awarded a GCSE certificate or other qualification and of the grade of the certificate or qualification
- the pupil's level of attainment in each subject and attainment target on NC subjects assessed under statutory arrangements and, in the case of technology, in each profile component
- comparative information about the GCSE examination results of 15-year-old pupils in the school and nationally.

End of KS1, 2, 3 and 4 – all pupils:

- where requested by parents, the pupil's level of attainment on the 1–10 NC scale by attainment target, if this has not already been statutorily provided
- a statement that the levels have been arrived at by statutory assessments
- a statement where a pupil has been exempted from any attainment target under s. 17, 18 or 19 of the 1988 ERA.

Reports to receiving schools

The results of statutory assessments of the pupil under the NC by subject and attainment target at all previous key stages and the school year in which the assessments were made.

The information must include that for key stages assessed by previous schools:

- the teachers' latest assessments of the pupil's progress against all applicable attainment targets since the last statutory assessment or since the pupil arrived at the reporting school (provided that the pupil was on roll for at least four weeks) whichever is more recent
- any public examination results, including the results of examinations leading to vocational qualifications.

Reports to school-leavers

- the subject and attainment target levels of every NC subject studied. The levels provided should be those achieved at the point at which the pupil was assessed in the subject for the last time under statutory arrangements
- the results of any public examinations, qualifications achieved and credits towards qualifications gained, including vocational qualifications or credits towards vocational qualifications
- 'brief particulars' of achievements in all subjects and activities studied as part of the school curriculum.

Report formats

1. **Reports to parents:** the format adopted should be consistent with meeting the minimum content requirements.
2. **Reports to receiving schools:** the format adopted should be consistent with meeting the minimum content requirements.
3. **Reports to school-leavers:** schools are required by the regulations to use the prescribed format.

KS2, 3 and 4 must include Standard Attainment Tests (SATs):

- results
- position within school
- PSE/work experience
- teacher assessment
- contributions to life of the school
- achievements
- pupil opportunity.

National Record of Achievement (NRA)

Changes to practice 14–19 are continuing at speed. In principle, the Records of Achievement (ROA) for end of KS4–5 should include:

- the subject and attainment target levels of every NC subject studied
- the results of any public examinations, qualifications achieved and credits towards qualifications gained, including vocational qualifications or credit towards vocational qualifications
- 'brief particulars' of achievements in all subjects and activities studied as part of the school curriculum.

These details should cover the pupil's achievements during the school year preceding his/her leaving school. In sum, the key principles of assessment of all pupils are:

1. Assessment should be an integral part of teaching and learning which means:
   - assessment should provide feedback to pupils about their learning
   - assessment should emphasise positive achievements and identify future learning needs
   - pupils should be provided with a broad range of experiences.

2. Assessment is the teacher's judgment of the evidence of pupils' achievements which means:
   - observing; asking questions; viewing pupils' products
   - listening; teachers support and foster pupil learning and can interpret this as evidence of achievement.

Policy

In addition to managing the implementation of government guidelines on assessment and reporting, middle managers will also participate in determining the school policy for assessment and reporting. As shown, assessment should be interpreted in its widest sense and not only in the context of the national curriculum. Assessment includes the gathering of evidence and the making of a judgment in order to provide feedback to the pupil to assist future learning and to award a qualitative value to the work or performance. The school policy for assessment and reporting should therefore:

- be understood by all participants
- begin with a review of current practice
- be developed and implemented incrementally
- support and promote equal opportunities within the school
- be integrated with or linked to schemes of work
- provide a framework for pupil continuity and progression
- be shared with all staff and governors.

A suggested framework for assessment and reporting policy is:

1. Identify the stages for development of a policy for assessment and reporting.
2. Identify achievable success criteria in order to evaluate the process of development and implementation.
3. Identify key personnel: assessment co-ordinator, heads of department/ subject co-ordinators, key stage co-ordinators.
4. Decide on the timescale.
5. Identify professional development and INSET needs for key personnel and whole staff.

6. Ensure that all INSET needs are reflected in the SDP.

7. Decide on a monitoring and evaluating structure.

Having considered the above, the policy for assessment and reporting should relate to the government's criteria. An assessment and reporting policy should indicate points of action, address key issues and contribute to school effectiveness by:

- supporting institutional development
- supporting institutional management
- supporting individual teacher development (CPD)
- promoting attainment
- enhancing quality of learning
- improving (changing) classroom practice.

Assessment is not an 'exact science' and should, therefore, be continually monitored and evaluated.

There are three stages in gathering and communicating evidence of a pupil's ability to learn: assessment, recording and reporting – all have been subjects of legislation. As an example of policy in practice, Figures 6.2 and 6.3 provides a basis for development of an assessment policy in your department.

**A POLICY FOR ASSESSMENT, RECORDING AND REPORTING
IN A SECONDARY SCHOOL**

Introduction

Assessment should be concerned with:

- making judgments about what pupils know, can do and understand
- making plans for pupils' progress
- valuing the achievements of pupils
- involving pupils and others in the assessment process
- identifying and helping to improve weaknesses.

The policy sets out to:

- make assessment continuous
- relate assessment to what is taught
- inform parents, colleagues and others (e.g. employers, colleges, etc.)
- strengthen curriculum planning by using assessment information to judge the success of curriculum aims
- measure performance by means of explicit criteria rather than comparing one pupil with another
- make use of assessment information provided by feeder schools
- recognise that pupils' achievement can be wide ranging.

To make this policy effective it is necessary to:

- make clear the learning objectives of a particular course
- develop assessment methods which allow pupils to show what they know, can do and understand
- develop the ability of pupils to review their own progress
- be positive in reporting achievement
- devise methods of recording and reporting which recognise the wide ranging nature of pupil achievement.

Figure 6.2: Secondary school assessment policy

DEPARTMENT MARKING POLICY

1. Marking should be done professionally and regularly. It is not necessary to mark every piece of work individually, especially if it is supervised classwork.

2. There should be oral feedback and time for reflection and/or correction or re-drafting by pupils.

3. Marks and grades are not necessary unless the teacher needs to use them to emphasise examination standards, or is marking objectively, e.g. in a 'Unit Test'.

4. The awarding of grades is encouraged in Years 10–13 in relation to published examination criteria.

5. A comment, preferably positive, should be used wherever possible, which will establish for the pupil their level of achievement and the extent to which they have met the objectives for an assignment.

6. Recording of marks/grades/levels/work seen is important, as is the disciplining of pupils for not doing work set or not handing in work for assessment. The use of assessment files allows rapid access to an individual pupil's achievement record.

7. The use of English should be assessed in geography and so should the use of mathematical/graphical skills. This should either be corrected or a notation used such as 'Sp' for spelling, or 'C' for missing capital letters, and pupils made familiar with their use. Good handwriting should be expected at all times.

8. Pupils should ideally be helped in the process of doing work by a pro-active style of teaching. This is at least as important as formal writing. Marking is seen to fulfil a formative as well as summative function.

9. Pupils should learn to write in sentences and in a style which does not require the writing out of questions that they are asked to answer (an exception may be when a question becomes the title).

10. Pupils should be aware of the marking scheme in use and encouraged to discuss the usefulness of marking and how it could better fulfil their learning needs.

Figure 6.3: Department marking policy

Inspection

In the context of administration, the inspection process is perhaps the most demanding of all events in the life of a school. This section will outline, in brief, the purpose of the school inspection and what it entails for the middle manager.

Background

Ormston and Shaw (1993a, p. 1) state:

The Office for Standards in Education (OFSTED) was set up in 1992 and has a statutory function to give advice to the Secretary of State for Education on the quality of education.

OFSTED inspections were intended to be very different from the previous HMI Inspections and LEA 'Team Review' type of inspections. In particular, OFSTED inspections were to be judgmental and not developmental. Vocabulary (such as 'good', 'satisfactory' or 'poor') was designed to describe the strengths and weaknesses (not successes and failures) of most areas of a school. Everything is open to inspection:

- documentation
- policy statements
- views of parents
- governor involvement
- school and individual planning records
- assessment procedures
- policy statements
- minutes of meetings
- budget forecasts
- resource levels
- accommodation.

The only exceptions are where a school has special circumstances: a voluntary-aided church school, for example, will have its RE inspected by the diocese rather than OFSTED.

Each school (primary and secondary) is to be inspected every four years by an inspection team which will publish its judgments to a wider audience. The framework for the Inspection of Schools (OFSTED, 1994c, revised 1996a) is the instrument by which schools are inspected and has the force of law (Chaplin, 1995, p. 143); the rationale being that each school is to be assessed on:

- *the standards it attains and the quality of learning and education it achieves*
- *its efficiency and the value for money it provides*
- *the spiritual, moral, social and cultural values it achieves.*

The process

As Ormston and Shaw (1993a, p. 31) indicate, the first impression the inspection team forms of the school will be via its documentation; this is listed in s. 2a of the OFSTED Handbook (see Ormston and Shaw, 1993a). Middle managers will participate in this process; each subject and pastoral team will need to ensure that its paperwork is in the most helpful form for inspectors.

Leading up to the inspection, middle managers will be required to either contribute to or develop:

- SDP
- school prospectus
- policy documents
- school timetable
- staff handbook
- schemes of work
- department handbook (including marking policy)
- department extra-curricular activities
- curriculum plan
- assessment and reporting procedures.

As a middle manager, it is important that all aspects of your work are well documented. The inspection team will know nothing about the structure, organisation and ethos of your pastoral or curriculum area. It is your responsibility to supply as much information as possible. There are several stages to the development of this process:

Stage 1

Gather information: *who has written these? who has copies?* List all documentation concerning your area, e.g.:

- policy documents
- schemes of work
- initiatives
- statistical data
- class lists.

Stage 2

Pastoral/subject area handbook: *identify strengths and weaknesses.* List all information that will be in the handbook, e.g.:

- curriculum/tutor groups
- staffing
- resources
- staff development – INSET
- differentiation
- extra-curricular, including visits, trips
- schemes of work
- lesson plans and evaluation
- policy documents.

Stage 3

Future planning: *identify key papers; identify key staff.* List ideas for the future:

- pastoral/curriculum initiatives
- government directives
- staff development.

Stage 4

Monitoring and evaluation: *identify strengths and weaknesses; identify opportunities and threats.* Prepare plan for review of all activities:

- set targets
- consult staff
- produce documentation
- cyclical.

A third dimension to inspection is what occurs beyond the classroom – the quality of the educational experience the pupil is receiving as a consequence of other aspects of school life:

- pastoral system
- primary/secondary partnerships
- school/HEI partnerships
- INSET
- cross-curricular links
- support
- extra-curricular activities.

Each inspection will aim to take into account all aspects of the educational experience. As a middle manager you have the opportunity to ensure that policy planning is being put into practice and to evaluate the success of that planning.

The majority of OFSTED teams are approved and OFSTED-Trained Local Authority Inspection Teams who bid for contracts to inspect schools. At present all schools must be inspected within a four-year timespan. This has provided a major boost to many local authorities, particularly those who have lost overall financial and administrative control of many of their schools through them becoming grant maintained (e.g. Lincolnshire). Due to the number of teams bidding for contracts and different specialisms of team members, few schools are inspected by local teams.

The inspection process should be viewed positively, as it provides the opportunity to recognise and celebrate good practices, and to develop new initiatives. When preparing for an OFSTED inspection, a middle manager should:

- be aware of what is required
- ensure that all curriculum/pastoral policies are well documented and that all information is accurate and up-to-date
- identify strengths and weaknesses – make the most of the strengths and work towards improving the weaknesses
- encourage the sharing of ideas in your team
- encourage a close working team
- examine the teaching and learning styles used by your team
- evaluate lessons in the context of schemes of work and policy-planning
- assess the positive and negative aspects of the learning environment you create for your pupils.

It is essential that, as a middle manager, you ensure that every member of your team is aware of the need to ensure that all preparation, planning and recording is detailed, up-to-date and in-line with departmental policy. In essence, the inspection process should work for you and your colleagues.

Inspectors will not wish to see documentation that does not reflect practice.

In addition to documentation, the inspection process involves observation. OFSTED's *pro forma* for lesson observation is predominantly concerned with the collection of data about the lesson *content*, the quality of *teaching*, the quality of *learning* and the standards of *achievement* displayed in the lesson (Ormston and Shaw, 1993a, p. 73). The inspector will grade what s(he) has observed:

- **very good**: many good features, some of them outstanding
- **good**: good features and no major shortcomings
- **satisfactory**: sound but unremarkable
- **unsatisfactory**: some shortcomings in unimportant areas
- **poor**: many shortcomings
- **conflicting evidence**.

The inspection process concludes with an inspection report delivered to governors, headteachers, staff and parents. The report is public property and has led to extensive media coverage of 'successful' and 'failing' schools. Grading categories 1–6 are currently being revised. The following case study will guide middle managers for future practice.

Case study: Head of Department (HOD)

The school received extremely short notice of inspection (three months). This caused a great deal of added apprehension, particularly in terms of administration for the senior management team and middle managers in producing updated handbooks. In this instance, the HOD having recently been appointed and there being no schemes of work or handbook, this proved to be a considerable burden. This also placed a strain on the inspection team themselves as they had little to read beforehand. This caused rather more meetings and explanation to take place than would otherwise have been the case. The OFSTED inspection team was further pressured by knowing they themselves were being inspected by HMI.

The HOD was apprehensive that a local team would be carrying out the inspection. He had no contact with his LEA subject advisor.

There is no doubt that there is a possibility that a local team could be biased – it may want its schools to look favourable or alternatively may be tempted to highlight more weaknesses since they would benefit from a school's need to 'buy in' advice locally. The HOD does not feel that local teams should inspect local schools unless it is the case for all schools, since this will always lead to apprehension before inspections.

The HOD believed that he had adequate preparation by the school, but in hindsight a departmental review by an outside agency may have picked up some minor planning issues. For example, 'Map skills' in Year 8 was criticised not because it was inherently wrong, but because it was not sufficiently integrated within the curriculum. It is useful to study the journals of the professional organisations and OFSTED's own report of the previous year's inspection findings, although there is no substitute for experience from a recently inspected colleague. The HOD was frustrated that the inspector could not see 'everything' and indeed was only in his department for two-and-a-half-days. He felt rather under-inspected but this is apparently common and is largely a sense of anticlimax after the build-up to the inspection.

The feedback was detailed, although the evidence base did seem small in terms of lessons observed. Nonetheless the department received an adequate and, in many aspects, very encouraging report, particularly as no member of the department had been in post for more than 16 months. The tasks for 'action planning' were predictable; greater use of differentiation and a wider variety of teaching methods to be used. It was a useful experience.

In the final report, statements were more general and the HOD was surprised to see just how different the other departments' reports were. For example, some received a paragraph or more on aspects such as management or special needs, while others received hardly a mention. Statements tend to be vague in places and terms such as 'sound or better' are not particularly helpful.

Comment

The OFSTED procedure is rather peculiar in terms of methodology. Large quantities of data are gathered, for example, from lesson observations. This is converted into a numerical score which only the headteacher sees. This data is then sorted into a series of broad qualitative statements such as 'outstanding', 'excellent', 'good' and 'sound'. The HOD would have liked better-defined results to help target-planning since these terms were not sufficiently precise. He would also have liked a common format for reporting. The HOD felt that staff and, particularly, parents received rather a disparate mix of analysis of departments.

The school maintained a close watch over the inspection, with staff requested to report all lessons observed and any concerns they may have had about their observed lesson. Detailed lesson plans were submitted to inspectors, although these were rarely commented upon. Overall the HOD was quite pleased by the inspection and certainly relieved, as the school will have to live with the public report for another four years.

The report was well received by governors and parents although poorly presented in the local press. This vividly demonstrates that, however positive an independent report can be on a school, the school is still in the hands of the media. What is published in a news report is read by many more people than will ever read the full report.

Post-inspection meetings

Following a formal inspection, the registered inspector is required to arrange two meetings to discuss the main findings of the inspection with school managers and governors before writing the report including:

- the headteacher and any member of the senior management team who wishes to be involved
- the governing body, with the presence of the headteacher.

Ormston and Shaw (1993a, pp. 102–3) offer the following advice:

Before the meeting
Prepare for the meeting in a business-like way. Hold the meeting in a comfortable, well-lit room with good acoustics. Take care of the environmental factors, such as temperature and coffee. Inspectors need to be able to set out their written information and both teachers and inspectors will wish to take notes.

There are two purposes of this meeting:

1. *To check the factual accuracy of the information on which the inspection team's judgement is based.*

2. *To hear clear and unambiguous judgements on the quality and standards of teaching and learning in the school, the factors that contribute to the quality and the standards and the issues that need to be addressed.*

During the meeting the senior management team are able to question the factual accuracy of the report. This includes (Ormston and Shaw, 1993a, p. 103):

- *clear and unambiguous assessment of the quality of the school and the standards achieved by pupils*

- *clear and unambiguous assessment of factors which contribute to the quality and standards*

- *clear and unambiguous assessment of the issues which need to be addressed in the school as the result of the inspection*

- *judgements based on factually accurate evidence*

- *all the judgements that are to be made in the written report.*

After the meeting the senior management team should agree what has been said by the inspection team, consider objective feedback and issues for action.

The written report

The inspection will be carried out under s. 9 of the Education (Schools) Act, 1992. The purpose of the document is to report on:

- the educational standards achieved in the school
- the quality of education provided by the school
- whether the financial resources made available to the school are managed efficiently
- the spiritual, moral, social and cultural development of pupils at the school.

The findings of the inspection will contribute to the annual report of Her Majesty's Chief Inspector (HMCI) of Schools to the Secretary of State for Education. The report will contain the following basic information about the school:

- name of school
- type
- status
- age range of pupils
- name of headteacher
- school address

121

- telephone number
- name and address of appropriate authority
- local authority area
- DFE school number
- name of registered inspector
- dates of the inspection.

The detail of the report will include:

Intake of pupils and the area served by the school

1. **School data and indicators** – number of pupils in each year group.

2. **Special educational needs** – number of pupils having statements of special educational needs.

3. **Free school meals** – number of pupils eligible for free school meals.

4. **Teachers and class** –
   - full-time equivalent teachers
   - pupils to teacher ratio
   - percentage class contact ratio
   - average teaching group size.

Teaching time per week

Pupil attendance:

	Percentage attendance figure for each year group for third week in the term prior to the term of the inspection:		
	Actual attendance	Authorised absence	Unauthorised absence
Overall percentages			

Number of exclusions in the last 12 months:

	Fixed period		Permanent		Number from ethnic minority groups	
	Boys	Girls	Boys	Girls	Boys	Girls
Totals						

National curriculum assessments results:

Key stage – number in year group			
LEVEL	ENGLISH	MATHEMATICS	SCIENCE

KS4

Public examination results – GCSE:

	School results			**School results**		
GCSE examination	Calendar year			Calendar year		
results	Boys	Girls	All	Boys	Girls	All
Percentage of pupils:						

	LEA Area 2			**England 2**		
GCSE examination	Calendar year			Calendar year		
results	All			Boys	Girls	All
Percentage of pupils:						

Sixth form examination results:

	School			**England**		
Examination	Calendar year			Calendar year		
results	Boys	Girls	All	Boys	Girls	All
Percentage of pupils:						

Other 17+18+ examinations or accreditation

What pupils do on leaving the school:

Figures show the percentage of the year group:

	FE or school	Employment	Training procedure	Other
End of Year 11				
End of Year 12				
	Further education	Higher education	Training procedure	Other
End of Year 13				

Financial information:

INCOME (£)	Last full financial year	Current year
Balance brought forward		
School budget share		
Specific or special purpose grants curriculum/staff development		
TVEI funding		
Other income managed by the school, lettings, funds raised, etc.		
TOTAL		

EXPENDITURE (£)	Last full financial year	Current year
Teaching staff		
Other staff		
Educational resources		
Premises costs		
Curriculum and staff development		
Other expenditure		
TOTAL		

Total expenditure per pupil (£)		
Expenditure per pupil on educational resources (£)		

Record of the evidence base of the inspection

1. The team consisted of ____ inspectors.

2. During the inspection, ____ lessons were inspected, as well as registration, tutor group sessions, assemblies, a meeting and other activities.

3. ____ planned discussions were held with members of staff and other adults associated with the work of the school as well as with members of the governing body.

4. Inspectors looked at the written work of many pupils. All the available written work from a representative sample of ____ pupils covering all year groups was inspected.

5. Planned discussions were held with these pupils.
6. Other less formal discussions took place frequently with both staff and pupils, mostly in the normal course of visiting lessons.
7. A large amount of documentation provided by the school was analysed both before and during the inspection.
8. The Registered Inspector held a meeting attended by ____ parents prior to the inspection.
9. A questionnaire sent to parents prior to the inspection was analysed and letters were received from some feeder primary schools and from employers.

Following the report, a summary of the main findings and key points for action will be presented:

Main findings and key points for action:

- main findings
- standards of achievement
- quality of education provided
- efficiency of the school
- pupils' spiritual, moral, social and cultural development.

Key issues for action:

- what the school now needs to do to comply with statutory requirements.

Standards and quality:

- standards of achievement
- quality of learning
- efficiency of the school.

Pupils' personal development and behaviour:

- pupils' spiritual, moral, social and cultural development
- behaviour and discipline
- attendance.

The national curriculum and other curriculum provision:

- English
- mathematics
- science.

Technology:

- design and technology
- information technology
- history
- geography
- modern foreign languages
- art
- music
- physical education
- religious education.

Factors contributing to these findings:

- quality of teaching
- assessment, recording and reporting.

The curriculum:

- quality and range of the curriculum
- equality of opportunity
- provision for pupils with special educational needs
- accommodation
- pupils' welfare and guidance
- links with parents, agencies and other institutions.

The concluding section of the report will identify key issues for action.

Key issues for action

Middle managers will need to consider this section of the report. It will contain a list of aspects of the school which the inspection team felt to be in need of action. All points will be expanded later in the report. This will be a post-OFSTED action plan, examples of which are given in Figures 6.4 and 6.5.

POST-OFSTED ACTION PLAN

Middle Managers (Strategic Management and Planning)

KEY ISSUE: Middle Managers (Strategic Management and Planning)

What tasks need to be tackled?

1. Provide opportunities for HODs and HOYs to be involved in strategic management and identification of whole-school priorities.
2. Show costings (time and money) in development plans at all levels.

What action will be taken?

Initiative Group to be established consisting of SMT and volunteer HODs and HOYs.

Group to 'brainstorm' on current and future levels of involvement, share good practice at school/departmental level, propose changes to job descriptions, share group's ideas with other HODs/HOYs, put into practice.

What are the performance indicators?

Revised job descriptions showing clearer strategic role for HODs/HOYs.

Group to set own targets.

How will progress be monitored?

By Initiative Group – regular reports to HOD meeting.

Group to monitor and re-set targets after 6 months then annually.

Personnel Committee and/or Liaison Committee to receive reports.

Lead person:	People to be consulted:	People to be kept informed:		
Others:				
SMT + approx. 10 HODs/HOYs				
Key deadlines (dates):	Meetings to report to	SMT HODs	GOVS	AGM
April 96: starts		Yes	Yes	Yes
Sep 96: 1st review				
+ March 97 and annually				

Resources to support development (people, time, INSET, equipment):

* INSET funding (matched 50:50) from Thames Valley Tech

Figure 6.4: Post-OFSTED middle management action plan

POST-OFSTED ACTION PLAN
Geography

KEY ISSUE: Teaching and learning strategies for the most able

---

What tasks need to be tackled?

Greater use of differentiated material for more able.

What action will be taken?

Development of teacher/dept planned extension tasks.
Some (very limited) book purchase for extension tasks.
Attempt to use pupils' own cultural experiences.
Training to write essays/enquiry skills in KS3 (work started already).

What are the performance indicators?

Examination/end of unit test results.
Pupil self-esteem/option choices.
Pupil self-assessment.
Achievement of targets – personal and teacher-led.

How will progress be monitored?

By end of unit test/exam/homework/classwork – levels (assessment by).
Moderation between teaching staff.

Lead person:	People to be consulted:	People to be kept informed:
	Humanities Liaison	Humanities Liaison
Others:	(inter-school)	(inter-school)
	Assessment Working Party	Assessment Working Party

Key deadlines (dates):	Meeting to report to	STAFF SMT GOVS AGM

| As specified in DDP Evaluations of units and as specified above. | Humanities Liaison Group | |
| | Assessment Working Party | |

Resources to support development (people, time, INSET, equipment):
- Time – to be negotiated re reduction in national curriculum time
- INSET – as occur
- Equipment – greater variation of resources (books, etc.)
- IT – e.g. more modern computer, use of CD ROM
- Library – more resources

Figure 6.5: Post-OFSTED department action plan

Changes to OFSTED's approach

A review was deemed necessary due to shortcomings that were inherent in the system and the rate of curriculum change. According to OFSTED, the main aims of the revision are to:

- make inspections more manageable for inspectors and schools
- increase the value to schools of the inspection process
- make the framework more applicable to nursery, primary and special schools
- sharpen judgments about quality of education provided (teaching in particular) and what is achieved
- require clear, readable reports which highlight strengths and weaknesses and which state more explicitly what the school staff and governors need to do to tackle weaknesses
- ensure attention is paid to a school's own evaluation of where it stands, and its own priorities.

The new OFSTED inspection material was published on 16 October 1995, following initial revision in May 1994. The package now contains three documents rather than the previous single document. These are: *The OFSTED Framework* (for all schools), *The OFSTED Handbook* (primary, secondary or tertiary) and an *Inspection Resource Pack* containing specimen documentation for guidance. The new framework applies from the beginning of April 1996.

Two major aims of the revision were to make inspection more manageable for inspectors and to reduce the burden on schools. Each handbook has been reduced to half its former size. More explicit recognition is given to the content of the school. Specific modifications are:

1. Standards of achievement – attainment and progress requiring pupils' progress to be judged in relation to prior attainment not to ability.
2. Three main outcomes specified:
   - attainment and progress
   - attitudes, behaviour and personal development
   - attendance.
3. 'Quality of learning' removed.
4. 'Contributory factors' re-grouped under the main report headings of 'quality of education provided or management and efficiency of the school'.

OFSTED (1996a) is engaging in a period of consultation regarding the new arrangements. In sum, the arrangements proposed are intended to:

- reduce the inspection burden on schools
- use data from the first inspection, allied with changes over time, to inform decisions about when schools should be subsequently inspected

- focus resources on those schools judged to be weak
- continue to provide a picture of the performance of the education system in line with the requirements of the 1992 Act
- provide data on all national curriculum subjects on a representative sampling basis.

Summary

There are 'peaks and troughs' of administrative activity that occur in every academic year. Timetabling, assessment and inspection are key events in each school's programme. Identifying when such events occur is essential to the successful management of a department or school. Middle managers need to understand the administrative processes involved if they are to operate effectively as a manager and teacher in a school.

An observable difference between classroom teachers and middle managers is the amount of paperwork that accumulates in their staffroom pigeonholes. In order to prioritise, a middle manager needs to know and understand the purpose of each document. A middle manager should always keep administration under control and not let it dictate your actions. Process all documentation by categorising each paper according to importance.

Since the national curriculum (DES, 1988a), middle managers have had increased responsibility for the timetabling of subjects. Timetabling is both an administrative and team management process. The national curriculum provides a curriculum framework for all schools. Middle managers need to be able to know and understand the concepts and procedures involved in timetabling and curriculum planning.

In recent years there have been many debates focusing on assessment and reporting issues in education. As a middle manager, you will be required to process documentation related to assessment and reporting. At the end of each key stage, a headteacher must fully comply with the arrangements for assessing pupils. While this is the headteacher's responsibility, in practice middle managers are employed to complete each task.

In the context of administration, the inspection process is perhaps the most demanding of all events in the life of a school. Each school (primary and secondary) is to be inspected every four years by an inspection team which will publish its judgments to a wider audience. The framework for the inspection of schools (OFSTED, 1994c, revised 1996a) is the instrument by which schools are inspected and has the force of law (Chaplin, 1995, p. 143). As a middle manager, it is important that all aspects of your work are well documented.

7

■ ■ ■

The Planner

Introduction – what is planning?

Figure 7.1 illustrates the number of planning activities that currently exist in a secondary school. This demonstrates an unstructured approach which requires planning, implementing and managing.

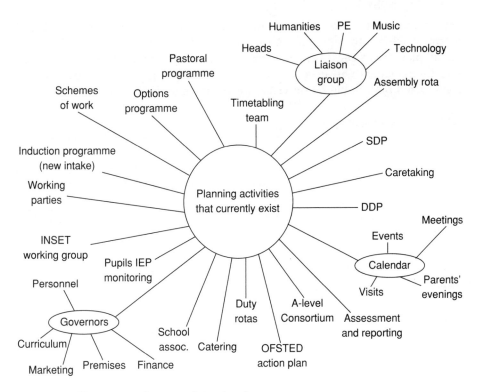

Figure 7.1: Unstructured approach to planning

Planning is a messy, repetitive and confusing aspect of a manager's life. As a *process,* planning consists of the following three elements (La Grave *et al.*, 1994, pp. 5–14):

1. **Objectives** – goals which are to be achieved in sufficiently detailed and precise terms to enable others to identify whether they have been achieved!
2. **Actions** – specification of the activities required to meet the objectives.
3. **Resources** – identification of what and who will be required to achieve the objectives and an indication of the timescale.

Planning may involve 'going around in circles' as you consider the various combinations of objectives, actions and resources that will provide you with your way forward. However, this is a necessary stage to ensure that all elements are considered.

Planning involves two aspects of practice that should be identified by a manager from the start:

1. **Analytical** – thinking things through involving calculation and individual reflection.
2. **Social** – motivating and drawing on the contributions and commitment from colleagues.

On balance, managers who spend time planning on their own will feel resentful when other people become involved and 'spoil' what had been a 'good' plan. However, an effective plan will not emerge from lengthy meetings. Middle managers will need to develop the skills required to prepare a well constructed plan. Table 7.1 describes the eight stages involved.

Table 7.1: Planning stages

Objectives	**Stage 1**	*Define the objectives*	What are you aiming to achieve?
	Stage 2	*Generate and evaluate objectives/actions*	What are the courses of action available? Which one will best achieve your objectives?
Actions	**Stage 3**	*Identify the actions*	What is required to implement your objectives?
	Stage 4	*Sequence the actions*	What is the best order?
Resources	**Stage 5**	*Identify the resources*	What resources are required?
Review	**Stage 6**	*Review the plan*	Will it work? If not, return to stage 2 or 3.
Preparation	**Stage 7**	*Prepare plans and schedules*	Who will do what and when?
Audit	**Stage 8**	*Monitor and evaluate*	Re-plan if necessary.

Specific points

When determining objectives be **SMART** (Tuckman, 1965). Remember, objectives should be:

Specific
Measurable
Attainable
Relevant
Timed.

Monitoring and evaluating plans will be considered in more detail in the final section of this chapter.

Problems and constraints

Planning can be challenging, enjoyable even; it can also be difficult (LaGrave *et al.*, 1994, pp. 5–24). Middle managers need to be able to plan a variety of events that happen in the life of the school, and specifically within their area of responsibility. The majority of middle managers will experience limitations on financial and other resources. There will also be time factors to consider in the preparation and implementation of the plan. It may be necessary to alter the plan in order to accommodate demands on equipment, space, staff and time.

Planning will also be constrained by the need to meet deadlines. This must be included in the development of plans. More specifically, problems may arise if objectives are vague, circumstances change, or you run into difficulties with people and politics.

Strategic and operational planning

The terms 'strategic planning' and 'operational planning' are relatively new concepts in school management. Previously, strategic planning was in the LEAs' domain, whereas operational planning happened in practice in the schools.

Strategic planning

A strategy is a broad statement which relates the overall approach and direction towards the achievement of a mission. Developing and maintaining a strategy involves establishing a framework within which an operational plan can take place.

Strategic planning is long-term planning, which takes into consideration the strengths and weaknesses of the organisation and external factors such as government directives. A School Development Plan (SDP) is a strategic plan, as shown later in this chapter.

Operational planning

Operational planning is about tasks and targets and directly relates to the role of a school's middle managers: who does what, when and how. It is concerned with making things happen in a short timescale, how to run a department or team over a short period of time, up to 12 months. Operational planning is detailed. It aims to achieve a particular set of objectives within a given time. A department development plan (DDP) is an operational plan.

School planning and management

John West-Burnham (1994b, p. 157, Figure 8.1) in *The Principles of Educational Management* defines effective management as a three-part process: plan, act, review (see Figure 7.2). In an earlier chapter West-Burnham (1994a, p. 79) explains:

> *Strategy, policy and planning are inextricably related management activities in that each requires the others in order to translate aspiration into action.*

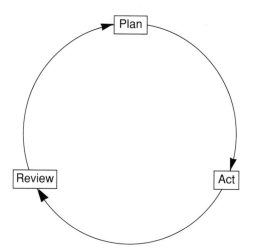

Figure 7.2: The management cycle

Strategic planning is therefore central to the process of managing. West-Burnham (1994a, p. 80, Figure 4.1) offers a valuable model for strategic planning in the school context (see Figure 7.3).

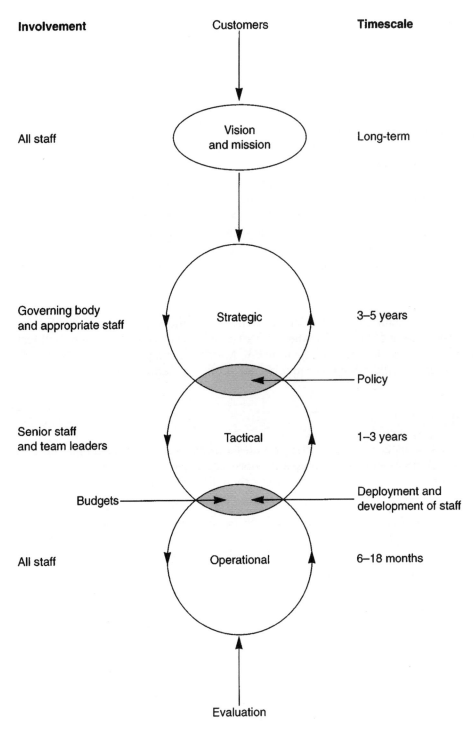

Involvement Customers **Timescale**

All staff Vision and mission Long-term

Governing body and appropriate staff Strategic 3–5 years

Policy

Senior staff and team leaders Tactical 1–3 years

Budgets Deployment and development of staff

All staff Operational 6–18 months

Evaluation

Figure 7.3: Strategic planning in context (West-Burnham, 1994a, p. 80; after Davies and West-Burnham, 1990)

The 'key features' of this model are (West-Burnham, 1994a, pp. 81–2):

1. *Everything is driven by the values and mission of the organisation and these have been developed and are owned by all staff.*

2. *Strategic planning has a three- to five-year timeframe, i.e. beyond the contingent and reactive, and is primarily the responsibility of senior staff and community representatives.*

3. *Once agreed, strategy has to be translated into a policy which serves as the basis of decision-making, notably for annual budgets and the deployment and development of staff.*

4. *Medium-term planning is primarily concerned with translating policies into action, most significantly through annual development plans, objective budgeting and planning for the deployment and development of staff.*

5. *This, in turn, facilitates the negotiation of short-term targets so that each individual is working to optimum effect.*

6. *Because the vision has been translated into individual activities, evaluation is based upon the aggregation of specific outcomes, allowing the matching of intention and actual achievement.*

Strategic planning in all schools will occur annually through the School Development Plan (SDP). The value of an SDP as an operational tool will rest with the senior management team. Middle managers, as West-Burnham indicates, will have greater involvement at the operational level.

The SDP — *Research*

All schools have an SDP that provides a framework for strategic planning in which they can identify long- and short-term objectives to manage themselves effectively. An SDP should relate clearly to the school vision or mission.

> *A School Development Plan is a plan of needs for development set in the context of the school's aims and values, its existing achievements and national and LEA policies and initiatives.*
>
> School Development Plan Project (DES, 1991b)

The SDP should be central to the management of the school, involving all teachers. The extent of a middle manager's involvement will be determined by the headteacher and/or senior management team. In practice, middle managers will need to know and understand the content of the SDP. As the management structures of schools change increased collaboration may lead to a greater involvement in policy-making for middle managers. Hargreaves and Hopkins (1991, p. 4) argue that:

> *The production of a good plan and its successful implementation depend upon a sound grasp of the processes involved. A wise choice of content for the plan as well as the means of implementing the plan successfully will be made only when the process of development planning is thoroughly understood.*

Middle managers, therefore, need to have an understanding of planning for effective management at operational level.

An SDP encompasses national, LEA and school initiatives, providing schools with a framework for strategic planning. The SDP will identify existing achievements and needs for development. Each school's aims – visions and missions – will be stated and reflected at every stage of the plan. The SDP enables schools to manage themselves in an effective coherent manner within both local and national contexts.

The main purpose of an SDP should be to improve the quality of learning for pupils. In practice, all management activities should relate to the SDP if they are to have a central role in school life. Effective middle management will depend on the knowledge and understanding of the SDP in directing the school towards its vision.

An understanding of the planning process is a necessary prerequisite to participation in the development of the SDP. A model of the planning process will aid development planning (see Figure 7.4).

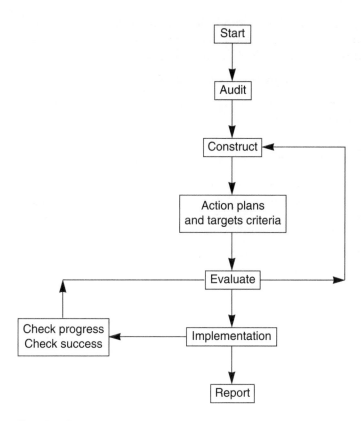

Figure 7.4: The planning process

137

It is critical that each SDP should be unique. As Skelton *et al.* (1991, pp. 166–7) state, the format for SDPs should:

- demonstrate involvement
- provide a focus for action
- provide a means of presenting the plan
- provide a means of assessing progress.

As stated, success of the development plan will depend upon the planning process. There are several examples in school management literature of what should be included in the SDP. Skelton *et al.* (1991, pp. 19–21) identify six key areas for development:

- *the developing curriculum*
- *the staff*
- *the school constituency*
- *buildings and sites*
- *organisational systems*
- *the climate.*

Fundamentally, all SDPs should identify strengths and weaknesses in each of these areas. In essence an audit will provide a basis for selecting priorities for development. The context of the audit will be:

- missions, aims and values of the school
- policies and initiatives
- inspections and reviews
- staff appraisals
- views of all stakeholders: staff, governors, parents, pupils and community.

A full audit will be time consuming; a programme of specific small-scale audits may be more practical and achievable within the school setting. As a middle manager you may be allocated responsibility for an area associated with your work. A comprehensive audit will include:

- interviews with colleagues
- lesson observation – where appropriate
- review of documentation
- writing up findings.

The outcomes of an audit should reveal strengths and weaknesses in order to provide a basis for action planning. The audit will also identify priorities for development. Having completed the audit, the next stage is to construct a plan which is manageable, coherent and achievable. The DES (1989a, p. 10) suggests that the plan should include:

- the aims of the school
- the proposed priorities and their timescale
- the justification of the priorities in the context of the school
- how the plan draws together different aspects of planning
- the methods of reporting outcomes
- the broad financial implications of the plan.

As a strategic plan, the SDP should consider the changes needed to improve the effectiveness of the school. Planners should recognise that the urgent and unavoidable linking of priorities will lead to increased collaboration between staff and other stakeholders.

Once the SDP has been completed, detailed action plans can be drawn up. This will involve middle managers and colleagues deciding on the way forward to implement the SDP. Action plans are a means of operationalising the strategy. Action plans should contain;

- the agreed *priority* area
- the *targets* – specific objectives for the priority area
- *success criteria* against which progress and achievement can be judged
- the *tasks* to be undertaken
- allocation of *responsibility* for tasks and targets – with *timescales*
- *resources* required.

Action plans should prepare the way forward for the implementation of the SDP. How this will work will depend on several factors. Hargreaves and Hopkins (1991, p. 65) identify the activities required to make the plan work:

- sustaining commitment during implementation
- checking the progress of implementation
- overcoming any problems encountered
- checking the success of implementation
- taking stock
- reporting progress
- constructing the next development plan.

People management is the key to successful implementation of the SDP. Middle managers have a critical role in this process.

Figure 7.5 is an example of a framework for practice in schools. In this scheme, middle managers are full members of the school development structure. Middle managers work with the headteacher and two deputy headteachers in the design and implementation of the SDP.

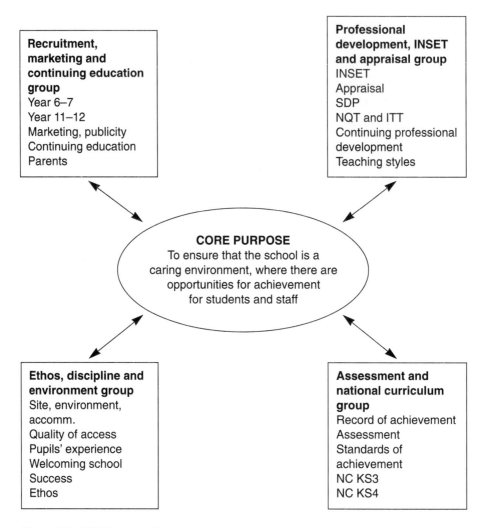

Figure 7.5: SDP framework

Department/team development

> *Whether a pupil achieves or underachieves is largely dependent on the quality of planning, execution and evaluation that takes place within departments.*
>
> (HMI, 1984)

If it is to be effective, the DDP should be placed in the context of the school, LEA and national planning. Figure 7.6 illustrates the position of the DDP within the school structure.

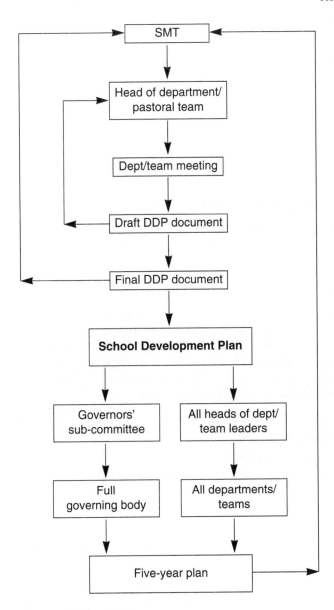

Figure 7.6: Position of DDP in SDP

A DDP is similar to the SDP. The DDP should reflect the aims of the SDP and provide an operational framework for implementing the action plans emanating from the SDP. In brief a DDP should contain the following:

- summary of the department's aims and objectives
- method of achieving the aims and objectives
- monitoring and evaluation.

141

The DDP should enable staff to work 'together' towards a common goal. As such the plan should have a sense of direction and purpose, the central aim being to improve the quality of teaching and learning within your area of responsibility. Points for consideration are:

- aims and values
- schemes of work
- policy documents
- teaching and learning
- assessment and reporting.

A DDP should also include statements on:

- special educational needs
- equal opportunities
- differentiation
- resources.

The process by which the DDP is constructed will reflect your style of management. Consulting colleagues may be time-consuming, however failure to do so may also be time-consuming. If a plan is to be effective it will need to be developed collaboratively. As Caldwell and Spinks (1988, p. 37) indicate in their model for *The Collaborative School Management Cycle* (see Chapter Three), staff as team members should participate in:

- goal-setting and need identification
- policy-making
- planning of programmes
- preparation and approval of programme budgets
- implementing
- evaluating.

The following example of good practice in a co-educational comprehensive school illustrates the need for a detailed DDP:

Creative arts development plan 1994–99

This framework is intended to focus the DDPs over the next five years. Towards this we propose to develop in four areas:

- to ensure that the creative arts are recognised as central to the school community
- to enable the creative arts to flourish within the department
- to ensure opportunity for all

- to monitor the resources and funding available to the department in ensuring this development.

Ensure that the creative arts are recognised as central to the school community by:

- raising the profile of the work done by students in the creative arts department through presentation, performance, exhibition and display
- providing the accommodation necessary for the creative arts and the study of the creative arts, and investigating the possibility of shared access to specialist designated arts facilities with other institutions
- providing useful academic and vocational courses and routes through the school, into post-16 and advice for beyond the school courses, in all areas of the creative arts
- providing career advice, work experience/COMPACT and information on further and higher education opportunities within the creative arts and cultural industries
- raising the standards of achievement and expectations among students in the work they produce
- supporting new types of creative art, new ways of presenting and interpreting the arts, working with new technologies and monitoring the existing work done in the department
- ensuring well-qualified, informed and trained staff are available to students, whether through staffing of specific short-term projects, or buying in experience for longer term and on-going projects; INSET to meet the needs of permanent staff, and full involvement of all staff in the department in its on-going development
- creating manageable teaching group sizes, through rationalising the delivery of the creative arts subjects to all pupils at KS3 and KS4.

Enable the creative arts to flourish within the department by:

- ensuring that opportunities to enjoy and participate in the creative arts are increased and spread more widely through the school
- promoting diversity and variety in the creative arts
- imaginatively managing the greater flexibility available within the curriculum, following the Dearing Report (1995) on the national curriculum, allowing the possibility of extending learning and a commitment within the school to the delivery of creative arts education
- encouraging pride and developing a critically appreciative audience for the creative arts
- encouraging artists-in-residence, student-led work, audiences within the school and participants to raise standards in the creative arts

- working with the LEA, local advisors and inspectors, and local and national bodies to develop new opportunities for creative arts projects, cross-curricular links and schemes of work within the creative arts and other departments at the school, and with other schools in the LEA
- maintaining, and extending where possible, instrumental music tuition, with particular attention to including instruments from different cultures
- an expectation that students will receive formal exposure and experience in all creative arts practice
- ensuring that all students have experience of professional specialisms, whether outside school, or through workshops and performances by individuals and groups within school.

Ensure opportunity for all by:

- promoting all forms of cultural diversity within the creative arts
- promoting all forms of participation in the creative arts
- developing and updating staff experience through INSET
- recognising the actual and potential contribution of community groups from ethnic minorities to the creative arts, and seeking ways of capitalising on this resource
- making more resources available to groups from ethnic minorities with the potential to extend their creative arts education
- building and developing links with these community groups.

Ensure greater funding for the creative arts from all sources:

- from the allocation of departmental budgets, curriculum development bids and TVEE funding, based on a clear set of costed options
- from the allocation of local educational grants and funding projects, and partnership with other schools and colleges of further and higher education
- from trust funds, grant agencies and other philanthropic sources
- from partnerships with the private sector, commercial and industrial organisations
- from broadcasting agencies, art centres, galleries, museums, exhibition and concert halls, and theatre companies.

As advised this also contains detailed aims and objectives for a five-year period:

Creative arts development plan aims and objectives related to school aims and objectives

Standards of achievement

To raise the levels of achievement of all pupils through a curriculum within the department that reflects and caters for the needs of an individual student in a multi-cultural, multi-ability school, irrespective of that student's starting point.

Assessment, recording and reporting (ARR)

To continuously develop and implement a departmental system of ARR in line with the whole school system of ARR which provides pupils, parents, staff and other agencies with formative and summative outcomes.

Curriculum

To have in place a curriculum within the department that fits the needs of the students at the school and which takes into account statutory orders and establishes a continuum that opens progression routes post-16.

Creative arts objectives relating to SDP – standards of achievement

Academic year 1995–6

GCSE, GNVQ and A level grades to be raised by 5 per cent on previous year. Improve pupils' grades at KS5, KS4, KS3 measured relative to their achievements at KS4, KS3 and KS2.

Building on existing development strategies to facilitate pupils' performances on the NC approaching the national norm at KS3.

Academic year 1996–7

GCSE, GNVQ and A level grades to be raised by 5 per cent on previous year. Improve pupils' grades at KS5, KS4, KS3 measured relative to their achievements at KS4, KS3 and KS2.

Building on existing development strategies to facilitate pupils' performances on the NC approaching the national norm at KS3.

To further implement strategies to facilitate students' performances on the NC approaching the national norm at KS3.

Academic year 1997–8

GCSE, GNVQ and A level grades to be raised by 5 per cent on previous year. Improve pupils' grades at KS5, KS4, KS3 measured relative to their achievement at KS4, KS3 and KS2.

To have evidence that students' performances on the NC reflect or exceed the national norm at KS3.

Creative arts objectives relating to SDP – assessment, recording and reporting

Academic year 1995–6

To comply with examples of good practice in ARR and modify ARR policy as necessary.

To ensure department compliance with the whole-school ARR policy.

To assist in the evaluation of processes and outcomes of the pilot projects on self-assessment in the creative arts.

To assist in the implementation of the whole school (Year 7–12) National Record of Achievement (NRA) accreditation action plan.

Academic year 1996–7

To build upon and enhance the practice and process of self-assessment within the department.

To continue to monitor department assessment policy, practice and process.

To assist in the continued implementation of the NRA accreditation action plan.

Academic year 1997–8

To have a system in place to monitor and map the progress of a pupil through the department which provides formative and diagnostic feedback to pupils, parents and staff.

To have a system in place to monitor and map the progress of a pupil across the curriculum which provides summative feedback to pupils, parents and staff.

To evaluate the implementation of the assessment programme at KS3.

To have in place a reporting process which matches the school's NRA process that is fully accredited and meets externally validated criteria.

Creative arts objectives relating to SDP – the curriculum

Academic year 1995–6

To review what and how we teach at KS3 creative arts.

To establish a KS4 curriculum within creative arts which meets statutory NC orders.

To offer creative arts within the options that best meet the needs of pupils who choose these subjects.

To make short-term decisions about GNVQ Intermediate in Art.

To be fully involved in the monitoring and evaluating of the curriculum and to review the creative arts curriculum on a regular basis.

Academic year 1996–7

To establish a KS3 curriculum that improves the continuity of progression from KS3 to KS4 within the creative arts.

To evaluate transition and continuity from KS2 to KS3.

To review what and how we teach KS4 creative arts.

Academic year 1997–8

To establish a curriculum offer within the department at KS3 that improves continuity of progression from KS3 to KS4.

To evaluate the National (pilot) GNVQ (part one) for possible introduction at KS4 within creative arts.

Table 7.2 provides a further example of good practice of DDP in a secondary school.

Monitoring and evaluation

Monitoring and evaluation are critical to the successful implementation of plans at any level.

Monitoring

Monitoring is an essential stage in the planning process. Having implemented a plan, managers will need to monitor its progress. If plans are not monitored, it will not be possible to determine whether their objectives have been achieved. Monitoring will also enable managers to obtain the best results from the available resources. The process of monitoring will enable middle managers to lead their team towards agreed objectives. Once objectives have been agreed the department/team can move forward with confidence. From clear objectives comes a sense of purpose. It may be difficult to obtain co-operation and agreement when deciding on departmental objectives. However, it is important to reach agreement within your team if your plan is to work effectively.

Monitoring will also provide the basis for evaluating practice. Teams/departments will be able to measure and compare their performance against

Table 7.2: DDP

Area	1995 Autumn term	1996 Spring term	1996 Summer term
Curriculum	New KS3 syllabus introduced, incorporating post-Dearing changes. Timetable blocked with Years 8 and 9 (exception 8.1/2) 5 week blocks New GCSE course introduced Heavily revised Year 11 course in operation A level course commences in Year 12.	First term of revised KS3 course evaluated First coursework folio completed by Year 10 First term of KS4 evaluated Completion of presentation Year 12 scheme of work	Full evaluation of KS3 course Second coursework folio completed by Year 10 Adapt Year 8 programme in the light of changes in sub-programme
Resources	KS3 – all core texts increased to 30 per set GCSE – Key Geography 1 textbook included within scheme of work A level core text purchased/ library set up Resource area re-furbished/ stock catalogued Premises: refurbishment of Geog. Res. Area/Staff Office Improve environment of HU 4/5 and corridors	KS3-final phase of scheme of work initial development Introduction of further differentiated materials Inclusion of two units of 'geography-related' material as part of IT training Enter bid for screens/ new furniture HU 5/carpet for resource area/staff area Blackout for HU3/blinds for staff office	Increase number of books in pupil lending library Increased use of reprographics New chairs/staff office Continued production of differentiated materials Bid for personal computers for department
Management	Assessment: introduction of 'title-page recording' of pupil work New dept marking policy introduced Centralised recording system introduced 'Cause for concern' *pro forma* introduced	Evaluate 'cause for concern' *pro forma*	Recruit increased numbers for GCSE course 1996–8 Review Year 10 course
Other	Year 11 Seven Sisters visit Year 8 farm visits Head of dept commences MA	Year 12 Earth Surface Pro. Ctr. Year 8 Manufacturing Industry Year 9 Environ. visit	Year 8 Rivers/Year 10 Seven Sisters Year 11+12 res. fieldwork Year 11/12 Channel Tunnel

Area	1996 Autumn term	1997 Spring term	1997 Summer term
Curriculum	Year 11 coursework: folio 3 Year 11 geographical enquiry Timetable fully blocked (Years 8 and 9)	Evaluate GCSE coursework Revision sheet for new courses	First 'decision-making exercise' First MEG 3 examination Adapt Year 9 programme in the light of changes to sub-programme
Resources	Purchase of fieldwork equipment	Ensure efficiency of filing system – review	Identify textbook condition and bid for future purchase
Management	Full computerisation of assessment Department policy evaluation	Full knowledge for pupils as to how assessed Market new 'assessment culture' Second in dept to take greater role in unit revision and at A level Senior in dept to lead field trips	Evaluate KS3 and GCSE course and report
Other	Year 8 farm visits (inc. dairy) Full fieldwork programme	Year 12 Earth SPP Year 8 Man. Industry Year 9 Geo. Museum	Fieldwork as 1996 Senior in dept will lead some as part of continuing professional development

agreed criteria. Monitoring may also assist middle managers in the planning of staff development by providing an insight into the strengths and weaknesses in their departments/teams.

Most significantly, monitoring will provide a framework in which staff can reflect on their own practice, an outcome of which is enhanced job satisfaction. Monitoring is an on-going activity.

Evaluation

Evaluation is a component of development planning and an essential prerequisite to preparing any subsequent plan. The DES (1989a, p. 17) stated that the purpose of evaluating SDPs is to:

- *examine the success of the implementation of the plan*
- *assess the extent to which the school's aims have been furthered*
- *assess the impact of the plan on pupils' learning and achievement*
- *decide on how to discriminate between successful new practices throughout the school*
- *make the process of reporting easier.*

The process of evaluating the impact of a plan on practice is critical to the successful implementation of the plan. Evaluation is a collaborative exercise involving (Hall and Oldroyd 1990d, p. 34):

- asking **questions**
- gathering **information**
- forming **conclusions**

in order to:

- make **recommendations**.

In contrast to monitoring, evaluation encompasses reviewing the status of a plan's objectives. Through the evaluation process, managers will determine the need to change objectives, priorities and/or practice.

Hargreaves and Hopkins (1991) stress the importance of evaluation in enhancing the professional judgment of teachers. Evaluation can therefore lead to a change in teachers' perception of their practice. For middle managers, the evaluation of department plans can provide the basis for action. Hall and Oldroyd (1990d, p. 41) offer a checklist for planning and evaluation (reproduced by permission of the publisher, National Development Centre for Educational Management and Policy, School of Education, University of Bristol, 35 Berkeley Square, Bristol B58 1JA):

1. ***Purposes, broad guidelines, aims*** or ***objectives*** *for the subject under scrutiny which are:*
   - *clear*
   - *indicators of desired performance or outcomes.*

2. ***Questions*** *which are:*
   - *unambiguous*
   - *penetrating*
   - *useful.*

3. ***Information*** *which is:*
   - *accessible*
   - *related to questions*
   - *not too voluminous to handle.*

4. ***Conclusions*** *which consider:*
   - *conditions*
   - *effects*
   - *assumptions*
   - *alternatives.*

5. ***Reports*** *which are:*
   - *concise*
   - *focused on audience's need*
   - *likely to inform decision-making.*

6. ***A good evaluation brief:***
   - *specifying much of the above.*

The final stage in the evaluation process is to write the report. As a middle manager you may have to contribute to the evaluation of a SDP. It will be important for you to consider the purposes of the report as required. Essentially you will need to consider the following aspects of the evaluation process:

- purpose
- content
- process
- context
- outcomes.

Before disseminating your report, reflect on each and ensure that only necessary and relevant information is presented.

Decision-making

Planning involves decision-making, individually and collaboratively. If department planning is to be effective, middle managers will need to understand how to prioritise and how to make decisions. Warwick (1983, p. 3) states that:

> *Decision-making is so much part of daily life in any school that it can easily be taken for granted. Only when things go wrong; when bad decisions have been taken or the consultation process has broken down, do most teachers become aware of it.*

Hall and Oldroyd (1990b, p. 16) advise that *decision-making is intimately bound up with every individual manager's personal values, personal goals and management style.* Essentially middle managers have to 'think on their feet', making decisions at frequent intervals throughout the working day. In order to make quality decisions Hall and Oldroyd (1990b, p. 16) suggest that managers should have:

- *clear personal values*
- *clear personal goals*
- *problem-solving skills*
- *high creativity*
- *high influence.*

A middle manager needs to develop the skills and abilities required to determine when to act on his/her own or when to collaborate with others. Adopting a structured approach to decision-making will aid the process. This involves:

1. Clear analysis of the learning purpose:
   - context
   - resources
   - outcomes.

2. Clear specification of the criteria for the plan as determined by:
   - SDP
   - LEA
   - government initiatives.

3. Systematic research.

4. Testing decisions against likely outcomes to the quality of teaching and learning.

Deciding when to consult your team will affect:

- the quality of the decision
- staff's acceptance of the decision
- the amount of time involved in the decision-making process.

Fidler *et al.* (1991, p. 5) states:

Participation in decision-making has two major benefits:

a) an improvement in the quality of the decision.

b) improved motivation and commitment of those involved.

However, *participation is not without its drawbacks.* These include:

- *it is slower than autocracy;*
- *it consumes a great deal of staff time;*
- *the pattern of decision-making is less predictable;*
- *the pattern of decision-making is less consistent;*
- *the location of accountability may be less clear;*
- *some decisions are expected to be taken by senior managers and participation may be seen as abdication.*

In conclusion, middle managers should build on their team's ability to participate in the management of the school. A sudden transition to full staff participation will not happen, although middle and senior managers should be developing teachers' management skills within the context of CPD. The transition should be supported by appropriate training and a climate where risk-taking is accepted. Monitoring and evaluation of such processes are necessary for success.

Time management

Being a middle manager is a job in its own right, and a very demanding one; you will therefore need to have a clear view on how to manage your time and organise your workload (Shaw *et al.*, 1992). Middle managers will find that while responsibility can be appealing, in reality there are parts of the job that include vast amounts of daily administrative tasks. In order to manage your time effectively you will need to identify how you use your time and determine goals.

Middle managers need to adopt systems to aid personal and developmental organisation. The majority of middle managers have a full teaching commitment, consequently their organisations systems need to involve:

- day-to-day planning, diary keeping
- 'in tray', dealing with post and decision-making
- retrieval of information and filing
- organisation of the workspace
- department administration

- management of stock
- management of pupils' work
- organisation of lesson materials
- stress management.

Middle managers should also identify how time is wasted for example:

- procrastination
- delegating inefficiently
- mismanaging paperwork
- holding unnecessary meetings
- failing to set priorities.

Personal planning

As a player manager you will have many things to fit into a day's work. This section examines the quality of your time.

It is worth recognising which part of the day – or night – is the most productive for you – the time when you have your most creative ideas, or can concentrate best. For the majority of people, this time is early in the day, when they are freshest, and before the events of the day start to crowd in and push away ideas. A minority of people do their best work late at night.

It has been suggested that about 20 per cent of personal time is **prime** time, and that, used correctly, it should produce about 80 per cent of your most creative and productive work. The rest of your time is likely to be of lower quality and is nowhere near as productive.

Creative thinking, and the most difficult jobs, deserve high quality time. If you try to do them at times when you are likely to be interrupted a lot, or when you know that you are catching up, you will become frustrated. In this low quality time, you should plan to do things which are easy to pick up after interruptions – or jobs which you look forward to doing. Apart from the advantage to the individual in using prime time effectively, there are wider implications – for example, the timing of meetings. Important decisions need some of the team's prime time, not the traditional slot of low quality at the end of the teaching day. It is advisable for schools and colleges to timetable team meetings earlier in the day, when vital and creative thinking is needed.

Middle managers who realise the importance of incubation time for ideas ensure that their team members have had advance warning of issues to be discussed at meetings, so that they come able to participate fully and creatively. In sum:

- your prime time is when you do your best work
- seek to understand how **you** work, and then . . .

- plan your day accordingly as far as you are free to do so
- hold meetings, as far as possible, at the most effective times
- allow incubation time for the subconscious to work on problems, both for you and for your team.

Setting goals and priorities

One way in which you can improve your time management is to review the way in which you set goals or tasks. You may have some routine matters to attend to or some longer-term issues. Whatever they are, it is best to divide them into workable units of activity by once again using the acronym SMART. Your task needs to be *specific*, clearly defined. It needs to be *measurable*, so that it is easy to see when it has been completed. It should also be *attainable*. Unrealistic targets are depressing. They also need to be *relevant*, or appropriate, to current and future needs. And finally, your tasks should be *time-limited* with defined deadlines. Open-ended tasks have a habit of not getting done.

Once you have a SMART list of things that need doing, the next task is to prioritise them. If you do not, it is easy to feel helpless and stressed in the face of so many things that need to be done simultaneously.

Organising tasks into some sort of order not only makes it easier to finish one thing before going onto the next, but it also legitimises the fact that some of the things have to be put off until later.

The dilemmas arise when the urgent, but unimportant, regularly pushes out the important but less urgent. You have to readjust your schedules to fit new and urgent items in, but sometimes you need to be firm about the time you have planned for your important tasks. To add to the dilemma, your own perceptions of what is important may differ from that of others. In sum:

- make a list of your daily tasks
- prioritise the tasks according to their urgency and importance
- be ruthless with your order of dealing with the tasks
- examine why tasks are not getting done, and do something about it!

An example of good practice is the teacher's planner. Middle managers should use this to plan teaching and management time. Plan ahead, anticipate problems.

Handling interruptions

Interruptions are commonly given as reasons for schedules being upset and things not getting done. But in a job like teaching, constantly dealing with people, interruptions are a necessary part of your work.

A normal day in the life of a middle manager is full of interruptions. There are ways of handling interruptions that will give you more control over your time. The following list has been collected from many people. Some may be useful to you.

Keep interruptions as short as possible:

- keep to the point – do not get side-tracked into small-talk
- explain you new resolution to manage time better
- arrange to meet at a specified time later: after school may be too open-ended, unless a lot of time is needed; 10 minutes before a lesson-bell limits the time and focuses the discussion
- remain standing – do not settle down comfortably
- when summoned to consult, meet in neutral territory, or the other person's: it is easier for you to leave
- use non-verbal signals to give hints: stand up, body shift towards door, glance at watch.

Consider the interrupter's needs:

- give them your undivided attention
- do not interrupt, but get them to the point
- do not let your mind wander, it wastes time
- demonstrate that you have understood what is being said by paraphrasing the essence
- ensure, within reason, that they go away satisfied, perhaps with the promise of looking into it later, meeting again later, suggesting alternative support, even 'put it in writing' if necessary, but . . .
- be assertive in saying 'no' if they are asking too much.

Get back on track at once:

- do not use interruptions as an excuse to procrastinate.

If some of these sound harsh, remember you have the choice of how to handle interruptions. There will be occasions when you want to relax and indulge in small-talk, and when being time-conscious is less important than socialising.

Participation and delegation

Participation and delegation are two further time management mechanisms. These are discussed in detail in Chapter Two.

Summary

Planning is a messy, repetitive and confusing aspect of a manager's life. Planning may involve 'going around in circles' as you consider the various combinations of objectives, actions and resources that will provide you with your way forward. On balance, managers who spend time planning on their own will feel resentful when other people become involved and 'spoil' what was a 'good' plan.

When determining objectives be **SMART** (Tuckman, 1965):

Specific

Measurable

Attainable

Relevant

Time-limited.

Planning can be challenging, enjoyable even; it can also be difficult. Planning will also be constrained by the need to meet deadlines.

The terms 'strategic planning' and 'operational planning' are relatively new concepts in school management. A strategy is a broad statement which relates the overall approach and direction towards the achievement of a mission. Operational planning is about tasks and targets and directly relates to the role of a school's middle managers, who does what, when and how. Strategic planning is therefore central to the process of managing.

Strategic planning in all schools will occur annually through the SDP. An SDP encompasses national, LEA and school initiatives, providing schools with a framework for strategic planning. The main purpose of an SDP should be to improve the quality of learning for pupils. Once the SDP has been completed, detailed action plans can be drawn up. Action plans should prepare the way forward for the implementation of the SDP. People management is the key to successful implementation of the SDP. Middle managers have a critical role in this process.

If it is to be effective, the DDP should be placed in the context of the school, LEA and national planning. A DDP is similar to the SDP. The DDP should reflect the aims of the SDP and provide an operational framework for implementing the action plans emanating from the SDP. The DDP should enable staff to work 'together' towards a common goal. The process by which the DDP is constructed will reflect your style of management. Consulting colleagues may be time-consuming, however failure to do so may also be time-consuming.

Monitoring and evaluation are critical to the successful implementation of plans at any level. Having implemented a plan, managers will need to monitor its progress. Monitoring will also enable managers to obtain the best results from the available resources. Most significantly, monitoring will provide a framework in which staff can reflect on their own practice, an outcome of which is enhanced job satisfaction.

Evaluation is a component of development planning and an essential pre-requisite to preparing any subsequent plan. The process of evaluating the impact of a plan on practice is critical to the successful implementation of the plan. In contrast to monitoring, evaluation encompasses reviewing the status of a plan's objectives. For middle managers, the evaluation of department plans can provide the basis for action.

The final stage in the evaluation process is to write the report. As a middle manager you may have to contribute to the evaluation of an SDP. Before disseminating your report, ensure that only necessary and relevant information is presented.

Planning involves decision-making, individually and collaboratively. A middle manager needs to develop the skills and abilities required to determine when to act on his/her own and when to collaborate with others. Planning requires collaboration if planned objectives are to be achieved. Middle managers should build on their team's ability to participate in the management of the school. A sudden transition to full staff participation will not happen, however middle and senior managers should be developing teachers' management skills within the context of continuing professional development. The transition should be supported by appropriate training, and a climate where risk-taking is accepted. Monitoring and evaluation of such processes are necessary for success.

Being a middle manager is a job in its own right, and a very demanding one; you will therefore need to have a clear view on how to manage your time and organise your workload. Middle managers need to adopt systems to aid personal and developmental organisation. As a player manager you will have many things to fit into a day's work. Creative thinking, and the most difficult jobs, deserve high quality time. Important decisions need some of the team's prime time, not the traditional slot of low quality at the end of the teaching day. One way in which you can improve your time management is to review the way in which you set and prioritise goals or tasks.

8

■ ■ ■

Resource Management

Introduction

The 1988 Education Reform Act (ERA) radically affected the method of funding public sector schools. The measures included in the ERA have five elements:

- financial delegation
- formula funding
- open enrolment
- staffing delegation
- performance indicators.

The devolution of financial responsibility is known as Local Management of Schools (LMS). A direct consequence of LMS has been the introduction of a budgetary system in schools. Financial delegation has moved more of the decision-making on the use of resources away from the LEA. This includes the power of virement on the budget; schools are able to move (vire) spending from one item (such as maintenance) to another item (such as books). Financial delegation also includes the allocation of tasks, e.g. what maintenance work is to be carried out and when.

Background

Maclure (1989) described the introduction of LMS as *one of the most practical – and at the same time, least contentious – chapters in the Act*. He commented that the idea of financial delegation received general support. LMS was preceded by Local Funding Management (LFM) which was piloted in both Cambridgeshire and Solihull. Audrey Stenner (1988), a primary school headteacher, believed that headteachers would become better managers of education if they also managed resources. Nightingale (1990) also considered that *LMS should be of great benefit* although the *biggest concern over the budget has been the fear that any cuts in spending will simply be passed onto the schools to implement.*

The ERA did not prescribe any detail for implementing LMS; each LEA was to *prepare a scheme in accordance with the Act* (ERA, s. 33). Regulations for authorities to follow were issued in Circular 7/88. A report for the Department of Education and Science by Coopers and Lybrand (1988) was generally accepted as the unofficial guide to LMS. The report identified the implications of LMS for schools:

> *The processes required by all schools to exercise [. . .] new financial and managerial responsibilities [. . .] are those of:*
>
> - *management*
> - *planning and budgeting*
> - *financial control*
> - *management of information*
> - *administration.*

As Davies (1994, p. 327) indicates, if resources are to be managed effectively in schools, school managers will need to understand the budgetary process. This is not merely about spending money; budgeting involves management.

Davies (1994, p. 328, Figure 16.1) describes the position of budgeting within a cycle of educational management activity (see Figure 8.1).

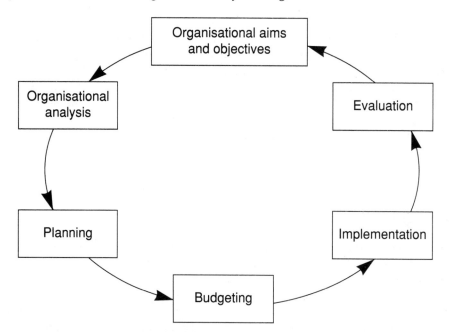

Figure 8.1: The educational management cycle

Description of LMS scheme

As stated, the basic principles of resource allocation were determined by the government in the ERA and Circular 7/88, these are :

1. All schools must have funds allocated to them on the basis of a formula.

2. The governing bodies of all secondary schools and larger primary schools must be given control as to how their allocation is spent.

The initial effect on the majority of maintained secondary schools in England and Wales was as follows:

1. The LEA determined the amount of money to be spent, known as the General Schools Budget (GSB).

2. The school was then allocated the Aggregated Schools Budget (ASB) which was determined by a formula.

3. The LEA withheld amounts from the GSB to meet certain types of expenditure, e.g. visiting instrumental teachers, staff salaries (teaching and non-teaching).

The formulae adopted by each LEA are based on those suggested in Circular 7/88, for example:

1. **Age-weighted pupil unit** – an amount of money allocated for each pupil according to age.

2. **Special needs** – allocated according to the number of pupils eligible for free school meals.

3. **School specific** – allocation related to specific circumstances, e.g. geographical area, support agencies.

4. **Small schools' protection.**

In practice the distribution of funds to schools was based on local factors which determined the focus for each school's expenditure. This was planned using headings identified by each LEA finance committee and later refined within an identified format, e.g. the Schools Information Management Systems (SIMS).

Budgetary process

Davies and Ellison (1990, p. 43) identified four stages of a budgeting cycle: budgeting review, budgeting forecasting, budgeting implementation and budgeting evaluation. In Davies (1994, pp. 330-4):

1. *Budgeting review:* assessment of the current financial position and the causal factors: key categories being income and expenditure.

2. *Budgeting forecasting:* assess the impact of future financial trends, and what will be required to resource the school.

3. *Budgeting implementation:* place current decisions in the context of the audit and future projections. A useful staged implementation process could be:
   - set out headings and sub-headings of the budget
   - allocate fixed costs to headings
   - allocate recurrent costs
   - bring forward items from the audit and forecast; establish priorities
   - decide between alternative projects and courses of action
   - put budget forward for approval by the institution's governors
   - set check points during the year for possible virement opportunities.

4. *Budgetary evaluation:* it is important that institutions do not ignore this vital part of the budgetary cycle. In order to produce an effective budget, evaluation is the key.

In practice, the budgetary process within schools is the responsibility of the headteacher and finance committee, a sub-committee of the governing body. The LEA allocates funds (schools allocation) to the school and the finance committee will then decide on the distribution of funds. The process of distribution is based on previous expenditure under headings prescribed by each LEA for the allocation of funds within each school:

- employees
- capitation
- premises
- contingency
- transport expenses
- client receipts
- supply and services.

Within this process the finance sub-committee of the governing body will review the previous years' figures and add known increases, e.g. 3–4 per cent for teachers' pay rise. In addition the finance committee must retain 1 per cent of the total budget as a contingency for over-spending and this figure must be shown in the accounts. The budgeting process should allow each school to plan, co-ordinate, control and evaluate its activities (Davies 1994, p. 329). Irvine (1975) comments:

> *A budget, as a formal set of figures written on a piece of paper, is in itself merely a quantified plan for further activities. However, when budgets are used for control, planning and motivation, they become instruments which cause functional and dysfunctional consequences both manifest and intent which determine how successful the tool will be.*

The draft school budget should then be presented to several groups from within the school community for discussion. Teaching staff should be shown the budget. The governing body finance sub-committee, as the official representative of the full governing body, is able to change the allocation of funds in the budget if necessary. The full governing body then has to approve the budget before it is returned to each LEA finance committee. Once set under the above headings, there is very little scope for the virement of funds, as the LEA will only permit 5 per cent within each heading of the budget. The process of determining the budget operates in a timescale of approximately three months. This process may be further complicated by a change in the ASB during this period. It is the duty of the headteacher to inform the finance sub-committee of any changes as they occur. The headteacher is also responsible for adjusting the amounts allocated under each heading within the budget, should the school's allocation be reduced.

A school's budget is recorded both centrally and locally. The headteacher will be sent a computer printout by the LEA; this is coded according to the pre-set headings. This document includes all payments made to the school or by the school. This will be overseen by senior management, as appropriate. Should the figures not agree with those on the school's SIMS computer, the headteacher will then contact the LEA finance department. All staff, teaching and non-teaching, are paid direct from the LEA and these payments are recorded in the document. In addition, the school has a cheque book to be used for local payments only.

Having planned the budget and received approval from the LEA, the headteacher then operates the budget. The senior and middle management teams are involved in the management of specific areas, for example:

- **material resources and systems** – e.g. SIMS computing system within the school dealing with income from the LEA
- **buildings and maintenance** – the allocation of tasks to the LEA, school and contracted specialists for the maintenance and servicing of the school environment. *Note*: the LEA is responsible for all exterior maintenance.
- **INSET** – teacher training, funded directly by the LEA.

The allocation of funds to subject departments and teams is determined by middle managers who prepare a budget on behalf of their teams.

The effects of the budgetary process

Nightingale (1990) concluded that Local Funding Management (LFM) enhanced children's education by:

- improved teaching provision
- improved level of staff support
- improved supply cover
- more resources

- a cleaner, better maintained environment
- a more open style of management.

There is also a vast array of literature which states that the devolution of funds has improved both the effectiveness and efficiency of resource usage within a school, e.g. Levacic (1989) and Chapman (1990).

Schools are not businesses. Educational organisations do need financial management, though this differs from business management and there are no simple means of marrying the two styles together. Handy and Aitken (1986) identified four of the principal differences between schools and businesses:

- *no time for management*
- *the 'pile' of purposes*
- *role switching*
- *the children.*

To elaborate further, Handy's descriptions focus on the difficulties faced by the managers of educational institutions whose primary function prior to LMS was to educate. Therefore 'no time for management' is rooted in the position of the headteacher as a teacher not as an administrator or manager of staff. An outcome of this is the 'pile of purposes', whereby the headteacher becomes a multi-functional individual faced with the problem of prioritising in order to achieve what is required to 'manage' the institution. A consequence of becoming multi-functional is 'role switching', when the headteacher no longer teaches but manages and administrates. This then removes headteachers from their initial primary function, to educate the children. Thus s(he) distances his/herself from the majority of people within the institution.

Handy also identified the need for structure in any organisation, whether the structure be 'tidy or untidy'. Arnold and Hope (1983, p. 264) state, *a vitally important task for the management is to co-ordinate various interrelated aspects of decision-making.*

There is substantial evidence that involvement in forecasting, planning, communication and evaluating increases motivation and therefore perform-ance. Schools could increase their effectiveness, in terms of the budget, if programme-planning through collaborative decision-making was adopted.

Budget systems

There are two systems of budget planning shown in educational literature: Chapman (1990) and Levačić (1989). The first is the Programmed Budget System (PBS). This involves budget by programme:

- development of an educational plan
- collection and appraisal of data
- preliminary expenditure plan
- preliminary review plan
- formal budget document
- adoption of budget
- administration of budget
- review and audit.

Early indications are that very few schools have adopted a formal PBS. However, it would be possible to produce similar results from a budget based on an SDP. It would then be possible to measure the effect of the budgetary process as determined by the model used for its design and operation.

Brockman (1972) explained that programme planning (PBS) is one facet of PPBS (planning, programming, budgeting system). He recommends its adoption for several reasons:

1. *Programme* [planning] *reflects an educational plan [. . .]*
2. [Programme planning] *is holistic rather than incremental [. . .]*
3. [Programme planning] *focuses on the programmes that are new as differentiated from programmes that are continuing [. . .]*
4. *All programmes affect all other programmes in the unit [. . .]*
5. *Incremental budgeting is eliminated [. . .]*
6. *Contingency funds will not be available next year [. . .]*

While each of the above is valid in the broader educational context, a change to PBS may be too radical for some schools. A more appropriate method of determining the budgetary process may begin with Brockman's basic planning questions:

- *What are we trying to do?*
- *Are there different ways to do it?*
- *How much will it cost to do it?*
- *How can we tell when we have done it?*

An alternative to PBS is Zero-Based Budgeting (ZBB). As Hartley (1979) states *the primary purpose of ZBB is to exert greater control over budgets requiring justification for every proposed expenditure, beginning theoretically from* [a base of] *zero.* ZBB could be seen as a means to allocate a reduced amount of resources.

Implications for middle management

Middle managers will have responsibility for determining and managing their department/team's budget. This should be included in the DDP (see Chapter

Seven). You will need to know and understand the budgetary processes involved in the school financial management.

Current practice may involve a bidding system, whereby middle managers will decide on the amount required to fund the running of his/her department for the next financial year. A useful method of preparing a bid is to compare financial statements from the previous year with similar departments/teams; look for areas where money could be saved, e.g. file paper and identifying the areas which need funding. Begin with basic needs and move to additional operational expenditure. Aim to spend all your capitation (the amount allocated from the school funds to your area for teaching materials), cost each item, then attempt to justify the cost. Make a copy of each list and circulate to colleagues for comment.

When completing financial documentation to be forwarded to senior management, ensure that you follow the 'house-style'. Summarise on one side of A4 paper. The headings given in Table 8.1 may be appropriate.

Table 8.1: Department/team annual capitation

Department/ team:	Cost:	Purpose:	Staff/room:	Item:	Essential/ optional:

This process will also lead you to prioritise expenditure within your budget. Once acquired, the management of resources will involve:

- a stock-take of each room's resources
- detailed accounts of each year's losses/gains
- estimated use of stock according to:
  - number of pupils in each room
  - curriculum activity, e.g. art will involve more consumables than drama
- identification of new materials/equipment related to specific activities.

The *pro forma* shown in Table 8.2 could be used to audit stock.

Recommendations

A useful method of preparing financial statements is to record materials used throughout the year. This will also avoid the additional administrative pressure of the annual 'stock-take'. Another possibility is the delegation of the stock-keeping to a member of your team.

A direct consequence of LMS is the change in relationship between teaching staff and management. There are examples of dysfunctional elements of LMS manifested in terms of distrust of managers by staff, with a tendency to resist, which

Table 8.2: Department/team stock audit

Room	Staff/ subject	Class	Materials/ equipment required	In stock	To order	Cost
		1				
		2				
		3				
		4				
		5				
		6				
		7				

may give rise to internal conflict. These are characteristics which have been identified by Marconi and Seigal (1989) within the context of behavioural accounting in response to the budgeting process. They also explain the benefits of participation. However, they warn of the dangers of pseudo-participation whereby the players are involved at both the planning and decision-making stages prior to operation of a budget, yet in practice the decisions are made by the controller alone.

In sum, financial managers should consider:

1. The development of a more open management style: Thomas *et al.* (1989) cite examples of the changed role of staff under LMS, which begins with the role of the headteacher.

2. The introduction of a structure which incorporates a collaborative decision-making process (Spinks, 1990).

3. The embodiment of the principles of programme planning within the budgetary process. It is possible to incorporate some of the important principles of the PBS cohort once a full LMS scheme is in place (Spicer, 1990).

4. The assessment of the success of the budgetary process in terms of what the institution can do for people (House, 1973).

Department/subject co-ordinators' budget

Middle managers should have control of capitation or capital funding for their subject/team area. An example of current good practice is as shown in Figure 8.2. Essentially this shows evidence of budget reviewing, budget forecasting and budget implementation. The subject co-ordinator/head of department has prioritised and indicated the purpose of each purchase.

CAPITAL BID

Geography Department – June 1995

There follows a prioritised listing of capital items which the Geography Department wants to purchase in the financial year April 1995 to April 1996.

However, purchases would be made on the understanding that they would also cover the financial year 1996–7 and will make the Geography Department self-sustaining for some considerable time in the future.

I believe, however, that the resources of the department need up-grading now so as to provide pupils with a sound long-term base of excellent materials.

Introduction

In the attached paper 'Proposed Future Plans for Geography at school A', I have set out in detail how I wish to see the Department develop over the next three years. I am particularly keen to expand upon the resource base in Year 9 where there are presently very few resources – 17 'Interactions' textbooks used by six tutor groups are the only fairly recent textbooks available in school. Similarly at GCSE, despite recent purchase, we only have 22 copies of 'Wider World' and 12 copies of 'Key Geography 2'. These are the only modern resources available for teaching three groups of 22 pupils in Year 10 and two groups (of 22 and 26) in Year 11.

I am pleased to report that no books have gone astray since September – four damaged KS3 books have been charged to the pupils found to be responsible.

Figure 8.2: Department capital spending (bid A)

1. Textbooks to facilitate teaching at GCSE and to support new MEG syllabus 3 GCSE course (similar changes would have been required even if we had kept with same board) in keeping with new syllabus development.		
14 copies of Key Stage Geography 2	@ £6.99 =	£97.86
30 copies of Key Stage Geography 1	@ £6.99 =	£209.70
1 copy Resource Pack KG 2	@ £41.50 =	£41.50
1 copy Resource Pack KG 1	@ £41.50 =	£41.50
3 copies of Wider World	@ £8.75 =	£26.25
30 copies of British Isles	@ £3.50 =	£105.00
2. Textbooks to add urgently to main stock at KS3		
8 copies of Foundations	@ £7.25 =	£58.00
5 copies of Connections	@ £7.25 =	£36.25
20 copies of Interactions	@ £7.25 =	£145.00
New material		
35 copies of Places	@ £7.25 =	£253.75
1 Teachers Resources Guide	@ £41.50 =	£41.50
Geography Eye Satellite Resource Pack	@ £22.20 =	£22.20
3. TV/video equipment (joint bid with History) – Granada (22–4 June)		
24″ Remote Control TV and Video	@ £250.00 =	£125.00
4. Fieldwork equipment		
1 Thermometer	@ £16.95 =	£16.95
1 Anemometer	@ £17.95 =	£17.95
5. Teaching equipment		
1 World Globe	@ £15.45 =	£15.45
Total capital bid	=	**£1253.86**
With discounts that I have discussed with all three possible suppliers, this figure will drop to £1000–1050.00. This would amount to a bid of £500 per year over two years.		

Figure 8.2: continued

Capital allocation

Within school A, all capital is 'drip fed' to subject co-ordinators at regular intervals during the academic year. This would appear to allow senior managers to retain control of all spending. It would be more manageable if capital funding were allocated to subject co-ordinators at the start of the financial year. Table 8.3 indicates the capital expenditure allocated to departments in a secondary school.

Middle managers may have the need or opportunity to bid for extra funds during the course of the academic year. Figure 8.3 is clear, concise and relates to the original bid (Figure 8.2).

Table 8.3: School capital allocation

Department	Maximum allocation	Allocation July	Allocation November	Remarks
English	1626	1076		
Music	52	52		
Technology	351	0		
Geography	337	337	212	Sixth form textbooks
History	376	267		
Soc. ed.	143	0		
Modern languages	1545	1545		
Maths	1094	674	460	B/F £87 + consumable adjustment £373
Art	54	0	150	Part of materials
Bus. ed.	27	0		
Science	1105	780	325	
Library	1027	633	294	Sixth form texts
Medical	696	0		
Hoy/Pastoral	18	0		
SEN	812	124	535	Computer (486)
S.11	10	0		
Drama	270	TBA	140	Textbooks and lighting
RE	24	0		
PE	92			
IT	40	0		
Total		5488	2116	

A level capital bid (revised) – Geography 13/10/95

The amount allocated so far is £101.00

Further to our recent conversation and bearing in mind this is a new course, the department would like to bid for the following:

4 copies 'Geography – an Integrated Approach' D.Waugh	£88.00
2 copies 'Population Geography' H.Barrett	£26.00
4 copies 'The Geography Settlement' P.Daniel/M.Hopkinson	£54.00
1 copy 'Process and Landform' A.Clowes/P.Comfort	£13.50
Reprographics though could be as re-arranged if 'capital'	£30.00
Total	**£211.50**

This represents a shortfall on the existing budget of some £110.50.

This is a realistic proposal of the minimum expenditure required to set up the course. All extra materials – videos, reproducible masters, journals, past papers, staff copies of texts – to be provided privately.

Figure 8.3: Capital spending (bid B)

Having completed the process of bidding for resources, records of purchase need to be retained as shown in Figure 8.4.

Consumables and reprographics must be included in all school budgets. Photocopying is expensive, all copies need to be recorded. An example of good practice is given in Figure 8.5.

Summary

The 1988 Education Reform Act radically affected the method of funding public sector schools. The devolution of financial responsibility is known as Local Management of Schools (LMS). A direct consequence of LMS has been the introduction of a budgetary system in schools. Financial delegation has moved more of the decision-making on the use of the resources away from the local education authority.

As stated, the basic principles of resource allocation were determined by the government in the ERA and DES Circular 7/88. The initial effect on the majority of maintained secondary schools in England was as follows:

1. The LEA determined the amount of money to be spent, known as the General Schools Budget (GSB).

ORDER FORM – Internal Use only

Department: *Geography*

Please complete legibly.

Please give: Prices VAT free

Unit Prices in £

Accurate descriptions

You do not need to calculate total prices. This order will be returned to you for your records.

Total debited

£..............................

Order No ....

Supplier

Delivery req'd by ....

Description	Exp. code	Unit Cost	Disc.%	Quantity
pack 9" ×7" ruled 8mm mar.	202663	£8.99		8
pack of A4 ruled 8mm mar.	202962	£6.90		8
pack A4 4 hole 8mm mar.	200011	£11.80		3
coloured crayons	143344	£1.08		6
30 cm rulers	190794	£1.40		2
protractors	189403	£0.60		2
compasses	115732	£2.68		1
pack 4" myer riser rails	150819	£0.37		22
A4 plastic wallets	166575	£2.45		2
BBC VHS E180 tape	357480	£1.85		10

Signed .... Head of Department   Date:.........................

For office use : Actioned by: ....

Figure 8.4: Team/department order form

2. The school was then allocated the Aggregated Schools Budget (ASB) which was determined by a formula.

3. The LEA withheld amounts from the GSB to meet certain types of expenditure, e.g. visiting instrumental teachers, staff salaries (teaching and non-teaching).

In practice, the budgetary process within schools is the responsibility of the headteacher and finance committee, a sub-committee of the governing body.

REPROGRAPHICS DEPARTMENT

Invoice for services purchased – Date(s) :   *December '95*
Department/Organisation: *Geography*
Teacher in charge/invoice to: *Head of Department*

1. **Photocopying services:**
   a) Reprographics Department service   @ .....pence/copy = £......
   b) Reprographics Key services   @ *5* pence/copy = £*1.95*
   Number of copies recorded   *39 copies*
   Total photocopying charges   = £*1.95*

2. **Duplicating services:**
   Total paper/card duplicating charges as price list = £*24.60*

3. **Other services as detailed:**

   Total for other services   = £
   For period stated, total charges owing/debited
   to departmental capitation account named : = £*26.55*

   Date of this invoice:

   Please direct enquiries connected with this invoice to department head

---

Figure 8.5: Record of consumables/reprographics

The LEA allocates funds (schools allocation) to the school and the finance committee then decides on the distribution of funds. The process of distribution is based on previous expenditure under headings prescribed by the LEA for the allocation of funds within each school. The draft school budget should then be presented to several groups from within the school community for discussion. Teaching staff should be shown the budget. The headteacher is also responsible for adjusting the amounts allocated under each heading within the budget, should the school's allocation be reduced.

A school's budget is recorded both centrally and locally. Having planned the budget and received approval from the LEA, the headteacher then operates the budget.

The allocation of funds to subject departments and teams is determined by middle managers who prepare a budget on behalf of their teams. Middle managers will have responsibility for determining and managing their department/team's budget. You will need to know and understand the budgetary processes involved in the school financial management. Current practice may involve a bidding system, whereby middle managers will decide on the amount required to fund the running of his/her department for the next financial year. A useful method of preparing a bid is to compare financial statements from the previous year with similar departments/teams; look for areas where money could be saved, e.g. file paper, and identify the areas which need funding. When completing financial documentation to be forwarded to senior management, ensure that you follow the 'house-style'. A useful method of preparing financial statements is to record materials used throughout the year.

A direct consequence of LMS is the change in relationship between teaching staff and management. There are examples of dysfunctional elements of LMS manifested in terms of distrust with a tendency to resist, which may give rise to internal conflict. As a middle manager you will need to be aware of resourcing issues as applied to your area.

9

■ ■ ■

Management of Change

Introduction – why change?

Management of change is a recurring theme in education. From the 1960s to the present there has been a continuous series of changes to the education system. Following Callaghan's Ruskin College (1976) speech, education has become more accountable for the way in which it serves society.

The reason for change is that education has to respond to the circumstances and events that happen in society. Schools, as organisations, need to develop, mature and adjust to both internal and external changes.

It is axiomatic that in society change is on the increase. Drucker (1980) states that:

> *All institutions live and perform in two time periods, that of today and that of tomorrow. Tomorrow is being made today, irrevocably in most cases. Managers therefore have to manage both today – the fundamentals – and tomorrow. In turbulent times, managers cannot assume that tomorrow will be an extension of today. On the contrary they must manage for change; change both as an opportunity and as a threat.*

Change is important and complex. Change can be unsettling, threatening and unpredictable. Introducing change can also be an opportunity for creativity and learning.

Before implementing change it is important to consider whether the change is necessary. Equally, there is always the danger that managers fail to see the need for change. In turn, change may provide:

- opportunities to acquire/practice new skills
- increased job satisfaction
- improved working practices
- opportunities to work with new people

- better use of your time and skills
- increased responsibility
- increased reward
- increased efficiency.

A middle manager is in a position that will enable him/her to identify and implement change as a positive tool in strategic planning. Initially teams will need to *own* change in order to implement it. Helping people own change will depend on a number of interrelated factors.

Change

Change will occur as a consequence of external pressures. Most innovations will occur due to social, technological, economic, political, market or chance factors. In education, innovations will involve a mixture of new 'things or conditions' as Hall and Oldroyd (1990b, p. 50) identified:

- *policies*
- *knowledge*
- *materials*
- *techniques*
- *skills or behaviours*
- *attitudes.*

Middle managers need to enable their teams to accommodate change. This should be a collaborative process involving innovation, implementation and adoption. Internal pressures for change are often a consequence of external pressures; this is self-evident in schools. The real problem is how to manage these changes effectively. As a middle manager you will encounter three types of internal pressures for change:

- top-down
- bottom-up
- expert.

Top-down

When someone in a position of authority introduces change, there is little the middle manager can do to influence the proposals. This scenario involves a clear statement by the decision-maker(s), followed by action and dissemination. The national curriculum is an example of the top-down approach. Leadership, collaboration and a willingness to take (not make) decisions will make the difference between poor and excellent practice. A top-down model will allow changes to be made quickly, efficiently and with authority.

Bottom-up

A consequence of collaborative management is a bottom-up approach to the management of change. This approach involves teams and will therefore concern middle managers when:

- the need is to address a problem which remains unclear to those not involved
- a school or department-specific solution is required.

A disadvantage to this approach is that it is time-consuming to plan and implement, as there is a need for consultation and agreement.

Expert

As a manager, you may approach an expert when you are unsure how to tackle an issue. The expert could be a member of the senior management team, colleague or external agent. The expert approach may offer a quick and cost-effective means of bringing about change. However, the introduction of an expert could mean loss of influence and control.

Middle managers need to take a broad view in order to achieve the best possible outcomes. Experts may be included in your team in order to maintain your team's and/or the school's objectives. You may wish to combine all three approaches, depending on the culture of the organisation.

Middle managers may be unable to effect change due to the constraints of their position. You will need to ascertain:

1. Who are the main players involved – staff, pupils, parents, governors?
2. Who will manage the change process – senior management, middle management, colleagues, external agents?
3. How will the change be evaluated – timescale, questions?
4. Does the change relate to school/department development plans?
5. Who will be responsible for recognising the need for change and making it happen?

Analysis of change

Change can take place at different levels, which need to be identifiable. The level of change will impact on those who are involved in the process of change. Factors influencing change may also create barriers to change (see Table 9.1).

Table 9.1: Factors influencing change

Factor	Result
Technical	Change in process or use of equipment, e.g. management procedures or computers
Social	Changes to beliefs and values, creation of a group, e.g. religion or football team
Power	Changes in political leadership at a macro- and micro-level, e.g. political party, head of school or head of department
Financial	Change in funding mechanism, e.g. availability of resources
Personnel	Change in status, family or own, e.g. marriage, divorce, children
Physical	Change in school site, e.g. condition of buildings, available facilities

Barriers to change

Some staff will be enthusiastic, while others may view change with fear, seeing it as a threat. As with other aspects of school management, staff reaction to change will reflect the culture of the school. Hall and Oldroyd (1990b, p. 63) identify that in settings where staff response was poor:

- *morale is low*
- *change agents are not respected*
- *there is a track record of failed innovation*
- *risk-taking is discouraged*
- *leaders are inflexible in their attitudes*
- *there is little outside support . . .*

*. . . teachers will be less motivated to support **change strategies** which:*

- *are unaccompanied by practical training and support [. . .]*
- *do not adapt to developing circumstances*
- *do not recognise local needs*
- *offer no sense of collective 'ownership'*
- *do not build a 'critical mass' for change.*

Neither will they commit themselves to innovations which:

- *are not seen as beneficial*
- *cannot be clearly understood*
- *are at odds with their professional beliefs*
- *are inadequately resourced.*

Middle managers should reflect on their own attitude towards change. This will influence those that work with you. Generally people who have a sense of commitment and are in charge of their lives will see change as an opportunity.

Those who are uncomfortable with their role will view change as a threat. Every school will have a combination of people who view change on a continuum from threat to opportunity! There may be individuals who will not be threatened by the change, but will feel threatened by the change process.

People will resist change, especially if it is someone else's change that has been forced upon them. Resistance to change can be a major restraining force that can be overcome with understanding. Change may incur resistance due to self-interest, misunderstanding, different assessments of the situation, or, as stated, a low tolerance for change. Common responses to change are 'political' behaviour, rumour, disagreement and/or excuses.

Westhuizen (1996, Appendix 1) identified the following resistance factors from his survey of all school principals (81) in secondary schools in the Free State Province of South Africa:

- *fear that change will cause a loss in job security*
- *the loss of established customs which provide security*
- *increased work pressure*
- *fear of the unknown*
- *the perception that change is not regarded as an improvement*
- *a disruption of the status quo (existing practices) which provides satisfaction*
- *fear that change will not succeed*
- *the absence of a need to change*
- *the lack of creative power*
- *the lack of courage to take risks*
- *an inability to handle uncertainty during the change process*
- *an irreconcilability of cultural characteristics with the proposed change*
- *a low tolerance for change*
- *the lack of resources to facilitate change*
- *insufficient evaluation of the progress of the change*
- *the lack of ethics to experiment at a school*
- *teachers who do not understand the aims/purpose of the change*
- *doubt about own abilities*
- *the lack of a positive climate for change*
- *unclear role definitions*
- *wrong timing for the implementation of change*
- *previous experience reveals no need for change*
- *application of the wrong strategy for change*
- *poor performance motivation*

- *the lack of support from the management team of the school during the change process*
- *weak strategies for managing resistance to change*
- *the absence of participative decision-making*
- *a high level of organisational conflict*
- *authoritarian leadership*
- *insufficient communication between the school principal and staff*
- *staff distrust in the management team of the school.*

Westhuizen (1996, p. 10) concluded that:

> When change is implemented in the school, a disturbance of the status quo occurs. The school as an organisation and more specifically, the teachers in the school react to the change by generating energy (resistance) to maintain the internal or existing equilibrium of the status quo. The energy that is generated at either the acceptance, but mostly at the rejection, upsets the balance. The result of the complex factors that give rise to this, is usually perceived as resistance to change.

Choosing a change strategy

In order to choose an effective change strategy a middle manager will need to:

- identify the level of complexity and time needed
- identify resistance and analyse
- select the method of overcoming resistance
- take account of his/her own attitude towards the change.

Strategies for implementing change can be summarised as follows:

- *directed* – imposing change by management, top-down, hierarchical
- *negotiated* – concedes everyone's wishes
- *action-centred* – as a consequence of action research.

Action research may provide the most appropriate way forward for managing change in a school. Action research involves identification of a practical problem/issue which is changed through individual or collaborative action, then researched. The problems may not be clearly defined and the change process may evolve through practice. As a mechanism for change, action research contains two key elements: collaboration and evaluation. By involvement, the team will try out a number of approaches to the problem and will learn from each; this will take time.

The choice of strategy adopted will be dependent on:

- the pace of change
- level of resistance
- level of status of the initiator
- amount of information required
- key players
- time available.

Schools, as organisations, should not ignore these factors. A common mistake is to move too quickly and involve too few people. Forcing change will have too many negative side effects. Equally, knowing and understanding change strategies will only go part-way to aiding/facilitating the change process. A manager can improve his/her chances of success by:

1. **Analysis:**
   - current situation
   - problems
   - possible causes of problems.
2. **Evaluation** – factors relevant to producing changes.
3. **Selection** – change strategy.
4. **Monitoring** – implementation.

As with all aspects of management, interpersonal skills are critical to successful and effective management of change.

Implementing change

Schools, as organisations, have the necessary structures and tools to successfully implement change.

INSET

Through a programme of education and training, schools can achieve change. An education and communication programme can inform and provide a platform for analysis in which resistors can engage in debate surrounding the implementation of change. This approach will require a lot of time and effort if it is to be effective. Middle managers can (and should) play an active role in the planning of INSET programmes if they are to be relevant to practice.

Participation and involvement

As team leaders, middle managers should encourage participation in the development and implementation process. Through participation, resistors become informed and are able to contribute to the outcome of change. The participation process can be difficult and time-consuming. When change is required immediately, it may not be possible!

Support

Another means of dealing with potential resistance to change is to be supportive through training, listening and providing time during busy periods. Support is most effective when fear and anxiety lie at the heart of resistance. Again, this can be time-consuming and does not always produce positive results.

Negotiation

A middle manager will need to be a skilled negotiator. Major resistance can be costly and is therefore best avoided. Negotiation can be a relatively easy way to avoid major resistance. However, managers must be sure of the parameters in which they are working to avoid a negative outcome.

Co-option

A form of manipulation is co-option, inviting resistors to join as change agents. Often the change will occur without the individual noticing. This will be difficult to maintain in the long-term as people do not enjoy being manipulated.

Coercion

This is a risky process, inevitably people will become resentful and the costs are high.

Successful approaches to change will often involve a combination of the above. Middle managers will require the knowledge and understanding, skills and ability to approach change.

Evaluating change

It is often difficult to test the outcome of change against the original objectives. There are often unintended outcomes, and defining criteria for success is problematic. If the objectives have been carefully constructed, evaluation should be possible. As change agents, managers should set objectives which can be measured after the change has been implemented. Evaluation can often proceed simultaneously with the change programme; this should not be left until the end. Strengths and weaknesses should be identified, as should opportunities and threats. In essence, evaluation should include:

- follow-up reviews – written and oral
- obtaining feedback from *all* who are affected by the change and change process
- communicating the outcomes.

Model

A model for implementing change in schools might be:

- identifying the need for change
- identifying alternatives
- deciding on the most appropriate change
- planning the change
- implementing the change
- consolidating the change.

Once change is in place, continue to monitor and evaluate, thus providing a framework for future change.

Summary

Management of change is a recurring theme in education. The reason for change is that education has to respond to the circumstances and events that happen in society. It is axiomatic that in society, change is on the increase. Change is important and complex.

Before implementing change it is important to consider whether the change is necessary. A middle manager is in a position that will enable him/her to identify and implement change as a positive tool in strategic planning.

Change will occur as a consequence of external pressures. Middle managers need to enable their teams to accommodate change. As a middle manager you will encounter three types of internal pressures for change:

- top-down
- bottom-up
- expert.

Middle managers need to take a broad view in order to achieve the best possible outcomes. Change can take place at different levels, which need to be identifiable. Some staff will be enthusiastic, while others may view change with fear, seeing it as a threat.

Middle managers should reflect on their own attitude towards change. People will resist change, especially if it is someone else's change that has been forced upon them. Westhuizen (1996, p. 10) concludes that:

When change is implemented in the school, a disturbance of the status quo occurs.

Action research may provide the most appropriate way forward for managing change in a school. As a mechanism for change, action research contains two key elements: collaboration and evaluation. Schools, as organisations, will have the necessary structures and tools to successfully implement change:

- INSET
- participation and involvement
- support
- negotiation
- co-option.

It is often difficult to test the outcome against the original objectives. In essence, evaluation should include:

- follow-up reviews – written and oral
- obtaining feedback from *all* who are affected by the change and change process
- communicating the outcomes.

10
■ ■ ■

Continuing Professional Development

Introduction

Schools are where pupils learn; schools should also provide a learning environment for all staff – teaching and non-teaching. Middle managers have a responsibility for members of the learning community.

As professionals, teachers should view the place in which they work as a place of learning. Within the framework of Continuing Professional Development (CPD), self-development and staff development are essential pre-requisites to effective management and effective schools. Equally, a pre-condition and an outcome of effective CPD policies is a culture that encourages reflection and development. This is often the antithesis of the teachers' experience of classroom and staffroom isolation (Ingvarson, 1990, p. 165).

This chapter examines CPD policies and practices, beginning with an introduction to Teacher Training Agency (TTA) and National Educational Assessment Centre (NEAC) initiatives, followed by a focus on staff development and middle management. A section on the place of CPD in schools leads in to staff appraisal. The chapter concludes with staff development in practice, through INSET and award-bearing courses.

Teaching Training Agency (TTA)

The TTA was established in 1994 by the government, to review and develop the training of teachers. Central to the TTA's work is the issue of school effectiveness set within the context of the government's school improvement programme. The TTA's Chief Executive, Anthea Millett, commented at the first

'Teachers Make a Difference' conference: *good teaching is what makes a difference to children's learning* (1996c, p. 18). Initiatives for the training of middle managers are currently high profile activities for government and professional agencies. The TTA and NEAC are developing schemes for the continuing professional development of teachers. As Earley and Fletcher-Campbell (1989, p. 87) state, *the developer must be developed*.

Educationalists and practitioners will not be surprised by this statement; they may however be surprised at the pace of the TTA's programme to develop a CPD strategy. In October 1995 the Secretary of State accepted the TTA's advice to establish a framework for the continuing professional development of teachers. Critically the TTA recognised the need for management and leadership development for aspiring middle managers. A major element of the advice was the development of national standards for teachers:

- newly qualified teacher (NQT)
- expert teacher
- expert in school management
- expert in school leadership.

An interesting distinction is made between management and leadership. Subject/pastoral team leaders are considered to be managers; in contrast heads of school are leaders. As indicated throughout this book, the author considers middle and senior managers to be both leaders and managers. At the initial stages of the development of the national standards for teachers, appraisal has been identified by the Secretary of State and the TTA as part of CPD for teachers.

Following the TTA's announcement to develop CPD there have been various consultation exercises encompassing:

- national teacher training
- appraisal
- Initial Teacher Training (ITT)
- National Professional Qualification for Headteachers (NPQH).

The results of the consultation process, involving practitioners from all sectors of education, will not be known until after the publication of this book. Middle managers should be aware of these initiatives and where possible participate in their development. Further discussion on the NPQH is included in Chapter Twelve.

Key points

A policy for the CPD of teachers is to be welcomed. If the central task of the TTA is to improve the quality of teaching, school effectiveness should relate directly to the development of schools as learning organisations.

New CPD initiatives should also relate to existing good practice and be introduced through SDPs. A strategic approach to the implementation of CPD is required if it is to be valued by professional teachers.

The majority of primary and secondary schools have established partnerships with Higher Education Institutes (HEIs). The development of CPD initiatives should reflect good practice contained in the key elements of these partnerships. CPD should therefore recognise and incorporate award-bearing courses within CPD. For many teachers, higher education has provided the platform to their professional development.

Accountability is of the essence if the profession is to be valued by all involved. All teachers should have access to CPD within the context of the national standards. Any practical outcome of the consultation process, i.e. implementation of CPD in schools, should be cost-effective, in terms of time and resources.

Essentially, the national standards for teachers should not be over-managerial or require extensive administration. If teachers are to have confidence in the process, time needs to be taken to create the appropriate culture within the school; this cannot be rushed.

The pivotal role of middle managers needs to be identified for the successful implementation of CPD and the national standards for teachers. CPD should be experienced from initial teacher training extending to 'expert' teacher manager or leader status in schools. A focused approach to management and leadership is required encompassing:

- strategic leadership
- organisational leadership
- teaching and learning
- community leadership
- staff appraisal and development
- school effectiveness.

The TTA has the opportunity to grasp the nettle of CPD for teachers through the proposed framework. At each stage of development, implementation and evaluation, new initiatives should involve practitioners. Teachers need to have confidence in the process. Middle managers need to develop the knowledge and understanding, skills and abilities to manage CPD in their schools.

National Educational Assessment Centre (NEAC)

In early 1996 the NEAC launched its first Middle Management Centre. This reflects the awareness of school governors, LEAs and school leaders of the need to develop the leadership and managerial skills of teachers in management positions. NEAC identified heads of department, heads of faculties and pastoral care heads in secondary schools, and subject/area co-ordinators and cross phase co-ordinators in primary schools, as middle managers who need to develop good leadership skills.

Based at Oxford Brookes University, NEAC was founded in 1990 to implement in the UK the assessment centre approach as a diagnostic tool for senior management in education. The process is adapted from a model which has been used for more than twenty years in America by the National Association of Secondary School Principals (NASSP).

In 1990, NEAC concentrated on competency-based assessment for head-teachers, both aspirant and in post. NEAC now recognises that a similar programme would be of benefit to middle managers in schools. Hewitt (1996b) identified the competencies to be assessed as follows:

Administrative competencies

1. **Problem analysis** – ability to seek out relevant data and analyse information to determine the important elements of a situation.
2. **Judgment** – ability to reach logical conclusions and make high quality decisions based on available information; to set priorities; to show caution where necessary.
3. **Organisational ability and decisiveness** – ability to plan and schedule effectively; to delegate appropriately; to recognise when a decision is required and to act upon it.

Interpersonal competencies

1. **Leadership** – ability to motivate others and involve them in the accomplishment of tasks; to secure general acceptance of ideas. Willingness to engage in pro-active behaviour.
2. **Sensitivity** – ability to perceive needs, concerns and problems from differing viewpoints and to act accordingly; to value the contribution of others.

Communicative competencies

1. **Oral communication** – ability to make clear oral presentation of facts or ideas.
2. **Written communication** – ability to express ideas clearly in writing; to write appropriately for different audiences.

In addition, stress tolerance and personal breadth competencies that focus on individual interests are needed. Motivation and educational values will also be commented on but not recorded.

In a middle management centre (a **process** not a **place**), four participants attend a location and are assessed during the course of the day by four experienced NEAC assessors (who have previously attended the course and have been assessed). A report is then prepared which poses appropriate questions relating to the participants' professional development. NEAC anticipates that participant schools will appoint a senior member of staff to act in a supporting/mentoring role, who will be present at the debriefing exercise. NEAC will have presented the senior management team with details and ensured that the process is understood prior to the assessment exercise.

All activities are work-related – discussion groups, in-tray, presentation, and a written response to a series of questions. The report presents a competency profile. The conclusion offers points for consideration in devising an action plan for development, and encourages participants to tackle them in a structured way.

Discussion

NEAC offers a highly structured approach to the development and training of middle managers. At NEAC's 1996 annual conference, Malcolm Hewitt, Director, commented on the need to develop a funding mechanism for the training of middle managers in education. This view was echoed by the TTA, which has encouraged practitioners to contribute to the development of their CPD programme for all teachers.

Middle managers and aspiring middle managers need to keep abreast of these developments and consider alternatives to the NEAC approach.

Developing your staff

New initiatives for the training of middle managers are one aspect of middle management; another is staff development. Earley and Fletcher-Campbell (1989, p. 105) deduced from their research that *desire for development was seen as one of the hallmarks of a successful department*. They also identified the increasing importance for middle managers to attend to this area.

Development is a term encompassing any experience or process which helps to bring out an individual's full potential. As a manager you should aim to improve the quality of your existing staff. You will be responsible for achieving targets and will only succeed if the people who work with you are competent. Therefore you should offer the members of your team sufficient training and development.

Staff development has been defined by the National Policy Board for Educational Administration (NPBEA) (1993, pp. 11–13) as:

> *Working with [. . .] staff to identify professional needs; planning, organising and facilitating programmes that improve [. . .] staff effectiveness and are consistent with institutional goals and needs; supervising individuals and groups; providing feedback on performance; arranging for remedial assistance; [. . .] participating in recruitment and development activities; and initiating self-development.*

Development experiences perform four major functions, they:

- enhance the personal and professional lives of teachers
- are remedial
- set the groundwork for implementing school aims
- introduce changes.

In general, middle managers have a responsibility to see that individuals develop new skills. Staff development should not mean an additional activity; often development activities will happen as a matter of course. Staff development includes personal development, team development and school development. You will need to be aware that staff development has a wider importance:

- promoting shared values
- implementing change
- promoting equal opportunities.

Shared role

The responsibility for developing staff is shared. The school as a whole has a responsibility to develop policies and provide resources for staff development. Depending on the size of the school a middle (or senior) manager may have responsibility for staff development. Maintained schools will also have the support and guidance of the LEA officers who are trained to provide courses for practitioners. Grant maintained and independently funded schools can purchase these services as required.

Middle managers have part of the responsibility for staff development. A middle manager will know his/her staff's work, experience and aspirations. As a player manager, a middle manager is uniquely placed to assist a colleague's development.

The individual also has a stake in his/her own development and should take some responsibility for it. Development cannot be imposed; individuals must own the development process or it will not happen. A middle manager can assist staff in their development in several ways:

- role model – staff will adopt your practices and attitudes
- specific guidance/training
- encourage reflection
- sensitive delegation
- promote development opportunities
- act as 'gate-keeper' for information and various opportunities as they arise.

Middle managers need to identify the development needs of their teams and aim to achieve each, collectively and individually. Recognising development needs is an on-going process involving formal (appraisal) and informal (observation) approaches. A detailed job description will provide a framework for identifying individual needs, equally applicable to current and future posts.

Development opportunities

Staff development, while important and desirable, is just one of many demands placed on a middle manager. Recognising that development involves on-the-job activities is critical to both the teacher and manager-teacher.

Induction is one such activity. When a new member of staff joins your team/school, identify (in advance) what your new colleague will need to know, for example:

- job description
- his/her position in the team/school
- school's aims (SDP)
- department's aims (DDP)
- relevant documentation including staff handbook
- reporting and assessment procedures
- members of his/her team – introduce colleagues.

Mentoring is a process whereby you can pass on to someone else your knowledge and understanding, skills and abilities. As a method of developing the knowledge and understanding, skills and abilities of teachers, it has proven qualities. There will be further discussion of mentoring in Chapter Twelve. However, before moving on, there are some possible drawbacks to mentoring. Mentors may:

- pass on bad habits
- not be qualified/able to impart their knowledge of their job
- lack the patience required
- be reluctant to pass on their skills
- be too closely involved to see their job from another person's perspective.

Further models of staff development include:

- self-development/team-development – a sharing of expertise
- action learning – identifying an area of development, sharing advice towards solving problems
- 'in-house' course – sharing expertise within the school
- job exchange – working in a different environment
- distance learning
- job-rotation – encouraging your team to share classes.

Within education the market place is saturated with providers of training and education for teachers, e.g. consultants who consider themselves to be 'experts in the field'. When considering how to identify suitable training, it would be useful to consider what areas of expertise are available within the school, LEA or partner Higher Education Institutions (HEIs).

Implementation

As the NPBEA (1993, pp. 11–16) advise:

> To be implemented successfully, staff development programmes must have an operational plan [headed by the senior management team].

A middle manager will participate in the development of an operational plan. Good operational plans set clear and specific objectives for each development activity and assign responsibility for those involved. Participation in staff development is critical to success. Appraisal is a means to assess staff needs and to measure short-, medium- and long-term results. An operational plan for staff development should also reflect the aims of both the SDP and DDP.

Once targets have been set, there must be adequate time, resources and follow-up support for development. Figure 10.1, based on American practice (NPBEA, 1993), illustrates the process of school development planning.

Staff development will only be successful with effective training, monitoring and evaluation procedures. It should be a continuous dialogue. As a middle manager you should identify your responsibilities in the process and participate! A collective approach to staff development will need to be time-consuming if it is to achieve its objectives.

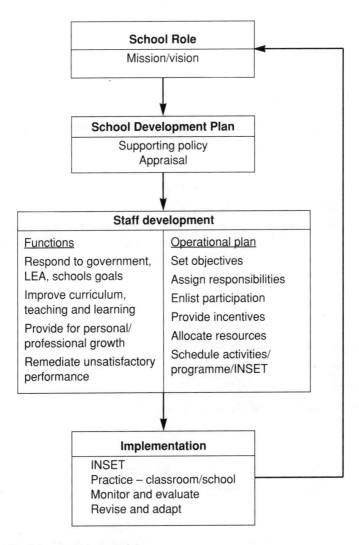

Figure 10.1: Staff development model

Appraisal

Appraisal has been a contentious issue in schools since it was first legislated in 1991. This followed a lengthy period of arbitration between the government and teaching unions from 1982–6. The original Advisory Conciliation and Arbitration Service (ACAS) (1986) agreement on which the pilot schemes were conducted stated that appraisal was intended to be a:

continuous and systematic process intended to help individual teachers with their professional development and career planning and to help ensure that the in-service training and deployment of teachers matches the complementary needs of individual teachers and their schools.

Statutory regulations (National Steering Group, 1991) state that the aims of teacher appraisal are to:

- improve skills and performance
- improve careers through appropriate in-service training (INSET)
- help teachers having difficulties with their performance
- provide references
- improve the management of schools.

Fidler (1994) found that middle managers have a restricted view of their role in appraisal. Appraisal has much to offer schools; middle managers have a vital role in achieving the benefits of an appraisal scheme. As a middle manager you will need to understand both the principles and the process of appraising staff as part of the school staff development programme. The purpose of this section is not to enter the appraisal debate, but to present appraisal as a means of identifying and fulfilling staff development needs in schools. This section will encompass the following:

- the purpose of appraisal
- management of appraisal
- practical issues
- appraisal review and development
- discussion.

The purpose of appraisal

The purpose of appraisal is to motivate and develop individuals. As a middle manager you will be involved in identifying a colleague's strengths and weaknesses, and the setting of targets which are attainable. Appraisal is *not* judgmental, but an audit or an evaluation leading to performance-related rewards or sanctions.

The primary purpose of appraisal is performance enhancement. An outcome of the appraisal process should be an action plan which identifies specific targets and training needs. Appraisal is a development process.

The 1991 regulations (Regulation 4) detail the aim of appraisal as:

> *in carrying out their duty under Regulation 3 (the duty to appraise) appraising bodies shall aim to improve the quality of education for pupils, through assisting school teachers to realise their potential and to carry out their duties more effectively.*

The statutory aims of appraisal were to:

- *recognise the achievements of school teachers and help them to identify ways of improving their skills and performance*
- *help school teachers, governing bodies and local education authorities (as the case may be) to determine whether a change of duties would help the professional development of school teachers and improve their career prospects*
- *identify the potential of teachers for career development, with the aim of helping them, where possible, through appropriate in-service training*
- *help school teachers identified as having difficulties with their performance, through appropriate guidance, counselling and training*
- *inform those responsible for providing references for school teachers in relation to appointments*
- *improve the management of schools.*

Appraisal procedures do not form part of any disciplinary or dismissal procedures, but appraisal statements may be used for the purposes specified in Regulation 14 (authorising Chief Executive Officers (CEOs) or designated officers/advisers to take account of relevant information when taking decisions on promotion, dismissal or discipline and exercising discretion in relation to pay).

In order that a developmental appraisal can survive, continuous evaluation is required of lessons from schools, LEAs, trainers, OFSTED, governing bodies and evaluators.

A working definition of appraisal is 'one professional holding him/herself accountable to his/herself in the presence of another professional'. As such a staff appraisal scheme should aim to:

- improve the quality of education of pupils through assisting staff and headteachers to realise their potential and to carry out their duties more effectively
- improve the management of teaching and learning within the classroom
- help staff and headteachers identify ways of enhancing their professional skills and performance and support them in the identification of achievable targets
- inform the process of developmental planning within the school
- assist in planning the professional development of staff individually and collectively within the framework set by the SDP and with reference to their role and function within the school
- enhance the overall management
- provide an opportunity to consider the effective management of change
- support the promotion of equal opportunities.

Management of appraisal

A middle manager should be aware of what is needed in schools in order for teacher appraisal to be managed effectively. Middle managers should have knowledge and understanding of the following:

- implementation plan
  - statement of aims of scheme
  - organisation of scheme
  - timetable/duration of cycle/frequency
  - documentation of scheme
  - personnel
  - resources
- SDP
  - process/cycle
  - availability/accessibility
- Job description
- Equal opportunities
  - awareness of staff of issues
- Staff development policy
- Professional development
  - co-ordinating
  - resources.

Ultimately the outcome of a staff appraisal scheme should be for members of staff: better understanding of the job, improved feedback and recognition, opportunity to regularly consider professional development needs, increased accuracy of references, greater awareness of career development factors and opportunities, support for work-related issues and greater job satisfaction; and for the school: school aims and staff aims co-ordinated, priorities clarified and determined, staff clarity about roles and responsibilities, professional development of management, school needs met through target-setting, improved communication, greater exchange of ideas and a more supportive environment.

To this end the principles of a staff appraisal scheme should be:

- that the process is open and based on the mutual understanding by all staff of the context, purpose, procedures, criteria and outcomes of the whole process
- that the process and procedures adopted should be fair and equitable, and by respecting equal opportunities, particularly in relation to gender and race

- that the progress and procedures supporting staff appraisal should be acceptable to all staff, headteachers, governors and LEA personnel and that all should benefit from participation in the scheme
- that it should give the opportunity for objective judgments to be made concerning the management of the institution
- that at all times the scheme should aim to avoid unnecessary bureaucracy and time-consuming administration by the maximisation of available resources, and that it should draw on data from a range of sources
- that it should be integral to the school's development strategy and attempt to balance the demands of professional development and public accountability
- that it should support development and improvement through a formative process.

Practical issues

Generating job descriptions for appraisal

Central to an effective scheme for staff appraisal is the preparation of job descriptions. A middle manager may by involved in writing a job description. Key features of a job description are that it should be jointly discussed and cover all aspects of the individual's work. A job description should state precisely to whom the individual is accountable and be broken down into areas of specific responsibility. Critically, it should be open ended and support development.

To be of value, a job description should include:

- appropriate personal details
- job title
- a statement of the primary function of the job which is clear, but brief, as to the overall role of the jobholder
- a statement of on-line responsibility which clearly specifies to whom the jobholder is responsible, and for whom the jobholder is responsible
- a detailed statement of the main duties which could be broken down into subsections and which may be used as a checklist to ascertain if the jobholder is satisfactorily performing the job
- a statement of duties.

The role of the appraiser is as follows:

- to oversee, co-ordinate and largely conduct the process of appraisal
- to be responsible for not more than four appraisees

- to be a party, with the appraisee, to the preparation stage of the process, with particular reference to agreeing the specific focus of the appraisal
- to agree what information will be gathered, by what method and from whom, in conjunction with the appraisee. The information collected should be focused on issues not on personality. The appraiser should provide a brief progress report
- to carry out classroom observation of the appraisee, using an agreed method of data collection and focusing on areas identified in conjunction with the appraisee
- to provide the appraisee with a written copy of the information to be collected, prior to the professional meeting
- to agree the date, venue and agenda for the appraisal interview; to carry out a review in that meeting and to agree targets with the appraisee. To agree and draft the written summary as a result of the meeting
- to agree a date, time and venue for the follow-up meeting
- to encourage the appraisee to follow the action plan agreed
- to agree any adjustments to the targets in the light of changed circumstances
- to monitor the professional development of the appraisee and determine, in consultation with the appraisee, what has been achieved.

Having considered the principles, the process of appraisal involves the following:

1. **Initial meeting:**
   - the purpose
   - date, time and venue for appraisal interview
   - date, time and focus of classroom observation
   - objectives of the interview
   - data collection/instruments to be used
   - what information is to be collected
   - who is to be approached
   - information to be available to appraisee prior to the interview.

2. **Staff self-appraisal:**
   - use of prompt sheet to support self-reflection on performance/role.

3. **Classroom observation:**
   - total of one hour on two or more occasions
   - specific focus: details of class/group work being carried out, teacher plans and preparation
   - questioning techniques
   - agreed methodology/format.

4. **Debriefing following observation:**
   - relevant data used to inform discussion, 'teaching analysis' within two weeks.

5. **Collection of any other relevant data:**
   - pupil-related, non-teaching duties
   - curriculum-based
   - carried out within half a term
   - relevant to past year's work
   - opportunity for feedback from areas of additional responsibility
   - data compiled during action research.

6. **Appraisal interview:**
   - clear agenda
   - comfortable environment
   - uninterrupted
   - adequate time
   - sharing documents prior to meeting
   - consideration of job description
   - review of work
   - identify successes, areas of development
   - identify constraints
   - identify expectations
   - professional development needs
   - identification of targets
   - only one interview per day
   - confidentiality and trust
   - nature of previous relationships
   - high priority by both parties and others.

7. **Preparation of an appraisal statement:**
   - recording main points: achievements, success and good practice
   - deficiencies, weaknesses and suggestions for dealing with them
   - requests for help and support
   - suggestions for professional development
   - comments about matters affecting individual's work.

8. **Agreed targets:**
   - should be stated clearly
   - should take the form of an action plan

- should be few in number
- should be challenging but attainable
- should be monitored and reviewed
- targets connected to: classroom strategies, school performance, career/professional development.

Copies to an appraisee and headteacher should be treated as confidential and permit those with access to draw on the information in making decisions concerning pay, promotion, disciplinary action.

The Director and designated Inspectors' targets to Chair of Governors should provide statements that are kept for up to two appraisal cycles, i.e. four years.

A review meeting should be held in the second year to review progress and reconsider appropriateness of targets, professional development/training career development and to raise any other issues.

A middle manager will need to be trained to develop the key skills of interviewing which are: questioning, analysing, summarising and reflecting, clarifying, giving and receiving feedback, problem-solving and target-setting.

The kind of information required largely determines the type of question selected in the appraisal process. For example:

- *open* – to encourage another person to explore matters of importance to them
- *reflective* – to encourage someone to explain his/her feelings or attitudes on an issue
- *leading* – to guide a person towards an answer which the questioner wants or expects to hear
- *hypothetical* – to encourage someone to step outside his/her current position, mental set or attitude and consider a matter from another standpoint
- *closed* – to gather very specific facts or obtain yes/no answers
- *probing* – to keep the person on the same topic but explore it in more depth.

Another key component in the appraisal process is classroom observation. During the observation it is important for the appraiser to concentrate on the pre-arranged aspects of the lesson (i.e. the agreed focus), record observations accurately, record data systematically, maintain the agreed relationship with pupils/teacher, be objective, defer judgment, and give an immediate response to the appraisee and thanks on leaving the lesson.

This is followed by a feedback session which should take place as soon after the observation as possible and be in a quiet and informal atmosphere.

The appraiser should allow the teacher to present an account and analysis while engaging in active listening and avoiding interruptions, then present the collected data and discuss its implications with the appraisee, encourage the teacher to identify areas for development of possible targets and conclude with an agreed written statement of the action to be taken.

Target-setting is a critical part of the appraisal process. A target is a statement of intent agreed by two or more people which refers to a desired state of affairs to be achieved in the future. In most circumstances it will concern a change resulting in an improvement of some kind.

Therefore targets should:

- aim to facilitate the teacher's own professional development
- be agreed in the context of the school's development plan and organisational goals
- be feasible and realistic in the light of available resources
- include some agreed performance that will help to illustrate the extent to which the target is being achieved
- be few in number
- include some indication of the support the appraisee will require/receive in order to achieve the target (the appraiser should accept responsibility for ensuring that support is provided)
- be reviewed in the follow-up meetings and modified as necessary.

A useful guide to target-setting is as follows:

S	–	**Specific**
M	–	**Manageable**
A	–	**Appropriate**
R	–	**Realistic**
T	–	**Time-constrained**
I	–	**Informative**
E	–	**Evaluated**
S	–	**Stimulating**

Issues

Since the introduction of teacher/headteacher appraisal, many practical issues have emerged which a middle manager needs to consider when implementing appraisal. Specifically, training needs to be near the point of implementation and greater emphasis is needed on higher order skills training for appraisers. There is also a need for an evolving pattern of guidance and documentation by the LEA. Critically, priority should be afforded to appraisal in the context of the OFSTED inspection system. Guidelines are required on linking appraisal to school development planning and school improvement. Issues arising from practice are shown as follows:

1. **Resources:**
   - time and human
   - funding to support outcomes

2. **Who appraises whom:**
   - who selects/allocates appraisers to appraisees
   - involvement of governors
   - support to appraisers' team

3. **Timing:** duration of cycle

4. **Frequency:** recommended only one appraisal interview per day

5. **Consistency:**
   - monitoring (school-based)
   - monitoring (LEA-based)

6. **Records/reports:**
   - ownership
   - duration
   - accessibility (LEA, governors)

7. **Outcomes:**
   - follow-up
   - additional support system

8. **Appeals:**
   - school system
   - LEA system

Appraisal review and development

Five years after the implementation of appraisal, there have been a number of reviews written focusing on the appraisal process. The most relevant to middle managers are those which have been completed by the Department For Education and Employment (DFEE), OFSTED and TTA. Significantly, OFSTED joined the TTA in its round of consultation conferences (May 1996). A possible outcome of this collaboration will be a new framework for the appraisal of teachers and headteachers.

An Evaluation of the National Scheme of School Teacher Appraisal (Barber *et al.*, 1995) revealed that for many teachers, appraisal has been a positive experience contributing to improved school management, the creation of a positive climate and better focused INSET and CPD. The report recommended the production of national guidelines on the management of appraisal to assist school appraisal co-ordinators.

OFSTED published a report on *The Appraisal of Teachers 1991–96* (April 1996) which was distributed to those attending the TTA's Appraisal Conferences (May 1996). In its conclusions, the report recommends that schools review their policies on appraisal, in particular the targets for individual teachers. OFSTED urged that appraisal is accountable and should be linked to pay or promotion as a matter of priority. It concluded that the appraisal system was functioning below its full potential and had slipped down too low on schools' list of priorities.

The TTA has identified appraisal within the context of CPD. In the future the TTA aims to make recommendations to the Secretary of State for Education focusing on how the appraisal system can be developed to improve teachers' performance, and the ways in which schools are managed, to promote staff development and school improvement. Areas for development following Barber *et al.*'s advice will focus on:

- collection of evidence
- target-setting
- relationships between teacher appraisal, staff development and school development planning
- links between appraisal, school self-review, OFSTED inspection and other systems of accountability.

Throughout the consultation process, the TTA has emphasised the need for a coherent approach to CPD. Appraisal, therefore, should have a greater impact in schools. The TTA acknowledges that there have been caveats of good practice; however there are startling shortfalls. The TTA's review of CPD (July 1995) found that 63 per cent of headteachers placed a direct link between appraisal and CPD, in contrast to 12 per cent of teachers.

Both the TTA and OFSTED consider that the appraisal process should have an impact on teachers, pupils and schools. During the conference debate on the future of appraisal, OFSTED and the TTA emphasised the model shown in Figure 10.2.

The TTA's perspective is to improve the quality of teaching and learning in schools. Teacher effectiveness is at the heart of the TTA's work, and it wishes to develop the materials and strategies for good professional practice. Its focus is on quality assurance; appraisal is the means of *gluing* the many facets of CPD together.

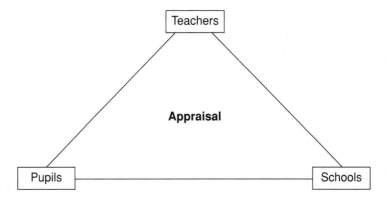

Figure 10.2: TTA/OFSTED appraisal model

Key issues to be considered by middle managers are:

- **process** – effectiveness?
- **outcomes** – what happens to targets?
- **appraisers** – confidentiality?
- **pay and performance** – should these be related?

Meanwhile practitioners and managers need to be aware of and participate in the appraisal debate.

Comment

Since its development, legislation and implementation in schools, appraisal has been evaluated by several agencies: university researchers, TTA and most recently OFSTED. In brief, all have stated the need for appraisal to be consistent with organisational values if it is to be of value (Fidler 1994, Wragg 1994, West-Burnham 1995). West-Burnham (1995, p. 117) emphasises the need for collaboration and support. Wragg (1994) focuses on helping teachers improve their teaching and performance. In contrast, OFSTED (1996b) introduces the notion of performance-related pay, the antithesis of appraisal as a development tool.

If appraisal is to work effectively there are enormous resource and financial implications. If teachers are to achieve their targets within two years, middle managers will need to plan the process within the framework of the SDP.

Ultimately appraisal should be a learning process, therefore appraisers (middle and senior managers) and appraisees (all staff) will need to identify what learning should take place and for what purpose. Appraisal can provide a unique opportunity to support the neglected learners in schools – teachers. Gunter (1995) commented on the potential for appraisal as a process to help facilitate the development of staff within a school.

As stated, the key issues are lack of resources and financial support for the initiative. If appraisal is to be both remedial and developmental there needs to be an investment of financial support, time and training. Middle managers need to know how to train staff and how to be trained. There is now a large body of literature on appraisal which highlights the need for trust, training, resourcing and commitment. Middle managers are central to the success of appraisal. Training opportunities should therefore be focused/allocated on middle management. An established method of staff development is the programme of INSET for teachers.

In-Service Education and Training (INSET)

As a middle manager you will need to be aware of the tensions that exist between personal professional development and school development. Senior managers have become more acutely aware of these tensions, with the increase of privatised consultancies delivering short courses to schools on any subject associated with education.

Continuing professional development for teachers has until recently been ignored in teacher education terms. The work of the School Management Task Force (SMT, 1990) and the emergence of the Teacher Training Agency (TTA) have led to a focus on the need for continuing professional development policies. In essence INSET has been the subject of much rhetoric and little planning (Williams, 1991).

The TTA's survey, focusing on CPD, carried out by MORI (1995) found that INSET represented a huge investment nationally of around £400m per annum. The need to produce an effective professional development policy is therefore self-evident. Middle managers should be aware of their team's needs and how these relate to the INSET provided by the school, LEA, local HEI and other agencies. Essentially all middle managers should keep a record of the INSET undertaken by staff. This should be monitored and evaluated in relation to the SDP and DDP.

In some schools there may be a Professional Development Co-ordinator (PDC), responsible for staff development and INSET. The effectiveness of continuing professional development will be dependent on management of:

- **information** – available for all staff concerning CPD, INSET and Grants for Education Support and Training (GEST)
- **planning** – collaboration between middle and senior managers in consultation with their teams
- **evaluation** – of all courses, needs analysis for individuals and the institution
- **resources** – 'experts' from school, LEA, HEIs and other agencies

- **networking** – the need for management to consult with teams and INSET providers.

Evidence from the review of recent OFSTED reports (Levačić and Glover, 1995) suggests that those responsible for planning professional development within schools need to follow a rational planning approach which links priorities for expenditure more closely to departmental or school aims. This should be followed by an assessment of alternative providers and their potential to offer value for money.

Evaluation of INSET needs to respond to the question of whether the programme enhanced pupils' learning and therefore teachers' ability to teach. However as Holt (1981, p. 153) comments:

The truth is there is absolutely no sure fire, incontestable way of evaluating an educational activity.

Critically, INSET evaluations should inform policy. In order to do so, these should include:

1. Aims that are clearly stated.
2. Performance indicators or outcomes that are SMART.
3. Questions related to 1 and 2.
4. Information arising from 1, 2 and 3 which is related to practice and accessible.
5. Conclusions that will inform policy.
6. Reports containing all of the above and understood by all participants.
7. An evaluation brief that will inform policy.

Figures 10.3–5 give an example of good practice in evaluating and planning professional development, management INSET, INSET and appraisal.

Professional Development, INSET and Appraisal (PDIA)

1. The department has contributed to the PDIA group's policies for teaching and learning, INSET appraisal, NQTs and student teachers.

2. Quality assurance has started in the department, in conjunction with inspectors and attached senior teachers, to begin to critically observe all teachers in the department and ensure the highest possible standard of teaching and learning.

3. The head of department keeps a database of INSET for members of the department, and plans are in place to identify the needs of all members of the department.

4. One member of the department has been involved in the NQT programme, and one member of the department has been involved in the mentoring INSET to support this programme.

Creative arts department aims relating to PDIA

School Development Plan:

To provide an action plan that offers a clear vision of the direction and the needs of the department, in line with the school's development planning groups and which fully exploits the finances and resources of the school.

Appraisal:

To assist in establishing a self-funding and efficient appraisal system that is complimentary to the running of the school and embraces all teaching.

INSET and staff development:

To ensure that the department has a system that allows staff as far as possible to attend INSET in relation to individual, departmental and school needs, focusing on the DDP, SDP and appraisal targets.

New staff and newly qualified teachers:

To assist in developing and maintaining a system that provides effective information and an induction programme for new staff and NQTs.

Student teachers:

To ensure a manageable programme of student teachers to the department which enhances and benefits the department.

Quality assurance:

To have in place within the department a system for quality assurance that will ensure the highest standards of teaching and learning.

Figure 10.3: Professional development model – creative arts

Creative arts objectives relating to PDIA

INSET and staff development

Academic year 1995–6:

- review the system of allocating INSET to ensure it is equitable and meets staff development needs while reflecting the DDP, SDP, QA programme and pupil priorities and needs
- review the system of INSET monitoring and recording to ensure accuracy and efficiency
- involvement in developing a programme of teacher placements in key departments to increase awareness of business and industry
- involvement in developing the induction and INSET programme for NQTs and new staff.

Academic year 1996–7:

- pilot a system of recording, monitoring and evaluating INSET that ensures efficiency, maximises available resources, and benefits students as well as enhancing staff development
- research – available sources for funding
- involvement in expanding the programme of teacher placements
- involvement in reviewing, evaluating and refining NQT and staff induction programme.

Academic year 1997–8:

- a system for INSET which reflects the DDP and SDP and enhances teaching and learning quality while enabling staff to maximise their professional development within financial resource limitations
- an efficient system for monitoring and evaluating INSET and utilising all possible funding sources, backed up within department
- full involvement in creating a programme of teaching placements extended to involve key departments and increasing awareness of business and industry
- involvement in effective induction programme for NQT and staff.

Figure 10.4: INSET and staff development model – creative arts

---

Creative arts objectives relating to PDIA

Quality Assurance (QA)

Academic year 1995–6:

- develop, in conjunction with the local inspectorate, a rigorous and efficient system of direct, critical observation of lessons. This must be systematic and provide feedback of the standards achieved using LEA and OFSTED criteria
- develop a monitoring system that records QA activity and informs INSET
- develop opportunities to observe and share good practice
- review and update department handbook to reflect DDP and SDP priorities, school and departmental policies and procedures
- review and update department handbook and schemes of work.

Academic year 1996–7:

- review and refine the process of lesson observation to the extent that it is entirely in-house with inspector input as required
- review and refine the monitoring system to record QA activity and inform INSET
- ensure opportunities to observe and share good practice
- review, update and refine SOWs and department handbook to reflect DDP and SDP priorities, school and departmental policies and procedures.

Academic year 1997–8:

- an efficient system that ensures that teaching and learning taking place throughout the department is of the highest order, ensuring that schemes of work and subject content are being followed and appropriately delivered to the maximum benefit of the pupils
- effective monitoring of the QA process with as many lessons as possible being good or better and resources targeted appropriately
- annual review of SOWs and department handbook with amendments as required.

Figure 10.5: Quality assurance development model – creative arts

As a consequence of self-assessment, SDPs, DDPs and OFSTED, management training has been identified as a priority in many schools. Figure 10.6 is an approach adopted by a secondary school. An alternative, school-based model (Figure 10.7) is provided by Forde, Reeves and Casteel (1996; reproduced by permission of Mrs V. M. Casteel, Head of Policy, Lanarkshire Department of Education, Municipal Building, Kildonan Street, Coatbridge ML5 3BT).

Middle management INSET day 15 April 1996

Here are my initial thoughts for the day with your managers. The overall aims and objectives for the project have been stated in our proposal; the specific aims of this day will be:

- to agree on the purpose and benefits of whole school planning and the strategic role of middle managers
- to review current processes, examples of good practice and ideas of all participants
- to agree the processes and systems to ensure effective development planning for the school
- to identify further action and training/development needs.

The whole day will allow maximum participation from those attending and should result in commitment to the ideas and actions and a move towards ownership of the school's strategic development. I would suggest four main parts to the day, each with some input from me followed by brainstorming to share ideas, experiences and to identify barriers:

1. The purpose of development planning. What is strategic planning? The purpose of planning and the benefits to be gained.
2. The planning process. Four-stage model (audit, construction, implement, evaluate). Review strengths and weaknesses of current practice at school. Explore experiences and ideas of the group. Agree outline process.
3. The role of middle managers in whole school planning. What is the strategic contribution that middle managers should be making? Explore issues and gain agreement. Review job descriptions.
4. Action plan. Identify and agree on action to improve the planning process/systems and the development of the middle management role. Set aims for remaining sessions with consultant.

Figure 10.6: Middle management INSET

The proposal

The original proposal had been to develop a package to support school-based management development but as the project proceeded, a number of purposes emerged which had to be taken into account. We moved rapidly from a 'package' to planning and writing the 'scheme'. Accordingly for each purpose identified a specific feature was incorporated:

Purpose	*Feature*
• to enhance management practice on a day-to-day basis	• school-based programme
• to develop skill in the use of sound and worthwhile management strategies	• adaptation of school management standards for the Scottish context
• to provide on-going support for the learner	• mentoring process
• to ensure a structured programme of learning	• self-study guide
• to sustain the programme of learning over a period of time (at least a session)	• outside support to the school through the role of the tutor
• to provide ways of demonstrating professional development through the option of accreditation	• validated programme at post-graduate level

---

Figure 10.7: INSET management training

In sum, as schools acquire greater management responsibilities middle and senior managers will require flexible approaches to providing support for individual and school development.

Summary

Schools are where pupils learn; schools should also provide a learning environment for all staff – teaching and non-teaching. Middle managers have a responsibility for members of the learning community.

The Teacher Training Agency (TTA) was established in 1994 by the government to review and develop the training of teachers. Initiatives for the training of middle managers are currently high profile activities for government and professional agencies. A policy for the CPD of teachers is to be welcomed. New CPD initiatives should also relate to existing good practice and be introduced through SDPs. Accountability is of the essence if the profession is to be valued by all involved. All teachers should have access to CPD within the context of the national standards. The pivotal role of middle managers needs to be identified for the successful implementation of CPD and the national standards for teachers.

Hewitt (1996a) identified the competencies to be assessed as follows:

- administrative competencies
- interpersonal competencies
- communicative competencies.

In a middle management centre (a process not a place), four participants attend a location and are assessed during the course of the day by four experienced NEAC assessors (who have previously attended the course and have been assessed). All activities are work-related – discussion groups, in-tray, presentation, and a written response to a series of questions.

New initiatives for the training of middle managers are one aspect of middle management; another is staff development. 'Development' is a term encompassing any experience or process that helps to bring out an individual's full potential. As a manager you should aim to improve the quality of your existing staff. You will be responsible for achieving targets and will only succeed if the people who work with you are competent. Mentoring is a process whereby you can pass on to someone else your knowledge and understanding, skills and abilities.

The responsibility for developing staff is shared. The individual also has a stake in his/her own development and should take some responsibility for it. Staff development, while important and desirable, is just one of many demands placed on a middle manager.

A middle manager will participate in the development of an operational plan for staff development. Good operational plans set clear and specific objectives for each development activity and assign responsibility for those involved. Once targets have been set there must be adequate time, resources and follow-up support for development. Staff development will only be successful with effective training, monitoring and evaluation procedures.

Appraisal has been a contentious issue in schools since it was first legislated for, in 1991. Fidler (1994) found that middle managers have a restricted view of their role in appraisal. The purpose of appraisal is to motivate and develop individuals. As a middle manager you will be involved in identifying a colleague's strengths and weaknesses, and the setting of targets which are attainable. Appraisal is *not* judgmental, but an audit or an evaluation leading to performance-related rewards or sanctions. A working definition of appraisal is 'one professional holding him/herself accountable to him/herself in the presence of another professional'.

Central to an effective scheme for staff appraisal is the preparation of job descriptions. The kind of information required largely determines the type of question selected in the appraisal process. Another key component in the appraisal process is classroom observation. Target-setting is a critical part of the appraisal process.

Since the introduction of teacher/headteacher appraisal, many practical issues have emerged which a middle manager needs to consider when implementing appraisal. Five years after the implementation of appraisal, there have been a number of reviews written focusing on the appraisal process. Barber *et al.* (1995) recommend the production of national guidelines on the management of appraisal to assist school appraisal co-ordinators. OFSTED (1996) concludes that the appraisal system was functioning below its full potential and has *slipped down too low on schools' lists of priorities.* The TTA has identified appraisal within the context of CPD. The TTA's perspective is to improve the quality of teaching and learning in schools.

If appraisal is to work effectively there are enormous resource and financial implications. If teachers are to achieve their targets within two years, middle managers will need to plan the process within the framework of the SDP. Training opportunities should therefore be focused or allocated to middle management.

As a middle manager you will need to be aware of the tensions that exist between personal professional development and institutional development. In essence INSET has been the subject of much rhetoric and little planning (Williams, 1991).

Evidence from the review of recent OFSTED reports (Levačić and Glover, 1995) suggests that those responsible for planning professional development within schools need to follow a rational planning approach which links priorities for expenditure more closely to departmental or school aims and is followed by an assessment of alternative providers and their potential to offer value for money. Evaluation of INSET will need to respond to the question of whether the programme enhanced pupils' learning and therefore teachers' ability to teach.

11
■ ■ ■

Recruitment and Selection

Introduction

Since the ERA (1988), schools have had increased responsibility for the recruitment and selection of staff – teaching and non-teaching. This has had an impact on all schools, primary and secondary. Having followed LEA guidelines and practice, school managers are now involved in this highly specialised and complex process.

As a middle manager it is likely that you will be involved in staff recruitment and selection. Generally, a large number of middle and senior managers participate in the appointment procedure.

When appointed to the post, a middle manager will inherit a team. Selection skills are only required when a vacancy occurs. It is critical to pick the right person for the job when the opportunity does arise. Before recruiting new colleagues you will also participate in job design, i.e. defining what is required for each post prior to appointment. This is a critical aspect of recruitment and selection; without a well designed job description you will not have a clear understanding of who will be required for the post.

Equal opportunities in education have created quite a stir in recent years. Equal opportunities are important because any unreasonable discrimination is unjust and will conflict with people's values and beliefs. Unreasonable discrimination will also waste potential talent thus undermining organisational effectiveness. Recruitment and selection involves reasonable discrimination, finding the best person for the job; equal opportunities is an important factor underlying the process.

Purpose of recruitment

Prior to any selection process the details of the vacant post will need to be clearly defined (Billsberry *et al.*, 1994, pp. 6–57). The need to appoint a member of teaching or non-teaching staff will be the result of:

1. **Change:**
   - government initiative
   - SDP (vision/mission)
   - restructuring
   - increased/reduced pupil numbers
   - curriculum plan.

or

2. **Maintenance:**
   - retirement
   - promotion – internal/external
   - maternity leave
   - transfer
   - resignation.

Change

There are a number of occasions which provide opportunities for considering the design or re-design of jobs. However, before implementing any change you and your team will need to be clear that the introduction of change can create ripples which will become tidal waves within the school as an organisation (see Chapter Nine).

As a middle manager, it will be inadvisable to embark on any major change without discussing this with others, i.e. your team and senior management. Any changes that will impact on the professional lives of others will require discussion prior to implementation.

Maintenance

As job descriptions are at the heart of any selection process, it is critical that they are an accurate reflection of what is required. If the need to appoint is due to a colleague vacating the post, it would be useful to ask them to analyse what the job entails. The problem with job descriptions written by those not in post is that they often give little indication of what is involved in practice. As Busher (1988, p. 100) describes:

> *Although the headteacher had issued a job description for heads of departments which itemised areas of responsibility in rather general terms, there was no available statement about what activities a head of department should actually perform in the school in managing a department. Nor was there available any rank ordering of these activities either by level of difficulty or by level of impact on department policy.*

The appraisal process may resolve these issues if it is fully implemented. Middle managers should, in practice, know and understand their role in the school as an organisation. A middle manager should also know and understand the roles of the members of their team. How each role is defined will depend on the aims of the school as defined in the SDP. Each role will be interpreted according to the expectations of the post-holder and his/her colleagues and managers. If a role is to be maintained it should be understood. A middle manager should, therefore, be aware of the requirements and expectations for each post.

Writing job specifications

Having analysed the purpose of the recruitment process, either change or maintenance, you will need to write the specifications for the post. Generally the latter will involve identifying qualifications, experience, knowledge, skills and attributes. When undertaking a job analysis, the model shown in Figure 11.1 will help.

From the job analysis, a job description can be written. This should describe the job, what the job holder is responsible for and what they will be required to do (Figure 11.2). An example of current practice is given in Figure 11.3 which describes a middle management post in a secondary school.

Person specification

The third stage in the process is to write a specification of the kind of person required to fill the job that you have just described. You will need to be as precise as possible about the skills, knowledge, qualifications and attributes which are required for the job (e.g. Table 11.1).

As a middle manager you will be involved in drawing up the specific points relevant to any vacant post within your team. When writing the job

Table 11.1: Person specification

Characteristics	Minimum	Desirable
Education		
Experience		
Training		
Communication skills		
Special circumstances		

1. **Key words:**
   - what is done?
   - when is it done?
   - why is it done?   } include teaching and
   - where is it done?   managerial details
   - how is it done?

2. **Responsibilities:**
   - responsibility for others – pupils and teachers
   - responsibility for resources
   - responsibility for budgets.

3. **Working relationships:**
   - relationships with superiors
   - relationships with colleagues
   - relationships with other departments and agencies
   - relationships with pupils
   - relationships with parents
   - relationships with team members.

4. **Job requirements:**
   - skills and experience
   - education and training
   - health
   - motivation and social skills
   - personal qualities.

5. **Working conditions:**
   - the school
   - the department/team
   - social conditions
   - funding and pay.

6. **Check up:**
   - check with the job holder
   - check with his/her manager.

Figure 11.1: Checklist for job analysis

specification, it is worth reflecting on how detailed you should be. If you want to attract a wide field, too much detail could deter the very applicants you would like to apply. Consider the following:

1. A detailed job description may make it hard to fill a post. It may be more advisable to be vague in order to identify the individual who will complement the team.

Job title: MIDDLE MANAGER

Grade:

Responsible to: Headteacher

A. Summary of main responsibilities and activities:
- subject area
- examination/pastoral
- age-range
- ability range
- special needs
- budgets
- inspection

B. Specific responsibilities:
- staff
- materials
- resources

C. Working conditions:
- school/LEA
- room

Figure 11.2: Job description

2. A vague job description may lead to confusion about what the post actually is. This could deter applicants or lead to problems when an appointment is made.

Internal job specification should promote professional development identification of personal qualities which may be as important as any description of what the job entails.

Responsibilities

As a middle manager you should clarify your responsibilities and authority in the recruitment and selection process. This will depend on the status of the school: independent, grant-maintained or LMS. In the UK, the Sex Discrimination Acts, the Race Relations Act, the Equal Pay Act, the Disabled Persons (Employment) Act, the Health and Safety at Work Act, the Rehabilitation of Offenders Act, the Trade Union Reform and Employment Rights Act and, in 1993, the Teachers' Pay and Conditions Document provided some indication of the scope of employment legislation that has a direct bearing on recruiting and selecting staff. Increasingly, school management involves knowledge of relevant legislation.

JOB DESCRIPTION FOR HEAD OF DEPARTMENT
(head of geography)

A) Responsibilities of all HODs

1. Leadership of a team of teachers within the department, including supervision of NQTs and student teachers, subject to agreement with deputy headteacher.

2. To ensure that the team of teachers within the department meets regularly according to the school calendar and is made aware of the school's policies.

3. To ensure that the departmental syllabus and schemes of work are being followed by members of the department and that agreed departmental and school standards of work and behaviour are adhered to.

4. To become familiar with the work being done by members of the department, to visit classrooms where practicable, to check pupils' work regularly and to ensure that homework is being set in accordance with the published homework timetable and is regularly marked.

5. To be the first person approached in cases of indiscipline within the classroom and to support his/her staff in dealing with difficult pupils.

6. To monitor the presence of staff within the department at the times and places prescribed and to check that there is a punctual start to lessons.

7. To be responsible for the allocation of pupils to sets where appropriate and to allocate classes to her/his team members, ensuring that colleagues have the opportunity to teach a cross-section of ages and abilities.

8. To be responsible for the submission of lists of candidates for public examination, together with estimated grades.

9. In consultation with SMT to arrange timetable, aid the supervision of students and take an active part in ensuring that newly qualified teachers are carefully supervised during their first months of service.

10. To be responsible for the spending of departmental monies in consultation with his/her team and to keep a stock-book as required by the headteacher.

11. To ensure that details of all learning resources within the department are available to the whole team, and to account for apparatus, equipment and stock in her/his charge.

12. To supervise pupils' assessments and school reports prepared by members of the department.

13. To participate in the selection and appraisal of teachers within the department.

14. To liaise with other departments, especially in respect of pupils with special needs, and thus support the co-ordination of topics delivered in more than one department, as well as encouraging others in cross-curricular work where appropriate.

15. To ensure that departmental representatives are allocated to and attend working groups as necessary.

16. To represent the department at HODs' meetings, and at other times when so requested.

B) Specific responsibilities

1. To plan and organise a full annual programme of fieldwork so that an opportunity to participate is provided to each student of the subject for at least one occasion each during KS3, KS4 and Post-16.

2. General supervision, in collaboration with Head of History/RE/Soc. Ed., of the humanities block, including locking between the morning and afternoon sessions as necessary.

3. To ensure the security and appropriate deployment of specialist equipment including computing and audio-visual resources.

4. To facilitate liaison with feeder primary schools.

5. To encourage staff and students in opportunities for curriculum enrichment, for example through cross-curricular activities or environmental/technical projects.

Responsible to: headteacher

Figure 11.3: Job description – head of department

Schools should have a recruitment policy that complies with government and (where relevant) LEA policies and legislation. A school policy will deal with any specific local issues, such as a middle manager's authority in the recruitment and selection process. When determining your responsibility and authority consider:

1. What policies and legislation should be referred to – school, LEA, government?

2. Who should be consulted – colleagues, SMT, advisors/inspectors?

Marketing

Before advertising, plan a schedule of dates to include:

- advertisement
- applications returned
- shortlist
- references
- interviews
- appointment
- starting date.

The timescale for each part of the process should be realistic, especially references.

Advertising

Once the documentation (job analysis, description and specification) has been completed the post will need to be advertised internally and/or externally. The LEA and/or school may have a specific policy for advertising. It is important to recognise that the cost of replacing someone in a job can be considerable and the cost of advertising will constitute a high proportion of this expenditure.

Key factors which determine an effective response:

1. The content of the advertisement:
   - key elements of the job
   - location
   - salary.

2. The media used:
   - *Times Educational Supplement*
   - *The Guardian – Education* (Tuesday)
   - local press.

3. The timing of the advertisement.

The advertisement should be factual, truthful and relevant, containing:

- job title – identifiable to the reader
- name, characteristics and location of school
- aims and responsibilities of the job
- aims of the department
- responsibilities of the previous job
- qualifications and experience needed
- salary (or salary range) and additions (e.g. London weighting)
- promotional prospects
- how the application should be made, for example:
  - send a CV
  - letter only
  - write/telephone for an application form and further information
- closing date
- name, address, telephone number of contact.

The content of the job description should encourage suitable people to apply for the job. The information contained in the advertisement should be taken from the job analysis and the job description. Advertising and recruitment in the UK should not contravene legislation.

Once the planning and checking has been completed, check that the advertisement presents the best possible image of the school. A means of communicating more information is by offering to send further particulars. These may include policy documents, SDP and the school prospectus. The focus is important: the department, school, training opportunities and full details of the job.

Application forms

Use the standard school/LEA application form or ask applicants to write a letter of application accompanied by a Curriculum Vitae (CV). Candidates will have to show in their applications how they measure up to the detailed job description/specification. Application forms facilitate the retrieval of information; a CV will also offer this information. The implications of LMS are that schools are increasingly using the letter/CV process; letters can be more personal and revealing. Take care not to ask applicants *for irrelevant information or information that contravenes current legislation. It will also be necessary to ask for referees at this stage.

Selection

A single advertisement could attract a large number of replies. As a middle manager you should consider that any slip-ups in the selection process could harm the school's public image. There are several points for you to consider:

1. Candidates will be anxious to know what is happening, so brief the school secretary and administration staff.
2. Application forms and further particulars should be ready to go out immediately. Records should be kept of people to whom they are sent.
3. Returned application forms should also be recorded and acknowledged by return of post, with some indication of what the next step will be.
4. Candidates selected for interview should be given as much notice as possible, and a name and phone number to contact in case of any queries or problems. They will also require a map, timetable for the day, information about any selection processes involved, details of expenses and any further information required.
5. Send those who have not been selected a courteous letter as soon as you are certain they are not required.
6. If references are required, letters should be sent at the earliest opportunity, so as to allow time for references to arrive before the date of the interview. Applicants may not want their present employers to know that they are applying for other jobs.
7. Detailed records of all correspondence should be kept at every stage.

Applicants will be intensely interested in the process. The selection process should be efficiently administered. Failure to do so can create an unfavourable impression.

Shortlisting

The number of applicants shortlisted will be determined by the time available for interviewing. The selection team, of which you will be a member, should ensure that the most suitable candidates are selected.

A shortlisting procedure should be drawn up, and several people should be involved. There may already be an established procedure for this process. When there are fewer (internal) candidates a less formal method of selection may be used. Those participating in the shortlisting process should approach the task systematically. Read the applications and place the applicants in rank order. It would be helpful to focus on two key requirements from the job specification. You may have to be quite ruthless; equally if there are too few candidates you may wish to re-advertise.

The involvement of a middle manager at the shortlisting stage is useful as s(he) will have an added insight into what type of individual will be most suitable.

References

Following shortlisting, references should be requested. Each candidate will have provided their current headteacher and one other referee. References can sometimes have limitations, as the referees will in most cases want to write a good reference or disguise the candidate's weaknesses. It is helpful for referees to be sent details of the requirements for the job and/or the job specification.

If time is short, a telephone reference may be used, followed by a written reference. The phone could be considered to be an inappropriate and informal referencing method. Conversations are too open and do not allow for carefully considered comments.

Middle managers should be involved in the reference reading/checking process. Many valuable insights into the personal qualities, skills and abilities of candidates are contained in references. The language may need 'decoding' in order to identify the indicators of performance.

It is essential that the recruitment and selection process is approached in a sensitive and professional manner. Candidates will make choices based on their first impression of your school.

The selection interview

The interview will play a dominant role in the selection process (Hall and Oldroyd, 1990a, p. 45). Middle managers will be fully involved in this stage. Many interviews are conducted by untrained personnel who fail to recognise the consequences of their decisions, or who base their judgments on first impressions. Selection processes are very expensive; it is worth trying to improve the process.

The primary aim of the selection interview is to determine whether the candidate is interested in the job and is competent to do it. Candidates may be compared against each other but more importantly they should be compared to the job specification. A selection interview will involve the following:

- a description of the school and the positive aspects of being a member of staff
- a description of the job in a realistic manner, including any induction processes
- ascertainment of the suitability of the candidate and his/her personal qualities
- setting out the expectations of the post-holder for the candidate and management team
- enabling the candidate to assess whether they want the job.

Interviewing is complex; as a middle manager you will need to prepare for the interview, conduct the interview and be involved in the decision-making process.

Preparing for an interview

Preparation is all important; candidates will have taken time to apply and will have a lot at stake, and you will want to select the most suitable applicant:

1. What you need:

- Fullest possible information about the job, job description, job/person specification, application form, references.

2. What the candidate needs:

- Candidates should be met on arrival with an offer of refreshments and shown the toilet facilities. They should be given the opportunity to 'see the school in action'. This should be supported by relevant literature: school prospectus, newsletter, school magazines, etc. All candidates should be provided with somewhere to wait in comfort and the opportunity to talk to someone about the organisation (a pupil or a teacher).

- Candidates will not want to be kept 'hanging around'; allow sufficient time for each candidate. Interviewing is extremely stressful and tiring; seeing more than six candidates in a day would mean that you will not be doing them all justice.
- Candidates should be advised of the structure of the day (prior to interview).

3. Location:

- A suitable room is essential and should be prepared in advance. The interview panel and candidate should be seated at the same level. Avoid low chairs, sunlight and excessive formality which will intimidate the candidates.

4. The interview:

- An interview plan will be required. A structured interview, organised in a series of discrete units, will achieve its purpose. The plan should provide a route through the interview and inform the panel on the way.

5. When planning an interview, identify:

- What you are looking for in the candidates; knowledge, intelligence, attitude or other personal qualities.
- How you will find out what you are looking for: qualifications, intelligence test, personality profiles, questions.

6. Effective questions and effective listening:

- The interview plan should identify who on the interview panel should explore specific areas of the candidate's experience. For example:
  - could the candidate do the job? (skills)
  - would the candidate do the job? (motivation)
  - would the candidate fit in? (personal qualities)
- A clear set of questions will help determine the above. Questions should be open, and lead or direct the candidate, providing the opportunity for the candidate to expand on a topic. Avoid closed or multiple questions that can be confusing. Essentially the questions should be:
  - capable of providing information
  - comprehensive and grouped in an organised way
  - able to allow interviewers to compare candidates with each other and the job/person specification.

Effective listening will involve listening actively, using words or body language to show that you are listening. It also involves recording relevant information that will assist the decision-making process. In sum, the interview will involve:

- the candidate talking for 70 per cent of the time
- controlling the flow of information
- listening and giving clear signals
- judgment – during and after the interview.

It is illegal to ask questions regarding:

- marital status
- family responsibilities
- sexual orientation
- political affiliation
- ethnic/disability status or attitudes.

When drawing the interview to a close, always provide the candidate with the opportunity to ask questions to clarify features of the job.

Decision-making

The drawing together of all information and decision-making are difficult processes. The evidence will be quite jumbled and will require processing in a logical manner. Your notes will be vital at this stage. Interviewers can make errors of judgment:

- stereotyping based on race, gender, class
- unsubstantiated judgment whereby a candidate is assumed to possess certain skills
- under-rating or over-rating all candidates.

A rating form prepared in advance of the interview will assist (Table 11.2). Any rating of candidates should be preceded by a detailed discussion. Selection is an important public relations exercise and the ground rules should be established at the start.

Table 11.2: Selection rating form

Specification	Candidates						
	A	B	C	D	E	F	G
Qualifications							
Education							
Experience							
Personal qualities							

Offering the job

This is a delicate process. The person appointed will be elated, the other candidates will feel deflated. The interview panel should provide all candidates with the opportunity to discuss the interview process and to evaluate strengths and weaknesses. These should be well considered and based on the evidence collated during the interview process. Sensitivity should be demonstrated at all times.

The new appointee will require further documentation:

- contract (including start date and time)
- staff handbook
- timetable
- classroom
- class lists
- reports
- schemes of work, etc.

This should be prepared by the middle manager in advance of the interview to enable him/her to take away relevant information.

The middle manager should then arrange times when the appointee can visit the school and department to meet new colleagues and pupils. A period of induction would provide support for a new colleague, as would a mentor. This should be planned carefully and reflect the needs of the appointee and school.

Summary

Since the ERA (1988), schools have had increased responsibility for the recruitment and selection of staff, teaching and non-teaching. As a middle manager it is highly likely that you will be involved in staff recruitment and selection. When appointed to the post, a middle manager will inherit a team. Selection skills are only required when a vacancy occurs. Prior to any selection process the details of the vacant post will need to be clearly defined. As a middle manager, it will be highly inadvisable to embark on any major change without discussing this with others, i.e. your team and senior management.

Middle managers should, in practice, know and understand their role in the school as an organisation. A middle manager should also know and understand the roles of their team. A middle manager should, therefore, be aware of the requirements and expectations for each post.

From the job analysis, a job description can be written. The third stage in the process is to write a specification of the kind of person required to fill the job that you have just described.

As a middle manager you should clarify your responsibilities and authority in the recruitment and selection process. Schools should have a recruitment policy that complies with government and (where relevant) LEA policies and legislation.

Once the documentation (job analysis, description and specification) has been completed, the post will need to be advertised internally and/or externally. The LEA and/or school may have a specific policy for advertising. The content of the job description should encourage suitable people to apply for the job. The selection process should be efficiently administered; failure to do so can create an unfavourable impression. The involvement of a middle manager at the shortlisting stage is useful as he/she will have an added insight into what type of individual will be most suitable.

Middle managers should be involved in the reference reading/checking process. It is essential that the recruitment and selection process is approached in a sensitive and professional manner. Interviewing is complex; as a middle manager you will need to prepare for the interview, conduct the interview and be involved in the decision-making process. Preparation is all important; candidates will have taken time to apply and will have a lot at stake and you will want to select the most suitable applicant.

The drawing together of all information and decision-making are difficult processes. Any rating of candidates should be preceded by a detailed discussion. Offering the job is a delicate process. The person appointed will be elated, the other candidates will feel deflated. The interview panel should provide all candidates with the opportunity to discuss the interview process and to evaluate strengths and weaknesses. These should be well considered and based on the evidence collated during the interview process. Sensitivity should be demonstrated at all times.

12

■ ■ ■

Where Next?

Introduction

As a profession, teaching has a limited amount of literature related to career development. Yet institutions and professions require occasional renewal to avoid stagnation. For the majority of teachers, applying for promotion can be a traumatic and lonely process. There are many factors involved. In brief:

- reflecting on current position
- deciding to move on
- identifying a suitable position
- completing an application
- the interview
- deciding to accept the job
- starting in a new school.

All professions are composites of knowledge and understanding, skills and abilities. However, for many years educationalists have focused their research on content issues. This emphasis has led to the creation of the TTA, a government agency which has within its responsibility, reviewing and developing the continuing professional development of teachers.

This chapter focuses on both practical and evaluative issues, and examines the TTA's National Professional Qualification for Headteachers (NPQH). It also considers award-bearing courses as a possible career move. The chapter concludes with a review of alternative directions for middle managers who wish to leave the profession.

Self-evaluation

The case for managers to work on their own development was made in a study by Constable and McCormack (1987) in Isaac (1995, p. 128). The report suggested that managers should:

- *own their own career, and positively seek out continuous training and development*
- *acquire the learning habit early in their career*
- *recognise when new knowledge and skills are required and seek them out.*

Self-development involves learning and understanding where you are within your job and career. You should, as stated, have a clear view of what your own job is about; the relationship between teaching and management, SDP and so on. You should also have an understanding of your position in relation to those you manage, as Isaac (1995, p. 133) commented:

Developing yourself as a manager depends on the extent to which you recognise issues from your reflection, and learn to change your behaviour.

As a manager, the process of learning is difficult. Managers face many demands including:

- government demands: deliver the curriculum, register pupils, parents' evenings
- senior management demands: implementation – action of school policy
- colleague demands: requests for assistance, information or help from others at a similar level or within your team
- pupil demands: to inform and liaise
- externally-imposed demands: social services, police, agencies which work for and with young people
- system-imposed demands: LMS, LEA, budgets, meetings, social functions which cannot be ignored.

In addition, there will be other demands such as family, friends, hobbies and social commitments.

Many teacher managers have recently been involved in the *Investors in People* programme which supports management development. In schools where time and funds have been given to the programme, middle managers have been encouraged to reflect on their own development.

Education management researchers have examined the Management Charter Initiative (MCI) standards in the context of schools. These have been clustered into four areas (Isaac, 1995, p. 36):

1. *Manage policy:*
   - review, develop and present school aims, policies and objectives
   - develop supportive relationships with pupils, staff, parents, governors and the community.

2. *Manage learning:*
   - review, develop and implement means for supporting pupils' learning.

3. *Manage people:*
   - recruit and select teaching and non-teaching staff
   - develop teams, individuals and self to enhance performance
   - plan, allocate and evaluate work carried out by teams, individuals and self
   - create, maintain and enhance effective working relationships.

4. *Manage resources:*
   - secure effective resource allocation
   - monitor and control use of resources.

Each of the above areas is described in earlier chapters. Specifically, middle managers should reflect on what choices are available within the context of self-development, identifying:

- what is required to improve performance?
- how this will be done?
- when this will be done?

Self-development is systematic; we never stop learning and developing. The art of self-evaluation is to be continually learning. As Senge (1990, p. 142) made clear:

> *People with a high level of personal mastery live in a continual learning mode. They never 'arrive'. People with a high level of personal mastery are acutely aware of their ignorance, their incompetence, their growth areas. And they are deeply self-confident. Paradoxical? Only for these who do not see that the journey is the reward.*

National Professional Qualification for Headteachers (NPQH)

By September 1997 the TTA will put into place a new NPQH, for those who aspire to headship. Middle managers, having been established as 'expert managers' (TTA national standards), will be trained for headship. The TTA is aiming to develop a strategic approach to CPD which will provide a better focused system of professional development for teachers. The fourth of seven aims listed in the TTA's *Corporate Plan 1996–7* (TTA, 1996a, p. 12) is:

To promote well-targeted, effective and co-ordinated continuing professional development.

The corporate plan clearly states that the headteacher must provide (p. 28);

professional vision, leadership and direction for the school and ensure that it is managed and organised to meet its aims and objectives.

For middle managers who aspire to become headteachers, the route to headship will be through the NPQH. This will be based either at regional training and development centres or distance learning from a national centre. Geographically there will be ten centres in England and two in Wales.

Key elements

Candidates will be required to complete a central compulsory module concerned with strategic direction and development, and covering the implementation, monitoring and reviewing of policies and practices.

The NPQH assessment centres will carry out initial needs assessment of all candidates and assessment for the overall award of the qualification.

NPQH funds will be allocated by assessment centres for those in grant maintained schools, and by LEAs for those in LEA-maintained schools. Prospective candidates are supported by other funds (school, TEC, self, etc.) and will be able to apply through NPQH assessment centres.

LEA and NPQH assessment centres will be required to use common selection criteria developed centrally through the TTA's NPQH management and development group.

The qualification may be gained within a year, particularly in the early stages of the scheme to allow experienced deputies who are close to headship to qualify. To ensure that evidence and training remains current, candidates will be given a maximum of three years to gain the qualification.

NPQH supported candidates will be required to spend the bulk of their grant at the NPQH training and development centres and the NPQH assessment centres. A percentage will be made available for supply cover and other registered training.

Allocation of NPQH funds will be guided by headteacher recruitment information; regions and LEAs will be given quotes indicating the minimum number of funded candidates required in the area.

Assessment

The TTA points out that rigorous assessment will be central to the success and credibility of the qualification both inside and outside the profession. To be awarded the NPQH, candidates will be expected to show that they have the appropriate level of school leadership and management knowledge, understanding, skills and abilities to perform the tasks required of headship.

Content

The draft national standards for headteachers set out five areas in which expertise is required:

- strategic direction and development of the school
- learning and teaching in the school
- people and relationships
- human and material resources and their development and deployment
- accountability for the efficiency and effectiveness of the school.

Each candidate will be required to develop the knowledge and understanding, skills and abilities needed for effective leadership and management in schools.

Access

The TTA indicates that the centres and distance learning provider(s) should be able to cope with a maximum volume of candidates from all funding sources of between 500–1000, varying according to region and demand.

Candidates embarking on the qualification will have very different experience and expertise. Regional assessment centres will have a critical role in the initial needs assessment of all candidates, helping them to judge their strengths, weaknesses and development needs in relation to the standards so that they can plan a coherent programme towards gaining the qualification.

All aspects of NPQH will be completed for no more than £2500. The balance between training and assessment is to be 80/20 although this may differ according to individual needs.

A list of NPQH training and development providers will be added to the HEADLAMP register, unrelated to regional centres. Candidates who attend courses directed by NPQH registered providers will do so 'at their own risk'. However, *all* providers will be working within the framework of the national standards.

Management

The managers of each centre and the distance learning providers will help develop the qualification through the TTA *National Management and Development Group*. As the qualification is developed, the TTA will ensure that leadership skills be emphasised as much as management skills.

In sum, throughout its work the TTA is encouraging the view that teaching is a high quality profession. Through its school effectiveness initiative, the TTA is securing a more effective professional development and career progression for teachers.

Mentoring

Mentoring is a term which is used in several different contexts in education today (Ormston and Shaw, 1993b). It generally means the positive support offered by staff with some experience to staff with less experience. This experience can extend over a wide range of activities, or be specific to one activity. Middle managers may engage in a number of mentoring relationships:

- mentoring of NQTs joining your team
- mentoring of colleagues to support them in their new role
- as a mentee, either by a middle manager or senior manager in preparation for a current or future post.

It is important to understand that mentoring is a continuous staff development activity which, once the system is in place, happens during normal school life. As a middle manager you will need to know and understand the essential elements of a mentoring relationship. These are:

- a recognised procedure (formal or informal)
- a clear understanding of the procedure and both roles
- trust and a rapport between both parties
- the credibility and genuineness of the mentor as perceived by the mentee
- confidentiality and discretion
- the relationship is based on the mentee's perception of his/her own needs
- a suitable range of skills used by the mentor: counselling, listening, sensitive questioning, analysis and handing back responsibilities
- an appropriate attitude by both parties, e.g. the ability of the mentor to challenge the mentee, and the self-motivation of the mentee to take action when necessary.

In addition, middle managers need to be aware of equal opportunity issues that will need to be addressed in the selection and training of mentors. The roles fulfilled by mentors can be categorised into:

1. **Vocational**: these roles help the NQT middle manager or new headteacher to adjust to changes in his/her career pattern, and in advancing within the profession.
2. **Interpersonal**: these roles enable the mentee to clarify a sense of identity and to develop a greater sense of competence and self-esteem.

Vocational roles include: educating through enhancing the mentee's skills and intellectual development, helping to develop a set of educational values, consulting in helping the mentee to clarify goals and ways of implementing them, helping to establish a set of personal and professional standards, networking and sponsoring by providing opportunities for the mentee to meet other professionals.

Interpersonal roles will include sharing and role modelling, allowing the mentee to gain an insight into how the mentor works in a professional capacity. A mentor should also encourage a mentee in order to build their self-confidence, recognising success. A mentor is also a counsellor who listens but does not tell the mentee what to do. Not all mentors will fulfil all the roles above, but the greater the number of roles the richer the relationship.

As a middle manager you will have a number of roles within the school and in relation to your team. You will need to decide who to mentor in the context of all your other tasks and responsibilities. Mentoring is time-consuming. As a mentee you should select your mentor on the basis of your professional needs, present and/or future.

Mentoring is a positive mechanism for developing management skills for both the mentor and mentee. As a process, mentoring should move through the stages shown in Figure 12.1. As a middle manager you should select a mentor who will assist your current practice and further your career.

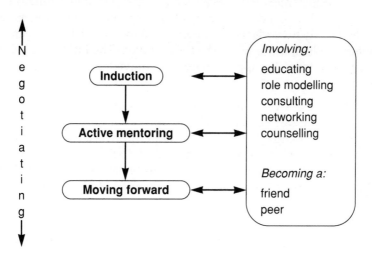

Figure 12.1: A model of mentoring

Masters and doctorates in education

Traditionally teachers have continued their professional development through award-bearing courses. Career advancement has been associated with further scholastic activity in a Higher Education Institution (HEI). Phillips and Pugh (1988, p. 16) summarise the meaning of the degree structure of a British university:

- a bachelor's degree shows that the recipient has obtained a *general* education
- a master's degree is a licence to practise
- a doctor's degree is a licence to teach in a university.

The majority of HEIs in England and Wales providing teacher education within Schools of Education offer masters' courses for practising teachers. Award-bearing M-level courses in education develop students' knowledge and understanding of education theory and research and thus inform practice. Some courses may focus on education management while others focus on specialist subject areas. Teachers can study at a university or opt for distance-learning packages.

Having successfully completed a master's course, teachers can continue with an academic education to doctorate level. There are currently two distinct approaches to doctorates for educationalists; the traditional PhD (Doctor of Philosophy) and the EdD (Doctor of Education). The former requires independent study towards the completion of a thesis which makes an original contribution to the knowledge of the field studied. The EdD is a modularised taught course offered by approximately 12 universities to senior education professionals.

As a middle manager you will be a busy professional. Working full-time and studying part-time can be very difficult. You will need to have full support from family and friends. You may also require financial support from your institution and/or LEA or school through GEST. Educational study and research should relate to practice and the needs of the school as identified in the SDP. Courses offer the opportunity to be challenged, stretched and excited in a collegial environment.

Before embarking on a course, try to gather as much information as you can. Visit the universities and talk to potential course leaders and supervisors. It would also be useful to read dissertations and theses in your area of interest to determine what will be required for the award.

If you are about to change job, move house or have any major family events in the near future this would not be the right time to start a course.

Academic study should relate to practice; be clear as to why you want to study and what you will do with the qualification. Think, 'what next?'

Research

Middle managers as player managers are active participants in school life at every level. Middle managers are in a position to influence and engage in educational research. Hargreaves (1996, p. 1) believes that teaching is not at present a research-based profession. Yet education researchers receive £35m per annum from the Higher Education Funding Council for England, the Economic and Social Research Council (ESRC), the Department for Education and Employment, the National Foundation for Educational Research and the TTA.

The TTA believes that teaching can and should be informed by high quality research. The TTA revealed that there are three core problems at the centre of education research (TTA, 1996b):

- too few research projects focus on classroom teaching or involve classroom teachers actively in the research process
- too much research stops short of working out the meaning of research findings for day-to-day practice
- traditional vehicles for reporting findings are not geared sufficiently to the needs of practitioners.

To help redress the balance the TTA is piloting a scheme, funding teachers to undertake up to 30 small-scale classroom-based research projects. The TTA has identified the need to (Millett, 1996b):

- increase the amount of classroom-based educational research relevant to improving the quality of teaching and learning
- raise awareness of what high quality research can contribute to teaching
- make research findings more accessible to teachers
- develop teachers' skills in conducting, interpreting and using research designed to foster improved classroom practice.

Middle managers should be aware of the opportunities to lead and participate in relevant educational research. Equally, middle managers should contribute to the development of teaching as a research-based profession.

Applications

This section, in contrast to the previous chapter, is designed to help you apply for your next job or course as you progress through your career. Middle managers may consider promotion, and will therefore need to be aware of the process of job hunting. In addition, many internal promotion opportunities will be treated as normal vacancies. You will require skills in completing a CV and/or application form and attending an interview. To be successful requires time and considerable effort. Before embarking on this journey reflect on the advantages and disadvantages of the new post, e.g. promotion prospects, curriculum area, travelling time and salary.

Preparing a CV

The purpose of a CV is to filter applicants, and in practice this may not be handled very well (Billsberry *et al.*, 1994, pp. 87–98). You must make sure that your CV will not be rejected: do not use coloured paper, list unusual hobbies or produce a book length document! A word-processed CV will allow you to adapt each application to match the job specification. In essence, there are no rules that dictate the content or structure of a CV. To begin with, create a database of your work experience and achievements (e.g. Table 12.1).

Table 12.1: Personal audit

	Job 1	Job 2	Job 3
Job title			
Employer			
School/authority			
Date joined			
Date left			
Education			
Qualifications			
Responsibility			
Achievements			
Positions of responsibility outside education			
Extra curricular interests			

After completing a personal audit, the next stage is to analyse what is wanted by the institution you intend applying to:

- what knowledge, skills and experience must the applicant possess?
- what additional training is required?
- what qualifications should they hold?
- what is the culture of the school/college?
- what personal qualities are required?

You are now in a position to match your CV to the post. Try to identify the key points you want to highlight, and the content of your CV will follow. Market yourself: your aim is to make the person reading your CV want to know more about you.

The length of the CV will be determined by the requirements of the post and the job specification. The CV and covering letter must communicate key facts about you, quickly, efficiently and professionally.

Presentation of the CV is critical to your success; use double space and consistent type face and alignments. Use the same style in the letter, CV and envelope.

Application forms

All application forms are different, in that each is for a specific post. As such, completing an application form is extremely time-consuming. Therefore you must know why you are applying.

Make several copies of the application form and answer each question in rough. Get someone to read through your responses, leave the rough copy and come back to it fresh. Fill out the form in black ink or type. Once completed, check the application form for spelling mistakes and inconsistencies.

The covering letter is your opportunity to highlight the main qualities of your application. Express yourself in a straightforward style and include any relevant information such as a reference number. Ensure that you include your contact number and address.

The interview

Interviews are stressful and tiring. You will require high energy levels to complete an interview successfully. Interviewers will find reasons to reject rather than reasons to accept. Candidates should prepare in advance the key points which they would like to communicate to the interview panel. Questions and answers must be selective and of quality.

Preparation is essential; find out as much as you can about the school and job. Try to talk to someone from the department before the interview; your research should give you some indication of how successful you will be.

Most interviewers will reach a decision very quickly; therefore the opening minutes of the interview are critical. First impressions do count! Make eye contact with everyone, shake hands firmly, speak clearly and slowly, and smile. Wear a suit and appropriate accessories. Interviewers will not remember the details of every candidate's response, so try to say something memorable. Do not say anything you had not intended to say; occasionally interview panels will remain silent in order to entice you into 'filling the gap'. Remain silent. You will not have to agree with the panel at all times; be professional in your response. You may wish to expand your replies where you have sufficient depth of knowledge and experience. Try to give specific examples of your skills. Try not to be too anecdotal or sound too defensive. If you cannot answer a question say so.

Consider in advance how you will deal with any form of discrimination which may manifest itself during the course of the interview. Be professional and do not ignore prejudice.

Tests

Increasingly, schools are introducing personality profiling and management tests to the selection process. These may also involve in-tray exercises, role play and discussion group exercises. It is unclear how relevant these are and whether they produce a valuable diagnosis. However, as a candidate you will need to approach such tests in a professional manner.

Read each question or direction carefully, manage your time and do not spend too much time on a particular part of the test. There are many different types of personality tests; the most common are questionnaires with multiple-choice responses. There are no right or wrong answers; the test is designed to reveal your personality. A number of questions will be aimed at each personality trait and some questions will check whether the subject is being consistent. You are best advised to answer truthfully.

Accepting the job

When you are waiting for the panel to reach a decision, examine the strengths, weaknesses, opportunities and threats of the job, team and school. You will only have a limited amount of information and should be as objective as possible. Most interview panels will ask candidates whether they would accept the job if offered. The majority of candidates will instinctively answer this positively; however, this may not be the most appropriate job for you. Consider where you have come from, i.e. your current post, and where you intend going to, i.e. your next job. When you have considered all relevant factors, make your decision. Prepare your response.

If you are offered the job and would like to accept, plan what happens next: contracts, timetable, team meeting, etc. You will also need to consider your letter of resignation and remaining weeks in your current post.

Rejection – debrief

At the point of rejection you will experience a mixture of feelings depending on the desirability of the post. Make use of the process, take with you as much advice as possible. Write down the key points to enable you to reflect on your positive and negative attributes. You may of course dismiss these comments. Use the process positively in order to plan for your next application.

Summary

As a profession, teaching has a limited amount of literature related to career development. Yet institutions and professions require occasional renewal to avoid stagnation. Self-development involves learning and understanding of where you are within your job and career. As a manager, the process of learning is difficult.

Self-development is systematic; we never stop learning and developing. The art of self-evaluation is to be continually learning. Middle managers, having been established as 'expert managers', will be trained for headship. For middle managers who aspire to become headteachers, the route to headship will be through the National Professional Qualification for Headteachers (NPQH).

Candidates will be required to complete a central compulsory module concerned with strategic direction and development, and covering the implementation, monitoring and reviewing of policies and practices. The qualification may be gained within a year, particularly in the early stages of the scheme to allow experienced deputies who are close to headship to qualify.

Candidates embarking on the qualification will have very different experience and expertise. Regional assessment centres will have a critical role in the initial needs assessment of all candidates. In sum, throughout its work the TTA is encouraging the view that teaching is a high quality profession.

Traditionally teachers have continued their professional development through award-bearing courses. The majority of HEIs in England and Wales providing teacher education within Schools of Education offer masters' courses for practising teachers. Teachers can study at a university or opt for distance-learning packages.

The TTA believes that teaching can and should be informed by high quality research, so it is piloting a scheme, funding teachers to undertake up to 30 small-scale classroom-based research projects. Middle managers should be aware of the opportunities to lead and participate in relevant educational research.

A word-processed CV will allow you to adapt each application to match the job specification. To begin with, create a database of your work experience and achievements. Market yourself; your aim is to make the person reading your CV want to know more about you.

All application forms are different in that each is for a specific post. As such, completing an application form is extremely time-consuming. Therefore you must know why you are applying.

Preparation is essential; find out as much as you can about the school and job. Most interviewers will reach a decision very quickly; therefore the opening minutes of the interview are critical.

When you are waiting for the panel to reach a decision, examine the strengths, weaknesses, opportunities and threats of the job, team and school. When you have considered all relevant factors make your decision. Prepare your response.

As stated, use the process positively in order to plan your next application.

Good Luck!

References

■ ■ ■

Adair, J. (1988) *Effective Leadership*, London: Pan Books.

Advisory Conciliation and Arbitration Service (ACAS) (1986) *Teachers' Dispute, ACAS Independent Panel: Report of the Appraisal Training Working Group*, London: ACAS.

Alexander, R. (1984) *Primary Teaching*, Eastbourne: Holt, Rinehart and Winston.

Armstrong, L., Evans, B. and Page, C. (1993a) *A Guide for Middle Managers in Secondary Schools, Vol. 1: Organisations*, Lancaster: Framework Press Educational.

Armstrong, L., Evans, B. and Page, C. (1993b) *A Guide for Middle Managers in Secondary Schools, Vol. 2: Relationships*, Lancaster: Framework Press Educational.

Arnold, J. and Hope, T. (1983) *Accounting for Management Decisions*, Hemel Hempstead: Prentice Hall.

Ball, S.J. and Bowe, R. (1992) 'Subject departments and the "implementation" of National Curriculum policy: an overview of the issues', *Journal of Curriculum Studies*, **24(2)**, 97–115.

Barber, M., Evans, A. and Johnston, M. (1995) *An Evaluation of the National Scheme of School Teacher Appraisal*, London: HMSO.

Bell, L. (1992) *Managing Teams in Secondary Schools*, London: Routledge.

Bell, J. and Harrison, B.T. (ed.) (1995) *Vision and Values in Managing Education*, London: David Fulton.

Bennett, N. (1995) *Managing Professional Teachers: Middle Management in Primary and Secondary Schools*, London: Paul Chapman Publishing.

Bennis, W. (1959) *Leadership Theory Administrative Behaviour: The Problem of Authority*, Administrative Science Centre, 22–3 April, University of Pittsburgh.

Bennis, W. and Nanus, B. (1985) *Leaders: The Strategies for Taking Charge*, New York: Harper and Row.

Billsberry, J., Clark, T. and Swingler, J. (1994) *Job Design and Staff Recruitment*, B600 The Capable Manager, Open Business School: Open University Press.

Blackburn, K. (1975) *The Tutor*, London: Heinemann.

Blackburn, K. (1983) 'The Pastoral Head: a developing role', *Pastoral Care in Education*, **1(2)**, 18–24.

Bradley, J., Chesson, R. and Silverleaf, J. (1983) *Inside Staff Development*, Windsor: NFER/Nelson.

Brighouse, T. (1991) *What Makes a Good School?*, Stafford: Network Educational Press.

Brockmann, F.J. (1972) 'Program Budgeting: Implications for Secondary Principals', *NAASP Bulletin*, **56(366)**, 34–42, Virginia: NASSP.

Brown, M. and Ralph, S. (1992) 'Towards the identification of stress in teachers', *Research in Education*, **48**, 103–10.

Brown, M. and Ralph, S. (1994) *Managing Stress in Schools*, Plymouth: Northcote House.

Brown, M. and Ralph, S. (1995) 'The Identification and Management of Teacher Stress' in Bell, J. and Harrison, B.T. (ed.) (1995) *Vision and Values in Managing Education*, London: David Fulton.

Brown, M. and Rutherford, D. (1996) *Leadership for School Improvement: The Changing Role of the Head of Department*, Cambridge: British Education Management and Administration Society (BEMAS) Partners in Change Conference (Cambridge), 22–7 March.

Burstall, E. (1996) 'What Really Stresses Teachers', *TES*, 16 February, p. 4.

Bush, T. and West-Burnham, J. (eds) (1994) *The Principles of Educational Management*, Harlow: Longman.

Busher, H. (1988) 'Reducing Role Overload for a Head of Department: a rationale for fostering staff development', *School Organisation*, **8(1)**, 99–104.

Caldwell, B.J. and Spinks, J.M. (1988) *The Self-Managing School*, Lewes: Falmer Press.

Calvert, M. and Henderson, J. (1994) 'Newly-qualified teachers: Do we prepare them for their pastoral role?', *Pastoral Care in Education*, **12(2)**, 7–12.

Calvert, M. and Henderson, J. (1995) 'Leading the Team: Managing Pastoral Care in a Secondary Setting' in Bell, J. and Harrison, B.T. (eds) *Vision and Values in Managing Education*, London: David Fulton.

Chaplin, B. (1995) 'Improvement through Inspection' in Bell, J. and Harrison, B.T. (eds) *Vision and Values in Managing Education*, London: David Fulton.

Chapman, J. (ed.) (1990) *School-based Decision-making and Management*, Basingstoke: Falmer Press.

Coleman, M. and Bush, T. (1994) 'Managing with teams' in Bush, T. and West-Burnham, J. (eds) *The Principles of Educational Management*, Harlow: Longman.

Constable, J. and McCormack, R. (1987) *The making of British managers*, London: BIME, CBI.

Coopers and Lybrand (1988) *Local Management of Schools*, London: HMSO.

Davies, B. (1994) 'Managing Resources' in Bush, T. and West-Burnham, J. (eds) *The Principles of Educational Management*, Harlow: Longman.

Davies, B. and Ellison, L. (1990) *Managing the Primary School*, Northcote House: Budget.

Davies, B. and West-Burnham, J. (1990) 'School governors – an effective management force or another bureaucratic layer of school management?' *School Organisation*, **10**, 2–3.

Department for Education (1992a) *The Education Reform Act: (National Curriculum) (Assessment Arrangements) Key Stage 1 and Key Stage 3 Circular 12/92*, London: HMSO.

Department for Education (1992b) *The Education Reform Act: The Education (National Curriculum) (Assessment Arrangement for English, Mathematics, Science and technology Order 1992) Circular 13/92*, London: HMSO.

Department for Education (1992c) *Reports on Individual Pupils' Achievements. The Education (Individual Pupils' Achievements) (Information) Regulations 1992 – Circular 14/92*, London: HMSO. .

Department for Education (1993a) *Reporting on Individual Pupils' Achievements, Circular 16/93*, London: HMSO.

Department for Education (1993b) *School Teachers' Pay and Conditions Document*, London: HMSO.

Department for Education (1995) *Reports on Pupils' Achievements in 1994/95, Circular 1/95*, London: HMSO.

Department of Education and Science (1988a) *Education Reform Act*, London: HMSO.

Department of Education and Science (1988b) *Education Reform Act: Local Management of Schools, Circular 7/88*, London: HMSO.

Department of Education and Science (1989a) *Planning for School Development: Advice for Governors, Headteachers and Teachers*, London: HMSO.

Department of Education and Science (1989b) *School Teacher Appraisal: A National Framework*, London: HMSO.

Department of Education and Science (1991a) *School Teacher Appraisal, Circular 12/91*, London: HMSO.

Department of Education and Science (1991b) *Development Planning: A Practical Guide*, London: HMSO.

Drucker, P.F. (1980) *Managing in Turbulent Times*, London: Heinemann.

Duignan, P.A. and MacPherson, R.J.S. (eds) (1992) *Effective Leadership. A practical Theory for new administrators and managers*, London: Falmer Press.

Earley, P. and Fletcher-Campbell, F. (1989) *The Time to Manage ? Department and Faculty Heads at Work*, Windsor: NFER-Nelson.

Etzioni, A. (1964) *Modern Organisations*, Englewood Cliffs, NJ: Prentice Hall.

Evans, A. (1995) 'Targets for Tonight', *TES*, 15 September, p. 27.

Everard, K.B. (1986) *Developing Management in Schools*, Oxford: Blackwell.

Everard, K.B. and Morris, G. (1985) *Effective School Management*, London: Harper and Row.

Everard, K.B. and Morris, G. (1990) *Effective School Management*, London: Paul Chapman Publishing.

Fidler, B. (1994) *Staff Appraisal*, State of the Art Review, pp. 61–70.

Fidler, B., Bowles, G. and Hart, J. (1991) *Planning Your School's Strategy: LMS Workbook*, Harlow: Longman.

Fidler, B. and Cooper, R. (eds) (1992) *Staff Appraisal and Staff Management in Schools and Colleges: A Guide to Implementation*, Harlow: Longman.

Forde, C., Reeves, J. and Casteel, V. (1996) *Supporting Management Development in Schools. A Partnership Approach*, British Education Management and Administration Society (BEMAS) Partners in Change Conference (Cambridge), 22–7 March.

Foy, N. (1981) 'To strengthen the mixture, first understand the chemistry', *The Guardian*, 2 September.

Fullan, M. and Hargreaves, A. (1992) *What's worth fighting for in your school?*, Buckingham: Open University Press.

Fullerton, H. and Price, C. (1991) 'Culture in the NHS', *Personnel Management*, **23(3)**, 50–3.

Greenfield, T. and Ribbins, P. (1993) *Greenfield on educational administration: Towards a humane science*, London: Routledge.

Gunter, H. (1995) *Appraisal and the School as a Learning Organisation*, Keele: Keele University In-service Education and Management Unit, School of Education.

Hall, V. and Oldroyd, D. (1990a) *Management Self-development for Staff in Secondary Schools, Unit 1: Self-development for effective management*, Bristol: NDCEMP.

Hall, V. and Oldroyd, D. (1990b) *Management Self-development for Staff in Secondary Schools, Unit 2: Policy, Planning and Change*, Bristol: NDCEMP.

Hall, V. and Oldroyd, D. (1990c) *Management Self-development for Staff in Secondary Schools, Unit 3: Team development for effective schools*, Bristol: NDCEMP.

Hall, V. and Oldroyd, D. (1990d) *Management Self-development for Staff in Secondary Schools, Unit 4: Implementing and evaluating*, Bristol: NDCEMP.

Hamblin, D. (1989) *Staff Development for Pastoral Care*, Oxford: Blackwell.

Handy, C. (1993) *Understanding Organisations* (4th edn) Harmondsworth: Penguin.

Handy, C. and Aitken, R. (1986) *Understanding Schools as Organisations*, Harmondsworth: Penguin.

Hargreaves, A. (1994) *Changing Teachers, Changing Times*, London: Cassell.

Hargreaves, D.H. (1996) *TTA Annual Lecture 1996 – Teaching as a Research-based Profession: Possibilities and Prospects*, London: TTA.

Hargreaves, D.H. and Hopkins, D. (1991) 'School effectiveness, school improvement and development planning' in Preedy, M. *Managing the effective school*, London: Paul Chapman Publishing.

Harrison, B.T. (1995) 'Revaluing leadership and service in educational management' in Bell, J. and Harrison, B.T. (ed.) *Vision and Values in Managing Education*, London: David Fulton.

Hartley, H.J. (1979) 'Zero-based budgeting for secondary schools', *NASSP Bulletin*, **63(431)**, 22–8 Virginia: NASSP.

Haynes, M.E. (1988) *Effective Meeting Skills*, London: Kogan Page.

Hedge, N., Mole, R., LaGrave, J. and Cartwright, B. (1994) *Personal Communications at Work*, B600 The Capable Manager, Open Business School: Open University Press.

Hewitt, M. (1996a) *Director's Address*, Annual Conference (Oxford Brookes University), National Education Assessment Centre (NEAC), 26 March.

Hewitt, M. (1996b) *Quality Assurance How and What?* Annual Conference (Oxford Brookes University), National Education Assessment Centre (NEAC), 26 March.

HMI (1984) *Departmental Organisation in Schools*, London: HMSO.

HMI (1988) *The New Tutor in School*, London: HMSO.

Holmes, G. (1993) *Essential School Leadership*, London: Kogan Page.

Holt, M.J. (1980) *Schools and Curriculum Change*, Maidenhead: McGraw Hill.

Holt, M.J. (1981) *Evaluating the Evaluators*, London: Hodder and Stoughton.

House, E.R. (1973) 'The Dominion of Economic Accountability' in House, E.R. (ed.) *School Evaluation: The Politics and Process*, McCutchon Publishing.

Hoy, W.K. and Miskel, C.G. (1991) *Educational Administration: Theory, Research and practice* (4th edn), New York: McGraw-Hill.

Hoyle, E. (1986) *The Politics of School Management*, London: Hodder and Stoughton.

Ingvarson, L. (1990) 'Schools: Places where teachers learn' in Chapman, J. (ed.) *School-based Decision-making and Management*, Basingstoke: Falmer Press.

Irvine, V.B. (1975) 'Budgeting: Functional analysis and behavioural implications' in Rappaport, A. (ed.) *Information for decision-making, quantitative and Behavioural dimensions*, (2nd edn) New Jersey: Prentice Hall.

Isaac, J. (1995) 'Self-management and development' in Bell, J. and Harrison, B.T. (ed.) *Vision and Values in Managing Education*, London: David Fulton.

Ketteringham, J. (1987) 'Pupils' Perceptions of the Role of the Form Tutor', *Pastoral Care in Education*, **5(3)**, 206–17.

Knutton, S. and Ireson, G. (1995) 'Leading the team – managing staff development in the primary school' in Bell, J. and Harrison, B.T. (ed.) *Vision and Values in Managing Education*, London: David Fulton.

LaGrave, J., Mole, R. and Swingler, J. (1994) *Planning and Managing Your Work*, B600 The Capable Manager, Open Business School: Open University Press.

Lang, P. (1983) 'How Pupils See It: Looking at how pupils perceive pastoral care', *Pastoral Care in Education*, **1(3)**, 164–75.

Levacic, R. (1989) *Financial Management in Education*, Buckingham: Open University Press.

Levacic, R. and Glover, D. (1995) *OFSTED Assessment of Schools' Efficiency*, Milton Keynes: Open University Press (EPAM Report).

Lifeskills Associates Limited (1995a) *Stress Levels*, London: Lifeskills Associates Limited.

Lifeskills Associates Limited (1995b) *Vision, Action, Results*, London: Lifeskills Associates Limited.

MacGilchrist, B., Mortimore, P., Savage, J. and Beresford, C. (1995) *Planning Matters*, London: Paul Chapman Publishing.

Maclure, S. (1989) *Education Reformed: A Guide to the Education Reform Act*, London: Hodder and Stoughton.

Marconi, H.R. and Seigal, G., (1989), *Behavioural Accounting*, Ohio: South Western.

Marland, M. (1989) *The Tutor and the Tutor Group*, London: Longman.

Marsh, J. (1992) *Total Quality Management in Education*, Avon: Training and Enterprise Council.

Maslow, A.H. (1943) 'A Theory of Human Motivation', *Psychological Review*, **50(4)**, 370–96.

Maslow, A.H. (1970) *Motivation and Personality*, New York: Harper and Row.

Mayo, E. (1933) *The Human Problems of an Individual Civilisation*, London: MacMillan.

McGregor, D. (1966) *Leadership and Motivation*, MIT: MIT Press.

McGuiness, J. (1989) *A Whole-School Approach to Pastoral Care*, London: Kogan Page.

Millet, A. (1996a) *Quality Teaching – A National Priority*, Address to North of England Conference (Gateshead), 5 January.

Millet, A. (1996b) *Chief Executive Speech – TTA Corporate Plan 1996/7 Launch*, London: TTA.

Millet, A. (1996c) 'Teachers make a Difference Conference', *TES*, 8 March, p. 18.

Mullins, L.J. (1993) *Management and Organisational Behaviour* (3rd edn) London: Pitman Publishing.

National Commission on Education (NCE) (1995) *Learning to Succeed*, London: Paul Hamlyn Foundation.

National Commission on Education (NCE) (1996) *Success Against the Odds*, London: Routledge.

National Leadership Network (1991) *Developing leaders for restructuring schools: New habits of mind and heart*, Washington, DC: US Department of Education.

National Policy Board for Educational Administration (NPBEA) (1993) *Principles for our Changing Schools*, Virginia: NPBEA.

National Steering Group (1991) *School Teacher Appraisal: A National Framework*, London: HMSO.

Nightingale, D., (1990), *Local Management of Schools at Work in the Primary School*, Basingstoke: Falmer Press.

OFSTED (1994a) *Primary Matters: A Discussion on Teaching and Learning in Primary Schools*, London: DFEE Publications Centre.

OFSTED (1994b) *A Focus on Quality*, London: Coopers Lybrand.

OFSTED (1994c) *Handbook for the Inspection of Schools*, London: DFEE Publications Centre.

OFSTED (1995a) *Guidance for the Inspection of Secondary Schools*, London: HMSO.

OFSTED (1995b) *Guidance for the Inspection of Primary Schools*, London: HMSO.

OFSTED (1996a) *Inspection of Schools (Revised)* London: DFEE Publications Centre.

OFSTED (1996b) *The Appraisal of Teachers 1991–6, A report from the Office of Her Majesty's Chief Inspector of Schools*, London: DFEE Publications Centre.

OFSTED (1996c) *Consultation on Arrangements for the Inspection of Maintained Schools from September 1997*, London: DFEE Publications Centre.

Ormston, M. (1996) *Leadership and Leadership Qualities*, Oxford Brookes University: School Of Education.

Ormston, M. and Shaw, M. (1993a) *Inspection: A Preparation Guide for Schools*, Harlow: Longman.

Ormston, M. and Shaw, M. (1993b) *Mentoring*, Oxford Brookes University: School of Education.

Peters, T. and Waterman, R. (1982) *In Search of Excellence*, London: Harper and Row.

Phillips, E.M. and Pugh, D.S. (1988) *How to Get a PhD. Managing the peaks and troughs of research*, Milton Keynes: Open University Press.

Pugh, D.S. and Hickson, D.J. (1989) *Writers on Organisations* (4th edn), Harmondsworth: Penguin.

Rutter, M., Maughan, B., Mortimor, P. and Ouston, J. (1979) *Fifteen Thousand Hours: Secondary Schools and their effects on children*, London: Open Books.

Sammons, P., Thomas, S. and Mortimore, P. (1996) *Improving School and Department Effectiveness*, British Education Management and Administration Society (BEMAS) Partners in Change Conference (Cambridge), 22–7 March.

Senge, P.M. (1990) *The Fifth Discipline – The art and practice of the learning organisation*, New York: Doubleday.

Shaw, M. (1994) 'Current Issues in Pastoral Management', *Pastoral Care in Education*, **12(4)**, 37–41.

Shaw, M., Siddell, T. and Turner, M. (1992) *Time management for Teachers*, Oxford Polytechnic: Oxford Centre for Education Management.

Skelton, M., Reeves, G. and Playfoot, D. (1991) *Development Planning for Primary Schools*, Windsor: NFER/Nelson.

Spicer, B. (1990) 'Program Budgeting: A way forward in school management' in Chapman, J. (ed.) *School-based Decision-making and Management*, Basingstoke: Falmer Press.

Spinks, J. M. (1990) 'Collaborative decision-making at the school level' in Chapman, J. (ed.) *School-based Decision-making and Management*, Basingstoke: Falmer Press.

Stenner, A., (1988) 'LFM in a Primary School' in Downes, P. (ed.) (1988) *Local Financial Management in Schools*, Oxford: Basil Blackwell Ltd.

Tannenbaum, R. and Schmidt, W.H. (1973) 'How to choose a leadership pattern', *Harvard Business Review*, **36(2)**, 95–101.

Taylor, F.W. (1947) *Scientific Management*, London: Harper and Row.

The Industrial Society (1982) *Delegation (Handout 4) Management in schools and colleges*, London: The Industrial Society.

Thomas, H., Kirkpatrick, G. and Nicholson, E. (1989) *Financial Delegation and Local Management of Schools; Preparing for Practice*, London: Cassell.

Torrington, D. and Weightman, J. (1989) *The Reality of School Management*, Oxford: Blackwell Education.

Trethowan, D. (1985) *Teamwork*, London: The Industrial Society.

TTA (1996a) *Corporate Plan 1996–7*, London: HMSO.

TTA (1996b) *Teaching as a Research-based Profession: Promoting Excellence in Teaching*, London: TTA.

Tuckman, B.W. (1965) 'Development sequence in small groups', *Psychological Bulletin*, **63(6)**, 384–99.

Wallace, M., Hall, V. and Huckman, L. (1996) *Senior Management Teams in Primary and Secondary Schools*, British Education Management and Administration Society (BEMAS) Partners in Change Conference (Cambridge), 22–7 March.

Warwick (1983) *Decision Making*, London: The Industrial Society.

West, N. (1995) *Middle Management in the Primary School*, London: David Fulton.

West-Burnham, J. (1992) *Managing quality in schools*, Harlow: Longman.

West-Burnham, J. (1994a) 'Strategy, Policy and Planning' in Bush, T. and West-Burnham, J. (eds) *The Principles of Educational Management*, Harlow: Longman.

West-Burnham, J. (1994b) 'Inspection, Evaluation and Quality Assurance' in Bush, T. and West-Burnham, J. (eds) *The Principles of Educational Management*, Harlow: Longman.

West-Burnham, J. (1995) 'Supporting staff through appraisal' in Bell, J. and Harrison, B.T. (eds) *Vision and Values in Managing Education*, London: David Fulton.

Westhuizen, P.C. van der (1996) *Resistance to Change in Educational Organisations*, British Education Management and Administration Society (BEMAS) Conference (Cambridge), 22–7 March.

West Sussex Advisory and Inspection Service (1994) *Head of Department as a Leader and Manager*, Sussex: West Sussex County Council.

White, R. and Lippitt, R. (1983) 'Leadership behaviour and member reactions in three social climates' in Cartwright, D. and Zander, A. (eds) *Group Dynamics*, London: Tavistock Publishing.

Williams, M. (1991) *In Service Education and Training*, London: Cassell.

Wragg, E.C. (1994) 'Under the Microscope', *TES*, 9 September.

Wragg, E.C., Wikeley, C.M., Wragg, C.M. and Haynes, G.S. (1994) *A National Survey of Teacher Appraisal*, Leverhulme Teacher Appraisal Project, Exeter: University of Exeter, School of Education.

Index

■ ■ ■